Conflicts
in Our Schools

Conflicts
in Our Schools

Lynn L. Weldon

Alamosa State College

Charles E. Merrill Publishing Company
A Bell & Howell Company
Columbus, Ohio

The Coordinated Teacher Preparation Series
Under the Editorship of

Donald E. Orlosky
University of South Florida

and

Ned B. MacPhail
Depauw University

International Standard Book Number: 0–675–09226–4

Library of Congress Catalog Card Number: 73–149004

1 2 3 4 5 6 7 8 9 10 / 76 75 74 73 72 71

Printed in the United States of America

Preface

Conflicts in Our Schools is intended to be a thought-provoking introduction to significant educational controversies. Some conflict areas, such as teacher strikes, federal control of education, teacher training, unionism, sex education, religion in the schools, cheating, and integration, are conspicuous. Less prominent, but probably more crucial in determining the future shape of American education, are fundamental disagreements in underlying problem areas: Which cultures should be supported in our schools, interpretations of human behavior, concepts of learning, irreconcilable governmental processes, and contradictory educational power systems.

This book is designed primarily for introduction to education and foundations and philosophies of education courses. In-service teachers and administrators also may find it helpful in familiarizing themselves with current educational issues. It provides brief, yet comprehensive, guides to the major controversies in each problem area, synthesizing each issue so that it can be analyzed and its facets compared and evaluated. Conflicting answers to five major questions are presented: 1. What kinds of students should the schools produce? 2. How should this be done? 3. Are the schools producing the results we want? 4. If we are dissatisfied with the present system, what others could we try? and 5. If we should wish to change to another system, how could this be done? This book is future oriented; many traditional beliefs are challenged and "Utopian" problem solutions are explored. Appropriate thought aids and bibliographies in each chapter are designed to stimulate thinking and to provide the reader with resources for further study.

The author has made a sincere attempt to summarize many of the conflicting issues in education in an equitable manner. While endeavoring to clarify significant facets of the issues, it has sometimes been necessary to make rather broad generalizations in order to cover major aspects of the conflicts thoroughly enough in the space available, so very specific qualifications generally have been omitted. It should

v

be recognized that the author does not imply that all persons subscribing to a particular point of view necessarily adhere to all the distinguishing qualities ascribed to that position.

Many of the concepts presented in this work result from the stimulating tutelage of Dr. Ernest E. Bayles, whose perceptive examination of much of the manuscript and his helpful suggestions in its preparation are deeply appreciated by the author. Thoughtful suggestions by Ralph P. Tharp, C.P.A., also have been helpful.

The main section of Chapter 7 appeared, practically unchanged, as "Cheating in School—Teachers Are Partners in Crime," *The Clearing House,* April, 1966, pp. 462–463. An abbreviated version of Chapter 12 originally appeared as "Is Teacher Education An Illusion?" *The Journal of Teacher Education,* Summer, 1968, pp. 193–196. The National Education Association's "Code of Ethics of the Education Profession," which was adopted by the NEA Representative Assembly in July, 1968, is reproduced in Chapter 17. The main section of Chapter 19 was published, practically unchanged, as "Teacher Loyalty Oaths—Good or Bad?" *Colorado Education Review,* December, 1967, pp. 12–14.

Contents

1

On What Culture Should Our Schools Be Based?

Educational systems usually are designed to serve the needs of the culture in a particular society. However, there appear to be at least five cultures competing for general acceptance in our society. 1. Perennialists are regressivists who would go back to the eternal truths or "Great Ideas" of classical culture and would inculcate these specially privileged truths into students' outlooks. 2. Essentialists are conservatives who would preserve, conserve, and transmit the essential, enduring truths of our American heritage through indoctrination. 3. Existentialists are individualists who are striving to achieve a culture based on individual freedom. They believe that schools should foster student freedom and self-direction. 4. Reconstructionists are radicals who believe that a cultural upheaval, fostered through indoctrination of collectivism, will inevitably usher in a socialistic, future-centered, "new social order." 5. Pragmatists foster reflective thinking. They would set up, perpetuate, and change cultural institutions on the basis of reflective study of the suitability of such institutions. Which of these cultures should provide the basis for our schools?

PERENNIALISM (REGRESSIVISM)

The perennialists would like to go back to the principles and values of ancient and medieval cultures. To them, the eternal and universal truths of past cultures are significant for all times and all situations; they are perpetual, enduring, and everlasting. These perennial truths are to be found in the works of the great thinkers of the past; they are concentrated in the "Great Books," the classics, which have persisted from ancient and medieval times. For example, the thoughts of Socrates, Plato, and Aristotle have been contemporary in every age. These thinkers raised questions that are as timely now as they were two thousand years ago.

Robert Maynard Hutchins and Mortimer J. Adler, among other classicists, have led the movement to raise the present culture to the level of the intellectual achievements of the past through editing the ageless *Great Books of the Western World*. In this series, many scholars have gathered what they consider the greatest ideas of the Western World into 54 volumes containing 443 works by 74 authors. As may be expected, these volumes emphasize the classics, which are as timely today as they ever were and no doubt will continue to be. These books will be universally contemporary because all mankind has been and always will be the same. The school curriculum should emphasize the classics because classical truths are always and everywhere the same; the educative process should, therefore, be the same for all mankind.

To most perennialists, an adequate general education would consist of the study of the great books and a thorough mastery of the arts of reading, writing, speaking, and reasoning. Perennial or permanent studies would include grammar, rhetoric, logic, and mathematics, particularly Euclidean geometry. The perennialist teacher indoctrinates eternal values; his task is to transmit the absolute and unchangeable truths. Since intellectual or mental development is the central focus of education, social, vocational, and physical development are not of prime importance in perennialist schools.

Perennialism has been criticized as regression or retreat from the challenging problems of present society. Opponents claim that the great men of the past were great because they fostered their vast intellectual powers on the cultural problems of their own times. Therefore, critics claim that modern education should give major emphasis to present problems.

ESSENTIALISM (CONSERVATISM)

Essentialists are conservatives in education who find value in the "eternal verities," the basically changeless values of American culture which have been proven by past experience. These conservatives tend to be opposed to socialism in its many forms. They support business competition, the American Legion, the National Association of Manufacturers, the American Medical Association, the Daughters of the American Revolution, the Chamber of Commerce, and patriotism. They are opposed to "governmental planning" and favor the profit motive, capitalism, and economic individualism. Essentialists feel that such enduring American cultural values, which provide the stability and order required to keep society on an even keel, should be preserved.

An essentialist education would present to students only those cultural ideals and values that are widely accepted. Teachers would be required to sign loyalty oaths—declarations that they will uphold the Constitution and traditional Americanism. Thus, teachers should teach the cultural *status quo* and should condition children to be opposed to "radical" theories or social change. Since human knowledge is cumulative, true progress can occur only when schools transmit to each successive generation of students the funded American cultural heritage. Education should develop respect for long-standing American institutions.

The word *essentialism* is derived from the belief that there are certain essential and fundamental ideals and abilities which all students must acquire. The traditional curriculum is considered the best type of subject-matter organization since it is composed of logically organized, systematic, and sequential learnings. The "exact and exacting studies" of classical languages and mathematics are emphasized. Effort, discipline, rigorous subject-matter mastery, and strict teacher-control of the learning process are necessary for effective learning. Essentialists are opposed to the "soft" curriculum, informal activities, "life-adjustment trivia," and the general permissiveness of "progressive" schools. The study of contemporary affairs is of minor educational importance, since such studies only supplement what is basic—transmission of the American cultural heritage. Since the school is a creation of the existing social order, not the creator of a new order, teachers should teach the cultural heritage as it is, resisting those who would promote social reform.

Although essentialists are not in complete agreement among themselves, the following skills are generally accepted as necessary: reading, writing, computation, and oral expression. Among the essential learnings would be basic historical facts of Western Civilization, basic American governmental processes, basic American economic patterns, primary facts of world geography, and the established laws and findings of modern science. These primary skills and learnings are to be mastered through repetition, practice, and drill, regardless of student interests and purposes. All other skills and learnings, being nonessential, are "fads" and "frills," and would be excluded from the curriculum if their inclusion hindered concentration on essentials.

EXISTENTIALISM (INDIVIDUALISM)

The progressive education movement was the dominant individualistic influence on American education during the first half of the twentieth century. The followers of William H. Kilpatrick set up child-centered, activity schools in which each student carried out his own projects based on his spontaneously-felt needs and interests. Each student individually purposed, planned, executed, and judged his own activities. However, by the 1950's the progressive education movement had gone into eclipse. Seemingly, its position on the individualistic side of the cultural-educational spectrum has been taken over by the existential movement.

Existentialists emphasize the "in here," personal, individual, private, subjective, and psychological world of the existing self. Essence is *esse* (to be) *ness*. First a person *is;* then he embarks on the task of making personal choices which determine *what* he is. In brief, "Existence precedes essence."

Determining one's own essence is not finding out what it is, but is making it. The existing self undertakes the responsibility of determining and building essence through the choices made each day. In this self-directing and self-determining process of choice, each person is his own designer or essence-giver. "What is man?" is an open-ended question, since man is like an actor for whom no part has been written. Fashioning his own essence is each person's life project. Through his "ad lib" choices, he builds his own essence, his own self-reality, from the building blocks of self-determinism.

The external world contains no meanings since the individual invents or creates his own meaning. The world is open—a world of freedom. In an existential culture, each person is totally free to choose what meanings he will give to the external world, as well as being totally free to choose his own developing essence. Only the individual can make the ultimate decisions as to what culture is the correct one for him.

Existentialists agree that the individual choosing of values is their "magnificent obsession." Existentialism is based on the postulate that all cultural beliefs must pass through an individual's own value system. To be, to exist, means to be engaged in choosing, in valuing. Existentialists emphasize personal values, which are baseless and arbitrary since each person creates his own value system. He has the ultimate freedom and responsibility to choose what he will devote his life to. Even the question of God's existence is beside the point since, regardless of the presence or absence of God, each man still must choose how he is to live his own life.

A person's freedom and responsibility to choose his own values is thwarted and restricted when he exists in a culture in which he is dealt with as an object rather than as a subject—a free, autonomous, and independent self. When a person is treated as an object, thing, instrument, or gadget, he is not a free being. In a depersonalized culture he is a thing to be manipulated. Existentialists fight against a disease rampant in our modern technological society—the disease of dealing with human beings as objects, not subjects.

The center of the existential educational process is the individual self as choice-maker. In contrast, contemporary education is glaringly antiseptic. Students are rarely asked to make value choices. Existentialists would turn the traditional educational process inside out. The curriculum is not to be mastered, nor is it to be experienced. It is to be personally created. Curriculum areas that tend to provide this subjective freedom of choice include music, drama, philosophy, poetry, creative writing, literature, dance, painting, and the creative arts. In brief, the true subject matter is the personal subjectivity of each student. Curricular activities are undertaken only on the individual student's own terms, not on those predetermined or set in advance.

A teacher's role shifts from the traditional one of transmitting predetermined knowledge to that of being a provocateur of the self—an inquirer, a researcher, and a facilitator of subjective, artistic expression. A teacher is to awaken, to jar, each student into awareness of and involvement in the poignant moral dilemmas of life: injustice, kindness, cruelty, tenderness, pain, suffering, warmth, neurosis, disease, love, death, and caring. Existential teachers provide time for private student reflection and private personal judgment about these moral dilemmas.

The paradigmatic existentialist school probably would be A. S. Neill's Summerhill school in England. For more than forty years, Neill has attempted to conduct a free and open educational society in which there are no rules, no requirements, no tests, no grades, no social rules, and so forth. Each student is an autonomous self, completely responsible for his own learning, self-directing and self-moving. Through using his freedom of choice, each student becomes responsible and authentic, freely determining the meaning and essence of his own life.

RECONSTRUCTIONISM (RADICALISM)

During the great economic depression of the 1930's, a number of pro-gressivists criticized the individualism, planlessness, and lack of social orientation of the progressive movement. Progressive education was taken to task for lacking a vital sense of direction. The critics cham-pioned the idea that the schools should lead society in establishing a new, more suitable, social order. George S. Counts' book *Dare the School Build a New Social Order?* was one of the rallying banners of this movement. Teachers and students were to be social planners, turning out the blueprint of the new social order. Since reconstruc-tionists believed that capitalism, individualism, economic competition, and free enterprise were self-evident failures, the new culture was to be based on collectivism or socialism. Consumer cooperatives, old-age security, and the Tennessee Valley Authority are current American cultural patterns that reconstructionists did and would applaud.

Reconstructionists believe that the present transitional and chang-ing culture is not adequate; therefore, they try to foresee clearly and concretely what the future should be. It is obvious, for them, that a designed or planned socialistic culture needs to be created. Social revolutions are forcing the emergence of economic controls by and for the common people. A planned and well-ordered collectivistic cul-ture would dispel the chronic vacillations and confusions embedded in the present social order. To certain critics of reconstructionism, the unstated but logical consequence of this line of thought is that the planned, collectivistic culture of the future will be a settled and basi-cally changeless one.

Reconstructionists are on the frontiers of culture, thinking about the new social order which "ought to exist," and assisting in the birth of a radically new cultural design. Harold Rugg's "frontier-thinkers" concept is consistent with reconstructionism. Choosing the writings of "frontier thinkers," Rugg tabulated the concepts contained therein and developed a description of the collectivistic culture that "ought" to exist.

A frontier-thinking teacher's major task is to advocate and promote loyalty to the emerging frontier culture, conditioning students to value a future, socialistic *status quo*. Students should be enthusiastic about building this new social order; they are expected to foster the emerging age of collectivism.

Many conservative groups, such as the American Legion, have actively criticized the indoctrinative methods implicit in the recon-structionist educational program. However, these conservative groups are not opposed to indoctrination. They oppose the "wrong type" of indoctrination—the reconstructionist type. Such "wrong" indoctrination indicates the "flaws" in laissez-faire capitalism and emphasizes the "glories" of the coming age of international collectivism.

PRAGMATISM (REFLECTION)

Pragmatic educators oppose both autocratic indoctrination, as exemplified by perennialism, essentialism, and reconstructionism, and the anarchistic individualism of existentialism; instead, they emphasize reflective studies of cultural patterns. Such studies involve dealing with problems which cannot be immediately answered, yet which the participants feel must be answered. Solutions arrived at through reflective investigations of cultural problems, like detective-story solutions, come at the end of study. Reflective study begins with an interruption of a significant thought-line, and is concluded when continuity in the thought-line is restored. Progress beyond such points is dependent on thoughtful examination of possible directions in which to go.

Prior to reflective study, pragmatists would not insist that any particular cultural patterns should be either accepted or rejected. They do insist that all cultural patterns may be subjected to criticism and appraisal. They would examine present cultural patterns to determine what aspects, if any, they would retain and what, if any, they would change or abolish. This does not mean that all cultural patterns must undergo constant study. It does mean that, when for some reason any cultural institution is suspected of being faulty, that institution may legitimately be subjected to reflective evaluation.

The pragmatic approach to the acceptance of culture may be distasteful to authoritarian groups, since it offers no guarantee of preserving hallowed cultural institutions. Pragmatists do not assume that any institution is inherently immune to critical examination. However, they do believe that cultural institutions, all of which are assumed to be mutable, should receive equal opportunity for their merits to be supported in the light of relevant criteria. For example, reflective examination of the Federal Constitution might disclose that certain sections tend to foster dictatorial governmental processes. On the basis of such study, the citizens could then vote on making changes.

A teacher's role in perennialist, essentialist, or reconstructionist schools is to advocate student acceptance of the respective cultural values. In existential schools, the teacher's role shifts to that of an evoker of student self-expression. In contrast, in pragmatic schools, a teacher's role primarily is that of serving as chairman or moderator of investigational class groups. Emphasis in the educative process shifts from explanation to exploration; it depends not on teacher advocacy of the rightness of beliefs basic to past, present, or future cultures, and not on encouraging students to do as they please, but instead on developing student abilities to make thought-out choices and to be aware of the consequences of choice-making.

In order for students to have the desire to seek answers to cultural problems, the problems presented must be ones which the students feel need to be answered. In order to incite students to participate in reflective studies, questions they cannot immediately answer, yet would like to answer, must confront them.

Perennial, conservative, and radical teachers tend to treat cultural conclusions as permanently fixed or finalized, never to be questioned. They tend to give favored treatment to certain cultural beliefs. In contrast, pragmatists take the conclusions reached through the reflective process as the way stations for thought, rather than terminal points. Not only are the conclusions to be reached considered tentative, but the reflective process itself is taken to be a way station which, after examination, may continue to be used, or may be rejected or changed. In summary, pragmatic educators emphasize the progressive resolution of cultural problems through use of the reflective-thought process.

CONCLUSION

Perennialism, essentialism, and reconstructionism seem to be basically totalitarian, since they foster the indoctrination of "right" cultural patterns. For perennialists, the right patterns are to be found in ancient and medieval cultures. For essentialists, "truth" is in the conservative elements of the present American culture. For reconstructionists, the true, collectivistic culture is yet to be. Existentialists emphasize individual freedom, which is in harmony with the anarchistic cultural assumption that each person should be free not only to believe as he chooses but also to do as he pleases. Reflective study by the pragmatists of seeming inadequacies and self-contradictions in the culture is compatible with the democratic assumption that all of a people should have the right to participate equally in determining how they will be governed.

Many educators appear to be eclectic in their cultural assumptions. The eclectic is not concerned with whether or not beliefs logically fit together, nor does he give serious thought to harmony of outlook. Instead of adopting one of the systematic cultural positions, eclectics accept personally appealing features of two or more cultural positions without ascertaining if the various features that they embrace are mutually compatible. For example, an educator may hold: 1. the perennialist belief that teacher advocacy of traditional Christian virtues of honesty and chastity is central to good education; 2. the essentialist belief that teaching students to love the free enterprise system is necessary; 3. the reconstructionist belief that social security and consumer protection should be advocated by teachers; 4. the existentialist belief that major emphasis in the schools should be placed on allowing each student to have time to be by himself; and, finally, 5. the pragmatist belief that central emphasis in the classroom should be given to thoughtful examinations of apparent discrepancies in cultural postures. It becomes obvious that many educators have absorbed mutually contradictory cultural beliefs without realizing it.

SELECTED REFERENCES

Bayles, Ernest E., *Democratic Educational Theory*. New York: Harper & Row, Publishers, 1960, Chaps. 15 and 16. A pragmatist offers a perceptive examination of American education.

Benjamin, Harold, *The Saber-Tooth Curriculum*. New York: McGraw-Hill Book Company, 1939. With the help of several tequila daisies, Dr. J. Abner Peddiwell lectures on the history of paleolithic education. A delightful satire on American education. (Also available in paperback.)

Brameld, Theodore, *Philosophies of Education in Cultural Perspective*. New York: The Dryden Press, 1955. An erudite and highly readable presentation and analysis of progressivism, essentialism, and perennialism. The references are excellent. Brameld presents his own philosophy of reconstructionism in *Toward a Reconstructed Philosophy of Education*. New York: The Dryden Press, 1956. Brameld's philosophy is examined by this author in "An Analysis of Theodore Brameld's Philosophy of Reconstructionism" in *Educational Theory*, 9, No. 2 (April, 1959), pp. 88–96.

Goldwater, Barry, *The Conscience of a Conservative*. Sheperdsville, Kentucky: Victor Publishing Company, 1960. A lucid statement of the conservative viewpoint. (Also available in paperback from Hillman Books and MacFadden Books.)

Great Books of the Western World, eds. Robert Maynard Hutchins and Mortimer J. Adler. Chicago: Encyclopaedia Britannica, Inc., 1952. Note that William James and Sigmund Freud are the most recent writers included in this perennialist compilation of classical writings.

Kneller, George F., *Introduction to the Philosophy of Education.* New York: John Wiley & Sons, Inc., 1964, Chap. IV. An excellent introduction to perennialism, essentialism, and reconstructionism.

Morris, Van Cleve, *Existentialism in Education.* New York: Harper & Row Publishers, 1966. A precise and very readable introduction to the educational implications of existentialism.

_____, *Philosophy and the American School.* Boston: Houghton Mifflin Company, 1961, Part V, "Five Philosophies in American Education." Basic cultural positions are examined.

Neill, A. S., *Summerhill—A Radical Approach to Child Rearing.* New York: Hart Publishing Co., Inc., 1960. A challenging approach to education which is applauded by certain existentialists.

THOUGHT AIDS

1. What cultural viewpoints, other than those presented in this chapter, might be found in the United States? For example, how would you classify the cultural beliefs of the Communist Party, the Black Panthers, the Black Muslims, the John Birch Society, and the SDS?

2. What cultural viewpoints do you believe are most prominent in the United States? Defend your choice.

3. Debate the issue: Resolved, as modern society becomes more complex, Americans must accept an increasingly collectivized economy.

4. Discuss the question: Should schools lead or follow society?

5. Read the books by Theodore Brameld listed at the end of this chapter and then evaluate the strengths and weaknesses of the description of reconstructionism presented in this chapter.

6. Indicate the various ways the following question might be answered by supporters of each of the five cultural viewpoints presented in this chapter: Should teachers in the American public schools attempt to reform society?

7. Some critics have claimed that most American public school teachers are content to support the *status quo.* Indicate the reasons why you think teachers might be content to do so. Which of these reasons do you believe are justifiable? Why?

8. Read Harold Benjamin's *The Saber-Tooth Curriculum*. Report to the class on the amusing principles of paleolithic education and indicate how they might be applied to contemporary education.
9. Some educationists recommend adopting an eclectic view in regard to conflicting cultures. Eclectics would adopt some of the more personally acceptable beliefs held by the rival cultural systems described in this chapter. Indicate possible strengths and weaknesses of eclecticism.
10. Perennialists, essentialists, and reconstructionists seem to expect to achieve security through fostering fixed or immutable cultural patterns. What are possible strengths and weaknesses of this concept of security? May mankind also find security in changing cultural patterns?
11. Collect criticisms made of American education. Examine the validity of each criticism on the basis of the conflicting cultural views presented in this chapter.
12. Is advocacy a valid teacher role? Why or why not?

2

How Should We Interpret
Human Nature?

Many teachers believe that certain subjects, such as mathematics, should be studied because they serve to "discipline the mind." To be good, education has to be difficult for a student; it must consist of what the student hates to do. This type of teaching is consistent with the "bad-active" concept of human nature. Badness is dynamic and progressive, not static; it actively and continually gets worse. Human beings, therefore, tend to go wrong when allowed to do what they like to do. Therefore, they must be forced (disciplined) to do what they don't like.

Many teachers who accept the "bad-active" belief about human nature also hold the contradictory belief that students should be allowed to pursue their own interests, particularly during "free play" or "free time" periods. This anarchistic "do-what-you-desire" belief is in harmony with the "good-active" concept that, if persons are allowed to do as they wish, they will do good. This belief directly opposes the "bad-active" belief that people will go astray if not coerced in the "right" direction.

Often such teachers also value programmed learning; that is, they believe that students should be allowed to go at their own speed through small and easy steps as they learn correct predetermined information. Under the logic of this position, students are held to be "neutral-passive," moldable chunks of protoplasm into which right sense impressions are to be drilled. In the words of an old hymn: "Thou art the potter; I am the clay; mold me and make me after Thy will."

In further contradiction, these very same teachers sometimes advocate putting students in thought-provoking situations out of which they must then thoughtfully extricate themselves, such reflective thought being consistent with the "neutral-interactive" concept of human nature.

Many teachers may be found simultaneously holding to two or more of these beliefs about human nature, apparently unaware that they logically result in mutually contradictory types of teaching practice.

THE BAD-ACTIVE CONCEPT

According to some interpretations of Christianity, the fall of Adam injured human nature. Adam fell from his exalted and Godly nature and the stamp of his original sin is on all his descendants; they are depraved and inclined toward evil. An enemy of God, man is born in sin and iniquity and, unless his life direction is corrected, he is naturally going down a wide open road to Hell. Unless forcefully restrained, mankind would actively drop away from the true, the good, and the beautiful.

Christian groups disagree as to the degree of human depravity. Some hold, with John Calvin, that man's nature is utterly corrupt and depraved, essentially sinful in all of his acts. At the other end of the spectrum is the Roman Catholic doctrine, from which viewpoint Adam was created with natural and supernatural natures. When he rebelled against God, he was punished by being deprived of his supernature, but this did not affect his strictly human nature. Without supernatural grace, man is disposed to do evil as a result of being deprived of perfect control of his human desires. The natural or carnal man is weak-willed and is inclined toward disorderly actions.

Bad-Active Education

New England colonial schools accepted Calvin's assertion that human nature is utterly corrupt. Since children are naturally inclined to indulge in evil actions, their natural impulses and interests must be thwarted. Because children had hellish impulses, Puritanic teachers literally had to beat Hell out of them. Students were full of the Devil, who had to be forced out. As the Bible said, "Folly is bound up in the heart of a child and the rod of correction shall drive it away." [1] The Puritan compulsory school-support act of 1647, the "Old Deluder Satan Act," established schools to frustrate the evil designs of that old deluder, Satan. Since the natural impulses of children had to be restrained and thwarted, education tended to be unpleasant, even cruel. As Finley Peter Dunne had Mr. Dooley say, "I don't care what ye larn thim so long as tis onpleasant to thim." [2] A Puritan teacher was expected to be a harsh dictator in a disagreeable prison.

Although outside of parochial schools the religious assumption of original sin is usually ignored in American education, the disciplinary aspect of Puritan education has persisted in "faculty" psychology. Faculties of the mind such as will, reason, and memory were to be developed through exercise and discipline. Subject-matter areas such as mathematics and foreign languages were to be studied for the sake of discipline.

Although the transfer-of-training assumptions underlying faculty psychology generally have been discredited in educational circles, the assumption persists that for education to be effective it must be difficult. Contemporary pronouncements that fads, frills, and easy courses should be tossed out of American public schools seem to be consistent with the bad-active assumption that easy education—education which follows the natural impulses of students—is harmful. Teacher-dictators must force students to climb the difficult path to knowledge.

THE GOOD-ACTIVE CONCEPT

In contrast to the assumption that the nature of man is inherently vicious, some persons assume that, by nature, man is good and getting better. As Jean Jacques Rousseau said in championing his "back to nature" movement, "Everything is good as it comes from the hands of the author of nature." [3] "Let us lay it down as an incontrovertible rule that the first impulses of nature are always right; there is no

---

[1] Proverbs 22:15.

[2] Quoted in Ernest E. Bayles, *The Theory and Practice of Teaching* (New York: Harper & Brothers, 1950), p. 86.

[3] Quoted in R. L. Archer, *Rousseau on Education* (London: E. Arnold, 1912), p. 55.

original sin in the human heart; the how and why of the entrance of every vice can be traced." [4] "When our natural tendencies have not been interfered with by human prejudice and human institutions, the happiness alike of children and of men consists in the enjoyment of their liberty." [5] There are kernels of goodness innate in man and these kernels will unfold naturally if restraints are removed. Since native impulses and desires are good, they can be trusted and should be respected.

Good-Active Education

As Rousseau said, "The spontaneous development of our organs and facilities constitutes the education of nature." [6] The aim of good-active education is to remove restraints so that students may freely and spontaneously express their fundamentally good natures. Although Friedrich Froebel's concept of a kindergarten—a children-garden where children naturally grow like little plants—was a step in the direction of good-active education, the activities in his kindergarten were strictly supervised. In a consistently good-active kindergarten, all restraints on children would be removed, and the children supposedly develop according to their own latent patterns. The enfolded kernels of goodness freely unfold as the self-activity of the children gives expression to their inherent interests and abilities. The gardener-teacher removes all restraints and the children develop freely, pursuing their own spontaneous interests and activities. If teachers restrain or discipline natural impulses, the free development of naturally good natures is hindered.

Each child determines his own curriculum by his spontaneous needs and interests. Since children naturally like to play, and since whatever is natural is good, play is good. Therefore, as in Froebel's kindergarten, play is the center of the good-active curriculum. Good-active or student-centered schools are based on the impulses or what one critic termed the "transitory whims" of children; the child is all-sovereign.

In contrast to the harsh dictator-teacher of bad-active education, the good-active teacher tends to be a protector. Rather than guiding

---

[4] Jean Jacques Rousseau, *Emile* (New York: E. P. Dutton and Company, 1911), p. 56.

[5] Rousseau, *Emile,* p. 49.

[6] Archer, *Rousseau on Education,* p. 56.

the development of children (positive education), the teacher removes restraints on their impulses (negative education). The child does as he pleases, and anarchy, not dictatorship, is the prevailing classroom climate.

The good-active assumption was compatible with many aspects of the progressive education movement, which achieved eminence in the 1920's and 1930's. In progressive child-centered schools, freedom, felt needs, and individual interests were emphasized. Child interests determined the curriculum. The progressive, producer-project method of pupil purposing, planning, executing, and judging was consistent with good-active education. To reflect progressive education, the earlier quote from Mr. Dooley should be changed to, "I don't care what ye larn thim so long as tis *pleasant* to thim." In contrast to the bad-active assumption that natural impulses are harmful, progressive education glorified them. "It makes no difference what a boy studies just so he likes it." [7]

By the 1950's, however, the progressive education movement faltered. Its place on the individualistic-anarchistic side of the educational spectrum has been taken over by existentialist educators who emphasize allowing each pupil to be his own choice-maker. To existentialists, the curriculum is personally and subjectively created by each student. The teacher's major task is to awaken each student to determine what is valuable and to realize that he alone is ultimately responsible for the choices he makes. Each student must be completely free to determine the meaning and essence of his own life.

THE NEUTRAL-PASSIVE CONCEPT

John Locke criticized the assumption that there are inborn propensities in human nature. He assumed that human beings are born without innate inclinations toward either good or evil. Man's nature is neutral and passive. A newborn infant's mind is "tabula rasa," a blank tablet; his pliable nervous system is yet to be molded. The child conforms passively to his environment which actively impresses itself on his pliable mind.

The human mind is molded by the sensations conveyed to it by the sense organs. Since mind is passive, it cannot actively accept certain perceptions and reject others. As Locke said, "For in bare naked per-

---

[7] Frederick S. Breed, *Education and the New Realism* (New York: The Macmillan Company, 1939), p. 64.

ception, the mind is, for the most part, only passive; and what it perceives, it cannot avoid perceiving." [8] Sense impressions impinging on the mind establish patterns of thoughts or ideas, just as waves leave patterns on beach sands. Personality development is a passive accommodation to the environment, while knowledge comes through passive observation of it.

Neutral-Passive Education

Education is passive adjustment to environment. Children are like clay in the hands of a potter, their minds like wax tablets upon which teachers may write at will. Learning is a relatively inactive affair, since the teacher or environment register sense impressions on passive minds. The cultural heritage is written upon and stored up in passive minds; teachers put the right knowledge on the "cupboard shelves" in student minds. Teachers set up the proper environment and sense impressions from this environment make patterns in student minds. Education is a process of establishing right habits; they are stamped in or inculcated in the mind through repetition and drill.

Although neutral-passive education involves dictatorial indoctrination of what teachers accept as true, the dictator-teacher may be kind and loving. His is not expected to be harsh and cruel, like a Puritanical dictator-teacher. Since he does not have to fight constantly against the sins of the flesh, he may kindly and quietly indoctrinate student minds.

THE NEUTRAL-INTERACTIVE CONCEPT

From this point of view, man is not naturally getting better or worse, nor is he akin to a chunk of clay waiting to be molded by his environment. His knowledge of objects, persons, and events constitutes what might be called his "world of insight," the world of his own concoction. Phenomena which affect him, even without his awareness, might be referred to as his "world of effect." Obviously, his world of effect is more encompassing than his world of insight, consequently he seeks to expand his world of insight. Moreover, he wants his insights to enable him to predict accurately what will affect him and how it will do so. As a consequence, he conducts his behavior in ways intended

---

[8] John Locke, *An Essay Concerning Human Understanding* (New York: E. P. Dutton & Co., Inc., 1947), p. 51.

to promote desired outcomes and avoid undesired ones. The process of acquiring accurate insights is one of formulating and testing predictive accuracy by deduction and experimentation. Thus arranging one's world of effect in a manner designed to carry out the logical implications of an insight, and determining whether the outcome is the anticipated one, is an interactive process.

Human nature and personality develop through the interaction of individuals and their social and physical environments. In contrast to the neutral-passive assumption that passive human beings automatically respond to stimuli initiated by the environment, the neutral-interactive assumption is that persons not only react to their environments, but they also initiate actions that change them.

Neutral-Interactive Education

A student is neither completely dictated to by his environment, nor is he free to do as he pleases. Learning is not passive conformity to environmental stimuli; it is a dynamic process of organization and reorganization of insights developed through the interaction of a growing personality and its world. The goal of education is to help each student independently reconstruct his outlook on life so that he may continually make his own interactive world more adequate and more harmonious.

CONCLUSION

Most educators doubtless hold the belief that the nature of the learner must be recognized and honored if classroom practices are to be efficacious in promoting learning of a proper kind. However, there seem to be at least four conflicting concepts of human nature. According to the bad-active concept, human nature is naturally inclined toward disorderly, even vicious, behavior. Therefore, the natural impulses of students must be curbed. In contrast, the good-active concept holds that man has kernels of goodness innately enfolded within him and, in the state of nature, these kernels will naturally unfold. From the neutral-passive point of view, education is a process of imprinting right sense impressions on passive minds, thereby establishing right habits. To neutral-interactive educators, students are not naturally getting better or worse, nor are they passive, moldable nonentities. Each student's nature is an on-going product of his interactions with his environment. Therefore, learning is a dynamic process of developing and changing insights as each student interacts with his expanding environments.

Of the four assumptions, the neutral-interactive seems to be the only one that is compatible with the democratic ideal of developing individuals capable, of making their own decisions through the critical analysis of competing alternatives.

SELECTED REFERENCES

Bayles, Ernest E., and Bruce L. Hood, *Growth of American Educational Thought and Practice*. New York: Harper & Row, Publishers, 1966. An excellent historical presentation of educational programs based on conflicting concepts of human nature.

Bigge, Morris, and Maurice Hunt, *Psychological Foundations of Education*. New York: Harper & Row, Publishers, 1968, Chap. 3. An excellent introduction to conflicting concepts of human nature.

Brubacher, John S., *Modern Philosophies of Education*. New York: McGraw-Hill Book Company, 1962, Chap. 3. A brief but excellent presentation of the natures of man.

Golding, William, *Lord of the Flies*. New York: Capricorn Books, G. P. Putnam's Sons, 1959. An attention-compelling allegory on original evil.

Hansen, Kenneth H., *Philosophy for American Education*. Englewood Cliffs, New Jersey: Prentice-Hall, Inc., 1960, Chap. 9. A number of assumptions concerning the nature of man are analyzed.

Neill, A. S., *Summerhill—A Radical Approach to Child Rearing*. New York: Hart Publishing Company, Inc., 1964. A perceptive and thought-provoking report on a thoroughly student-centered school.

THOUGHT AIDS

1. Are there any areas of agreement between the four concepts of the nature of man?
2. Read Arthur Miller's play, "The Crucible," which is based on the Salem witch trials. Is "The Crucible" relevant to current social problems?

3. For further analyses of Locke, Rousseau, Froebel, etc., see history of education books such as Frederick Eby, *The Development of Modern Education*, and I. N. Thut, *The Story of Education*.

4. Read Charlotte Bronte's description of Mr. Brocklehurst in her book, *Jane Eyre*. What concept of human nature is best exemplified in Mr. Brocklehurst? Why?

5. Debate the issue: Resolved, the natural man is an enemy of God.

6. Indicate the differences and similarities between the Roman Catholic and Calvinistic assumptions about human nature.

7. Look into history of education texts for descriptions of the Puritan New England colonial schools.

8. The author assumes that the neutral-interactive nature of man is the only concept of human nature that is compatible with democracy. Present arguments for and against this assumption.

9. Indicate possible concepts which could be held by advocates of the four human nature assumptions in regard to classroom discipline and student motivation.

10. Read Golding's *Lord of the Flies*. Is his message valid?

3

Which Concept of Learning Is Preferred?

Since the turn of the century, two conflicting groups of thought systems have developed in educational psychology. One, the stimulus-response group, has emphasized mechanistic, objective, observational studies of human behavior, often spoken of as scientific. These "behaviorists" deal with stimulus-response behavioral associations, conditioned responses, and reinforcement of correct responses. To them, learning is the imbedding of correct behavior. In contrast, the goal-insight group has emphasized cognitive, insightful, and purposeful goal-seeking actions. To goal-insight psychologists, learning is a process of developing insights in order to achieve recognized purposes or goals.

Many teachers apparently are not aware of the differences between the stimulus-response and goal-insight thought systems. They attempt to expose their students to good, not bad. As examples, English students are exposed to "good" literature, and music students listen only to "good" music. The emphasizing of desirable stimuli is based on the behavioristic or stimulus-response psychological system which holds that learning consists of impressing correct reaction patterns on pliable and passive students. Yet many teachers who organize their classes in such a manner also believe that students learn best the things which they see as being of major importance to them. This belief is based on the cognitive or goal-insight school of psychology which holds that learning is a process of catching insights, not of drilling in correct behavior. For example, teachers may employ linear programmed materials in their classes, in order to make sure that correct facts and concepts are transmitted step by step to their students; almost simultaneously, they may create situations in which students are required to attempt, through insight, to clarify puzzling situations. Thus, teachers foster student abilities unquestioningly to accept "correct" sense impressions, and also foster student abilities to question and possibly reject so-called "correct" sense impressions. Such teacher behavior can be likened to that of a carpenter who, being paid to build a house, strenuously works at building it in the mornings, and then demolishes his work in the afternoons. Such inconsistent teachers need to become aware of incompatibilities between stimulus-response and goal-insight thought systems.

THE STIMULUS-RESPONSE CONCEPT OF BEHAVIOR

A number of psychological schools of thought are grouped together under the heading of stimulus-response psychologies. The first is the conditioned-reflex group, which built upon the observations made by the noted Russian physiologist, Ivan Pavlov. Pavlov's classic example of neural conditioning was that of the dogs who, in anticipation of food, learned to salivate when a bell was rung. Rigidly mechanistic behaviorists, such as John B. Watson, derived many of their assumptions from Pavlov's work. Another school of mechanistic-behavioristic thought was the connectionist group led by Edward Lee Thorndike. Thorndike asserted that the reflex arc in the nervous system is the hereditary unit of behavior. Since most contemporary S-R associationists have, in certain respects, departed from Watson and Thorndike, perhaps the most appropriate term to apply to them is neobehaviorists. Leading neobehaviorists are E. R. Guthrie with his contiguous conditioning, C. L. Hull with his deductive behaviorism or reinforcement theory, K. W. Spence with his quantitative S-R theory, and B. F. Skinner with his operant conditioning. Because of its significance in contemporary programmed learning and teaching machines, Skinner's operant conditioning will be given the greater attention. However, the references at the end of this chapter include extensive presentations of the unique formulations of these and other leading psychologists.

For purposes of continuity, the traditional emphases of S-R associations will be presented first, and then the neobehaviorists' departures, if any, from these emphases will be noted.

For the historical groups of S-R associationists, the conditioned reflex was the basic unit of behavior. Conditioning was considered to be the establishing and strengthening of neural paths or reflex-arc connections or bonds through repetition of stimuli and responses. Behavior is a response to some form of stimulation. The most adequate explanation of human behavior and learning is supposedly on a purely mechanical, situation-response, conditioning basis. Conscious behavior, purposiveness, and intelligent experience are rejected as invalid assumptions in this highly mechanistic thought system. Quantitative data and objective measurements are emphasized and, through precise control of behavioral studies, laws of human behavior will be discovered. Psychology in this context is an engineering field, strictly devoid of theorizing.

To stimulus-response psychologists, behavior is changed through conditioning. Conditioning is a process of modifying stimulus-response habits; certain stimulus-response bonds are reinforced or strengthened. In classical conditioning, illustrated by Pavlov's teaching a dog to salivate at the ringing of a bell, an organism learns to respond to a new (conditioned) stimulus—the sound of the bell—in the same way it responds to an old (unconditioned) stimulus—the appearance of food—through both stimuli repeatedly being presented together. Repetition of the association of the two stimuli strengthens the bond between the new stimulus and the response—salivation. The new (conditioned) stimulus becomes a substitute for the old (unconditioned) one. Behavior is changed through stimulus substitution.

In operant conditioning, illustrated by B. F. Skinner's training of pigeons, behavior is changed through the reinforcement of certain responses. When a random response (pigeon pecks a button) is performed, it is reinforced by a reward stimulus (pigeon receives a food pellet). Such a reinforcement response increased the likelihood that the correct behavioral response will be repeated—pigeon will again peck the correct button. Thus, changes in behavior occur through response modification.

To the classical conditionist, man is a complicated machine whose behavior can be predicted and controlled with a high degree of accuracy and certainty if he is properly conditioned. In order to predict accurately how a person will act in a given situation, it must be known what environmental stimuli will be present and how the individual has been conditioned to respond to those stimuli. Proper behavior is caused by conditioned neural connections; complex acts are made up of additive combinations of simple, specific, conditioned-reflex arcs. To traditional behaviorists a whole is equal to the sum of its parts. Neobehaviorists, however, instead of talking about discrete and isolable links, tend to talk in more generalized terms about such things as "stimulus-response situations," "molar vs. molecular reactions," and "complex configurational reactions."

A human organism is a responding mechanism, passively awaiting stimulation by a stimulus-situation. The organism must be stimulated before it can act or respond. Human behavior is a set of psychological responses resulting from stimuli external to a self.

The Stimulus-Response Concept of Learning

Learning is said to occur when a specific neural bond or connection is established or strengthened between a situation and a response. As a consequence of Pavlov's studies, it was assumed that the whole complex of learned responses is developed through the acquisition of conditioned responses that become replacements for simple, unlearned responses.

How do neural connections become established or habituated? Earlier S-R associationists proposed that each stimulus-response neural impulse followed an exact, predetermined path through the nervous system. As each stimulus crossed a neural synapse, it slightly reduced synaptic resistance to its passage. Persistent, repetitive exercise of stimulus-response connections tends gradually to reduce synaptic resistance. Therefore, learning was considered to be a process of neural path-wearing in which resistance at the synapses was gradually reduced by exact repetition of acts. The greater the frequency of repetition of a reflex arc, the greater the learning.

Contemporary S-R neobehaviorists are not particularly concerned either with neural physiology or with the precise operations of the physical mechanisms which link stimuli and responses. They emphasize careful surveillance of observable behavior. Neobehaviorists appear to agree with Thorndike's assumption that learning is a process of conditioning which emphasizes the stamping in of correct responses. Habits are exact sequences of acts which are drilled into the nervous system.

A teacher initiates environmental stimuli that start nervous impulses in students and, in turn, automatically set off responses. When a teacher sets up the proper environmental stimuli, the students passively absorb the sense impressions, and these, in turn, form proper patterns in the students' minds. Rather than questioning the stimuli presented by the teacher, a good student accepts them. When proper behavior patterns are inculcated in student minds, actions will tend to become fixed and automatic, supposedly similar to the actions of a dial phone when the proper numbers are dialed.

Since all actions are determined by stimulus-situations, student actions are automatic and are not necessarily purposive. Therefore, student purposes and goals are not recognized in stimulus-response theory. Stimulus-response learning involves the identical elements theory that training will automatically transfer when previously conditioned neural connections are stimulated in later situations.

Since students automatically absorb sense impressions or stimuli, the teacher should set up the proper environment. Because bonds are strengthened by exact repetition of proper actions, exceptions should not be permitted because wrong bonds would tend to form. Students learn by doing right things through the habituation of proper actions. The repetitive, authoritarian system of education fostered by S-R associationists has been termed the "tell 'em" system. "All we seem to do is first tell 'em what we are to tell 'em, then we tell 'em, then we tell 'em what we have told 'em. Afterwards we give examinations in order to find whether they can tell us what we have told them." [1]

B. F. Skinner's operant conditioning seems to be a particular type of authoritarian learning process which has become popular in programmed instruction and teaching machines. In contrast to the work of earlier behaviorists who established correct responses to stimuli, operant conditioning is based on an organism first making a desired response, then being rewarded or reinforced for the response. The stimulus is a reinforcer which follows the response; the stimulus-reward makes the correct response more likely to reoccur. A teacher's task is to foster predetermined responses, rewarding correct acts for reinforcement. Behavioral objectives for students are divided into a number of very small sequential operants, or sets of acts, which are reinforced one by one as a student moves gradually toward fully correct behavior. Thus, in programmed learning, each student is led to construct a carefully prescribed order of responses, as each answer or action is immediately rewarded or reinforced.

---

[1] Ernest E. Bayles, "Democratic Education and Philosophic Theory," *Educational Administration and Supervision* 36, no. 4 (April, 1950), 217.

THE GOAL-INSIGHT CONCEPT OF BEHAVIOR

Gestalt, cognitive, organismic, topological, and field-theory psychologies are grouped under the goal-insight heading. Some of the leading exponents of insight-centered psychologies are Max Wertheimer, Kurt Koffka, Wolfgang Kohler, Kurt Lewin, George W. Hartmann, Raymond H. Wheeler, Boyd H. Bode, and Ernest E. Bayles. Kohler's study of apes led him to believe that his chimpanzees solved certain problems in ways that were inadequately explained by stimulus-response assumptions. In a flash of insight, the animals suddenly saw all the significant parts of problem-situations grouped together as meaningful wholes. Much of human behavior also seems to be controlled by insights. Situations are seen as purposeful patterns, as configurations leading to goals, and solutions to some problems seem to appear in a flash of understanding.

Every perception exists as a pattern or gestalt against a background. Gestalt is German for form, figure, or shape, and has been translated into American psychological terminology as pattern or configuration. Objects and events are seen and understood as part of a configuration against a background or frame of reference. Insight involves understanding what a thing is not, its background, as well as what it is. In using insight a person contrasts an object or event with its field or background to achieve his goals. Each person may initiate his own actions. In contrast, according to the stimulus-response viewpoint, each person, as a passive organism, reacts only when stimuli occur.

The emphasis of gestalt psychology is on purpose, whether overtly or covertly at work, as an integrating element in human experience. Since insightful human actions are purposive, specific acts can be interpreted and understood only in light of their goals and the consciously understood ways of achieving these goals. Emphasis is given to the unity or integration of experiences, not to a series of separate and unitary responses. Furthermore, actions are continuous, organized, intra-related wholes, the whole being greater than the additive sum of its parts; an integrative factor is present.

In order to predict what an individual will do in a certain situation, three basic factors must be known: 1. the situation; 2. the goals of the individual; and 3. the insights he uses so that his goals and the exigencies of the situation agree. Goal-insight psychologists invoke the principle of "least action" in their attempts to predict human behavior. This principle prescribes that an individual will attempt to achieve his goal in the way his insights indicate he can expend the least time and energy under existing conditions. In other words, a person will attempt to achieve his goals in the easiest, albeit the most adequate, way.

The Goal-Insight Concept of Learning

Learning is a process of developing new insights, of assigning new relationships. It is a process of formulating meanings rather than one of following neural pathways. Under the aegis of pattern-learning, emphasis in classroom procedures shifts from repetition to catching or developing a sense of bearing. Learning is involved in the reflective process of evaluating situations, analyzing what actions would seem to lead most efficiently to goals. Neither habit formation nor conditioning, learning is looked upon as a process of building insights and concepts. Learning is not simply the response of a passive organism to stimuli; it is the organization of behavior which flows from continual interaction between an individual and his world.

Since learning may occur as a flash of insight, learning may be gained without repetition of acts. Learning is not determined by how many times an action is repeated, but by the grasp a learner has of the meaning of the action. Practice, defined by goal-insight psychologists as a dynamic process of unique modification of actions, gives opportunities for gaining additional insights. Habit also has a place in goal-insight learning when it is defined as a non-hesitant, fluent, economical, and successful mode of accomplishing goals. Habitual action occurs when a situation and its meaning occur in the mind simultaneously. Although stimulus-response psychology emphasizes rote memorization and drill, goal-insight learning does not imply the complete absence of memorization. Memorization may be needed to accomplish a particular goal. For example, students may see a need to memorize the multiplication tables in order to use them fluently and successfully.

Insightful actions may be similar to previous actions, but they are never exact replicas. Even seemingly mechanistic actions, such as learning the multiplication tables, involve precise and unique adjustments as changing insights are developed. It is not how many times an act is performed that causes it to be learned, but what relationships are formulated during its performances.

Physiological studies of learning, including those made by Karl S. Lashley, have indicated that the human nervous system operates as a dynamic, integrated whole. Repeated nervous impulses do not seem to follow exact predetermined paths through the nervous system.[2] If the reflex-arc theory is inadequate and learning does not reduce synaptic resistance, what physiologically happens in the nervous system when learning occurs? As yet, both stimulus-response and goal-insight psychologists believe that a satisfactory answer to this question has not been found. Since Lashley's experiments cast doubt on the earlier stimulus-response beliefs, many neobehaviorists now hold the position that even though they do not know what physiological changes are associated with learning, repetition remains its most effective cause.

From the goal-insight point of view, transfer of training is accomplished by applying the principle of configuration. Students direct their learning toward their own purposes; hence learnings tend to be transferred when they are seen as positively related to one's purposes and goals. As Bayles notes, previous training will transfer if an opportunity for transfer is present, if a student is aware of the opportunity, and if the student believes that such transfer of training will foster achievement of his goals and purposes.[3]

Insightful analysis of conflicting alternatives appears to be the generalized method of democratic education. Democratic teaching would rule out the repetitive drill emphasized in stimulus-response psychologies. Goal-insight learning is consistent with democratic educational procedures because critical analysis of alternatives is encouraged through perplexing or problematic situations. Students and teacher together develop insights reflectively, as they contemplate possible solutions to problem-situations. There are no specially privileged insights, since all insights must stand the test of analysis based on appropriate criteria. In brief, democratic educational procedures emphasize reflective development of insights.

Insights may also be developed nonreflectively. Nonreflective development of insights is especially consistent with autocratic teaching procedures, though it may occur in democratic teaching. Students may be taught specially privileged insights, concepts, and relationships in an autocratic classroom unit. This is insightful thinking, learning relationships, on an understanding level. Although development of insights on an understanding level is not incompatible with democratic education, reflective development remains its special emphasis,

[2] See Karl S. Lashley, *Brain Mechanisms and Intelligence* (Chicago: University of Chicago Press, 1929), pp. 58–60, 173.

[3] Ernest E. Bayles, *The Theory and Practice of Teaching* (New York: Harper and Row, 1950), Chap. 6. *Also see* Bayles' *Democratic Educational Theory* (New York: Harper and Row, 1960), pp. 56–61.

whereas reflective development of insights is entirely incompatible with autocratic education.

CONCLUSION

B. F. Skinner's operant conditioning, which is the foundation of most of the currently popular programmed-instruction materials, is open to some devastating criticisms. Certain goal-insight psychologists point out that effective reinforcement of a "correct" response is dependent on whether a "reward" *is deemed as such* by the recipient. In Skinner's training of pigeons, a food pellet was rewarding to a hungry pigeon, but a shiny new dime would not be! Therefore, to these goal-insight psychologists, although goals and insights are ignored by behaviorists, they are still present and are what cause "reinforcement." Thus, reinforcement actually fits into the goal-insight thought-system and is in conflict with the stimulus-response system. Also, the mechanistic-behavioristic approach to learning tends to destroy the reflective abilities needed for effective participation in democratic societies. Stimulus-response learning is designed to thwart rather than to enhance student abilities to question and critically examine "right" behavior.

As noted in the introductory section of this chapter, both types of psychology of learning are often emphasized together in the classroom procedures of some teachers, who seemingly are unaware of the conflicting assumptions involved. Many teachers claim to teach in a democratic way and yet emphasize repetitive conditioning and drill in their classrooms. If teachers desire to teach in consistently democratic ways, it would seem that they should emphasize reflectively developed, insightful thought processes.

Many educational psychology texts seemingly tend to cloud the conflicts between stimulus-response and goal-insight psychologies. After analyzing approximately twenty educational psychology textbooks, Hunt and Metcalf came to the conclusion that a majority of the texts were eclectic and tended to mix and confuse the two outlooks.[4] For example, stimulus-response terminology was used to describe a goal-insight viewpoint. Most educational psychology textbooks fail to offer even a hint that stimulus-response psychology is in basic conflict with democratic educational procedures.

---

[4] Maurice Hunt and Lawrence Metcalf, *Teaching High School Social Studies* (New York: Harper and Brothers, 1955), pp. 16–18.

Over the past two decades, the goal-insight point of view apparently has suffered loss in popularity, perhaps at least partially through its success, since certain of its assumptions have been accepted by the neobehaviorists. The neobehaviorists presently are so much in the ascendancy that Ernest R. Hilgard has made the observation that "... the era of the 'great debate' among the major theories is over." [5] In contrast, Morris Bigge and Maurice Hunt make a strong case for the contention that the "great debate" between stimulus-response associationism and goal-insight learning theories is very much alive. [6]

A number of other contradictory beliefs may be found in the area of educational psychology. For example, although many teachers believe that learning involves the whole person, it is a rare teacher who deals competently with the psychic and emotional facets of his students. Why do many students who start as curious and enthusiastic first graders eventually turn into withdrawn and apathetic dropouts or hostile troublemakers who must be forced to learn? According to authorities in the field of counseling and psychotherapy, one of the necessary conditions for effective learning is the presence of a teacher who is genuinely concerned and involved with his students. However, in many teacher-education programs, the concentration of instruction is on developing "fact-givers" who are emotionally aloof and not personally involved with their students. Thus, we find teachers *claiming* to be interested in their students as persons, yet teaching and testing for informational tidbits rather than encouraging student self-development. They claim that self-awareness is important, yet how many of them are adequately self-aware? Do they encourage their students to be introspective, to consider deeply what they really want to do in life? They talk as if student initiative and maturity were very important, yet subtly shape their students to fit preconceived molds. Although they are ostensibly opposed to creating robots to be controlled by others, they fail to teach their students effective ways of resisting control or manipulation, particularly manipulation by these very same teachers themselves.

It is the desire of certain teachers to develop students who are capable of recognizing and dealing with their own emotions, yet how many of these teachers clearly recognize and effectively deal with

---

[5] Ernest R. Hilgard, ed., *Theories of Learning and Instruction* (Sixty-third NSSE Yearbook, 1965), Part I, p. 417.

[6] Morris Bigge and Maurice Hunt, *Psychological Foundations of Education* (New York: Harper and Row, Publishers, 1968), Part 3. *Also see* Bigge's "Theories of Learning," *NEA Journal* 55, no. 3 (March, 1966), pp. 18–19.

their own feelings of fear, anxiety, hostility, guilt, anger, sexual desire, and love? If certain educational psychologists are correct in their claims that the most significant factors in effective teaching are the teacher's perceptions of himself, others, and teaching, why in most teacher education programs are these perceptions not carefully examined? Since studies unmistakably indicate that threats and fear inhibit learning, it seems to be a paradox that teacher control of student classroom behavior is almost invariably based on such extrinsic methods. Although intrinsic motivation usually is the most effective, many teachers persist in emphasizing extrinsic devices such as grades.

SELECTED REFERENCES

Bayles, Ernest E., *Democratic Educational Theory.* New York: Harper & Row, Publishers, 1960, Chaps. 2 and 3. An excellent analysis of many of the concepts involved in educational psychology. For a comprehensive treatment of these concepts, *also see* Bayles', *The Theory and Practice of Teaching*, New York: Harper & Row, Publishers, 1950.

Bigge, Morris L., and Maurice P. Hunt, *Psychological Foundations of Education.* New York: Harper & Row, Publishers, 1968. An analysis of alternative psychological assumptions from a goal-insight viewpoint. The chapters particularly relevant to conflicting concepts of learning have been published as a separate volume: Morris L. Bigge, *Learning Theories for Teachers.* New York: Harper & Row, Publishers, 1964.

Hilgard, Ernest R., and Gordon H. Bower, *Theories of Learning.* New York: Appleton-Century-Crofts, 1966. An excellent review of the major theories of learning. Chapters range from Thorndike's connectionism to the technology of instruction.

Hunt, Maurice, and Lawrence Metcalf, *Teaching High School Social Studies.* New York: Harper & Row, Publishers, 1968, Chaps. 1 and 2. Important analyses of conflicting theories of learning and their relationships to democratic education. Also note the references at the ends of the chapters.

Packard, Vance, *The Hidden Persuaders.* New York: David McKay Co., Inc., 1957. An exploration of motivational research and its effects in conditioning public attitudes.

Theories of Learning and Instruction. Ernest R. Hilgard, ed. The Sixty-third Yearbook of the National Society for the Study of Education, Part I.

Chicago: University of Chicago Press, 1964. The first three chapters are particularly relevant to conflicting theories of learning.

The Psychology of Learning, Nelson B. Henry, ed. The Forty-first Yearbook of the National Society for the Study of Education, Part II. Chicago: University of Chicago Press, 1942. The conflicting theories of learning of conditioning, connectionism and field theory are presented. Each theory is defended by psychologists who espouse that position.

THOUGHT AIDS

1. To you, which type of learning is better, stimulus-response conditioning or goal-insight awareness of relationships? Why?
2. Why do you think the behavioristic viewpoint presently enjoys a much greater popularity among psychologists than the goal-insight viewpoint?
3. Examine B. F. Skinner's operant conditioning and the principles of programmed instruction based on operant conditioning. Do you agree with the contention that Skinner's educational program basically is an authoritarian learning process? Why or why not?
4. Do you agree with the assumption that democratic educational programs are in conflict with stimulus-response psychologies? Why or why not?
5. Do you agree with Ernest Hilgard's statement that ". . . the era of the 'great debate' among the major theories is over"? Why or why not?
6. Examine the meanings of key words in this chapter, such as conditioning, connectionism, behaviorism, associationism, drill, habituation, repetition, field theory, and insight as presented in the *Dictionary of Education*.
7. Evaluate the adequacy of the presentations in this chapter of conflicting theories of learning on the basis of Bigge and Hunt's *Psychological Foundations of Education*.
8. How valid to you is the argument that the best learning theory involves a combination of behavioristic and field theory assumptions? Why?

4

Are We Living in a Democracy?

To find the answer to the question, "Are we living in a democracy?" we must discover an acceptable definition for the term "democracy." It must be acceptable as a clear, logical, and non-self-contradictory definition which may be used in the educational process as a yardstick to determine whether or not we are preparing students for participation in a democratic society.

SOME DEFINITIONS OF DEMOCRACY

In the present cold-war clash among competing ideologies, many Americans believe that we are spending billions of dollars to make the world safe for "democracy." In contrast, the governments of various countries behind the Iron Curtain also claim to be "democratic," indicating that wide discrepancies exist in the definition of democracy. An examination of eleven currently popular American definitions of democracy may point the way to an acceptable definition.

1. *Majority Rule.* This popular definition of democracy has its roots in ancient Greece (*Demos*—the people, and *kratos*—authority).

The people are sovereign, their authority registered through majority decision. However, majority rule can be dictatorial; it may silence and even destroy minorities instead of democratically tolerating their viewpoints.

2. *Freedom and Liberty.* For many Americans, the words "democracy" and "freedom" are synonymous. To them, democratic countries are free and, conversely, totalitarian countries are enslaved. However, in the generally recognized "democratic" countries, such as Great Britain, Canada, Switzerland, Australia, and the United States, there are laws, rules, and regulations which limit and restrict the basic freedoms of speech, press, assembly, and religion. If democracy is freedom, it is fairly apparent that *any* laws are undemocratic since they place restrictions on personal freedom. However, such freedom, or lack of law, is also referred to as anarchy.

3. *Respect for Individuality.* Respect for the worth and dignity of the individual is emphasized in democratic countries, and often is used as a definition. However, it is possible that decisions made by democratic governments may promote, in certain specific areas, disrespect for individuality. Conversely, a benevolent despot may make decisions which foster respect for the individual. Seemingly, an end, respect for individuality, is being confused with democratic and autocratic means to achieve that end.

4. *Toleration of Minority Groups.* Like the previous definition, toleration of minority groups in democratic countries may foster certain intolerant actions toward minorities, making benevolent despots seem to be more tolerant toward minorities.

5. *Equality.* The United States *Declaration of Independence* asserts that "... all men are created equal ..." "Equal rights" and "no special privileges" are generally accepted as democratic principles. To some Americans, equal rights means the equal freedom of laissez-faire capitalism, the freedom of each American to conduct his business as he chooses. To other Americans, equality means the socialistic, equal distribution of economic goods. Since "equality" is given such contradictory meanings, it is not a clear definition of democracy.

6. *Inalienable Rights to Life, Liberty and the Pursuit of Happiness.* All of the generally recognized "democratic" countries regularly restrict or alienate the rights of criminals by jailing them. Inalienable rights would limit the sovereignty of a people to make decisions contrary to such rights, thus thwarting majority rule. Totalitarian governments may also decide that all citizens of their countries have inalienable rights to life, liberty, and the pursuit of happiness.

7. *Society Regulated by a Federal Constitution.* Many Americans believe that the United States *Constitution* is the foundation of their

democracy. However, England, a "democratic" country, does not have a constitution, while the Soviet Union, apparently a totalitarian state, does have a constitution.

8. *The American Way of Life.* Many Americans believe that the true meaning of democracy is to be found in the "American Way of Life." However, this phrase seems to have many varied, and often contradictory, meanings. To some Americans it means equal political freedom; to others, it means the right to carry on the traditional disenfranchisement of certain minority groups. Therefore, "The American Way of Life" is too vague and involves too many conflicting meanings to be a clear definition of democracy.

9. *Respect for Authority, Law, and Order.* Respect for authority, law, and order often is accepted as one of the cornerstones of democracy. However, totalitarian governments also often require respect for authority, law, and order.

10. *Shared Common Interests and Associated Living.* Governments in "democratic" countries may decide to hinder common interests and associated living. Conversely, a despot may make decisions fostering shared interests and associated living.

11. *The Golden Mean.* Emphasized by ancient Greek philosophers, the golden mean asserts that democracy lies midway between totalitarianism and anarchy, between oppression and license. However, defining democracy as lying somewhere between the extremes of oppression and license has merely compounded the problem of definition. Where does democratic control end and oppression begin and, conversely, where does democratic freedom end and anarchistic license begin. Even the totalitarian government of the Soviet Union allows certain individual freedoms, so the Russians can argue validly that their government is democratic because it is somewhere near the "Golden Mean."

Conflicts among various of these commonly held definitions may be noted. For example, majority rule can destroy the toleration of minority groups. Respect for individuality implies limitations on majority rule. Governmental regulations by a federal constitution are incompatible with the lack of restrictions implied by freedom and liberty. Respect for authority, law, and order may also conflict with freedom and liberty.

One of the major inadequacies of the previous definitions is that many of the claims could be made by dictatorial governments as well as by democracies. Apparently, defining democracy as a decision (such as to have a federal constitution), rather than as a way of making decisions, is self-contradictory.

DEMOCRACY AND ALTERNATIVES

Although there are a variety of democratic systems of governing—
the parliamentary form, the executive council system, and the presi-
dential system—the processes of making governmental decisions under
these systems have one basic similarity: the people are assumed to
have the power to make governmental decisions. Although totalitarianism assumes many forms—autocracy, monarchy, theocracy, plutocracy, oligarchy, and aristocracy—they have one clear element in
common—the decisions of a single person or a fixed group of people
determine what the entire people will do. No equality of opportunity
exists for the people as a whole to participate in making the decisions
by which they are governed. A third type of governing process,
anarchy, is an individualistic decision-making process in which each
person decides for himself what he will do. In contrast, both democratic and autocratic societies assume that the citizens must obey
enacted decisions. In a purely democratic society, the decisions would
be arrived at through equal participation in the decision-making
process, and in an autocracy through an unequal process.

In other words, in a thoroughly democratic society there would
be equal opportunity to participate in making group decisions, and
compliance with applicable decisions would be mandatory. In a totally
autocratic society there would be no equal participation in making
decisions but, again compliance with applicable decisions would be
mandatory. With an anarchistic government, each person would have
unlimited liberty to do as he pleased.

Many Americans agree that democracy involves sovereignty of the
people, responsibility before the law, and equal rights. It appears
that this consensus in regard to democratic traits is embodied in the
above definition of democracy.

Popular Definitions Reviewed

The popular definitions of democracy previously presented now
can be re-examined on the basis of the definition of democracy just
proposed.

1. *Majority Rule.* Voting is not an absolute necessity in a democratic decision-making process. If there are no declarations of opposition to a given proposal, why vote? Majority rule is brought into effect
only when a decision is not unanimous.

In terms of the definition of democracy just presented, majority rule means that the will of the people as a whole is expressed by those desiring to participate in the decision-making process. The people may make and enforce any decisions they desire, including a decision to end the democratic process. There are no "out-of-bounds" areas which the all-sovereign people may not invade. There is no tribunal higher than the people as a whole. Therefore, the possibility exists that a people may lawfully destroy democracy. Individual rights to participate in the decision-making process may be destroyed through actions of a majority of the group participating in the process. Majorities may destroy democracy by disenfranchising minority groups, thus prohibiting minority attempts to change the will of the majority. When minorities are denied participation, autocratic majority rule prevails.

Democratic majority rule does not require that every person participate actively in the making of a decision. The desire to refrain from participation is honored unless there is legal enactment to the contrary. However, even though a citizen does not actively participate in the decision-making process, he is passively participating in the sense that he tacitly indicates his unconcern about the decision to be made.

Democratic rule implies that smaller jurisdictional groups may not lawfully make decisions that conflict with larger jurisdictional groups to which the smaller groups are subordinate. For example, state laws must be in harmony with national laws.

2. *Freedom and Liberty* (Freedoms of Speech, Press, Assembly, and Religion). The terms freedom and liberty require clarification in their relationship to democracy. Basically, they most accurately describe anarchy (without rule), not democracy, since the latter implies that limitations on freedoms may be made through group actions. According to the foregoing definition, the only freedom implicit in the democratic process is the freedom to participate in that process. However, this freedom is not an inalienable right, since a democratic people has the sovereign power to limit freedoms, including the freedom to participate in the democratic process itself. This freedom must involve the right to criticize accepted decisions for the purpose of attempting to secure a following which will alter current policy. If the freedom to criticize is destroyed, equality of participation in the decision-making process is destroyed.

A dictator may allow the citizens of his totalitarian state to have a greater number of specific liberties than a democratically-governed people may give to themselves. Thus the degree or extent of freedoms does not determine whether a country is democratic or autocratic. The determining factors are the democratic and autocratic ways in which decisions about freedoms are made, perpetuated, and changed.

3. *Respect for Individuality.* Democratic decisions may tend to foster respect for individuality, but the people as a whole have the power to make decisions assaulting this respect. To many Americans, it seems wise to foster respect for individuality, but the democratic process does not guarantee wise decisions. Decisions in democracies, and also in autocracies, will only be as wise as those who participate in making the decisions. A wise dictator may make wiser decisions than those made by a people in a democracy. To some, democracy has been equated with "good" since, over the years, it has tended to foster those goals, such as respect for individuality, which many feel are the keystones of the culture. However, democratic majorities may make decisions which are intolerable, vile, disgusting, and barbaric; yet such actions are possible within the democratic process as long as the right to participate in decision-making exists.

4. *Toleration of Minority Groups.* Democracy implies toleration of minority groups only in terms of equality of opportunity to participate in making decisions. Democracy also requires that all individuals and groups must obey applicable democratically-made decisions; persons or groups who refuse to abide by legislated decisions forfeit their rights to respect or toleration when they use illegal means to impose their will.

5. *Equality.* The only equality implicit in democracy is equality of opportunity to participate in making socio-governmental decisions. As H. Clay Jent has indicated, as long as an individual abides by the democratic laws which are applicable to him, he may achieve whatever is within his desires and abilities.

> Democracy interpreted thus, instead of implying compensating special privileges for dull, indolent, or evil persons, implies that all individuals have equal opportunity to prove themselves—or fail—on merit. And, rather than implying equalizing special privileges for poor ideas, democracy provides equality of opportunity for all ideas, good or poor, to stand or fall on merit. Democracy implies that, if and when persons and ideas prove not to be equal, they should be regarded as unequal.[1]

Since the economic alternatives of socialistic equalitarianism and capitalistic laissez faire were discussed in the previous section on

---

[1] H. Clay Jent, "A Study of the Meaning of Democracy and of its Salient Implications for Teaching." Unpublished doctoral dissertation, School of Education, Univerity of Kansas, 1951, p. 333.

popular definitions, an analysis of the relationship of economic systems to democracy is in order. Capitalism, socialism, and communism are economic systems which may be chosen, perpetuated, and changed in either democratic or autocratic ways. For example, England, a basically democratic country, at times has adopted forms of socialism. The communistic economic system of the USSR was established and is perpetuated in an autocratic way. A communistic economic system may also be established and perpetuated in a democratic way. For example, the national parks and forests of the United States are owned by the government, yet they were established and are being perpetuated in a basically democratic way. A majority in any democratic country may decide that the people as a whole should own all the land and industries; if this decision is amenable to change by the people as a whole, it is consistent with the democratic process. Most Americans probably believe that such a decision would be unwise but, as was indicated previously, democracy does not guarantee wise or good decisions. Conversely, to specify that a people may accept only certain economic systems is to say that their sovereign will is powerless when they choose "unwise" economic systems.

6. *Inalienable Rights to Life, Liberty, and the Pursuit of Happiness.* H. Clay Jent succinctly states the conflict between democracy and inalienable rights.

> ... A member of a democratic society has the right to life if he does not break democratically enacted laws, violations of which provide for capital punishment. He must take his chances along with everyone else in military engagements if required by law to do so. A member of a democratic society has a right to liberty if he does not run afoul of democratically enacted laws, violations of which provide for imprisonment. He may pursue happiness in ways of his own choosing if his activities do not run counter to enacted laws. Obviously, other than rights specifically provided by law or those existing by virtue of absence of regulation, an individual in a democratic society has no rights whatever; none that might be called inalienable.[2]

7. *Society Controlled by a Federal Constitution.* Decisions to accept, perpetuate, and change federal constitutions may be arrived at through both autocratic and democratic means, but they are not necessarily a part of either democratic or autocratic decision-making processes. They are only potential, not mandatory, products of these processes.

---

[2] Jent, "A Study of the Meaning of Democracy," pp. 331–32.

Let us now turn to the implications of the Constitution of the United States. The long-standing argument as to whether or not the Constitution was established in a democratic way seems to be indecisive and will not be considered here. Whether or not the Constitution is being perpetuated and may be changed in a democratic way seems to be a much more relevant point for discussion. As specified by Article V of the Constitution, amendments must be proposed either by two-thirds of the state legislatures or by both houses of Congress, and such amendments must be ratified by three-fourths of either state legislatures or state conventions. These requirements necessitate an autocratic process, since, for example, if one less than three-fourths of the state legislatures desire to ratify an amendment to the Constitution and one more than one-fourth do not, the amendment will not be ratified. Thus, the will of a minority can prevail over the will of a majority. In contrast, democracy implies that, in situations in which voting is deemed necessary, simple majorities of those desiring to participate determine which decisions will prevail. Thus, two-thirds and three-fourths voting requirements are clearly autocratic; many Americans believe that such autocratic limitations on change are wise. However, such beliefs often seem to imply distrust of the competency of a majority of a people to make wise decisions. Such beliefs are in accord with the assumption that it is wiser for minorities to make decisions for the masses, rather than to permit the "tyranny of the masses." The autocratic assumptions implicit in such beliefs seem to be fairly obvious.

8. *The American Way of Life.* Democracy is a way of life only in the sense that the democratic process may be employed by any group. Democracy involves rules for governing a group, regardless of whether the group is the United Nations, a social club, a corporate board of directors, a school faculty, or a family. It is *one* way of life; there are others. "The American way of life" is not a valid definition of democracy; it is democratic only in the degree to which the democratic process operates in it. Certain aspects of the American way of life, such as restrictions on the voting rights of minority groups, seem to be clearly totalitarian.

9. *Respect for Authority, Law, and Order.* As was noted previously, autocracies may require respect and unquestioning obedience of autocratically-established authority, law, and order. Respect for authority, law, and order in a democratic system may be interpreted to mean that all members of the society who fall within the domain of a particular democratically-made decision are required to abide by that decision. However, these persons have the right to disapprove

the decision and may communicate their displeasure with the purpose of influencing a majority to change it.

10. *Shared Common Interests and Associated Living.* As with respect for individuality, shared common interests and associated living or social living are goals and decisions which may be established, perpetuated, and changed in either autocratic or democratic ways. Democratically-enacted decisions may or may not require associated living and the sharing of common interests. However, such decisions are only a small fraction of the many possible products of the democratic process and are not intrinsic aspects of the process itself.

11. *The Golden Mean.* On the basis of the definitions of democracy, autocracy, and anarchy previously presented, it is inadequate and inaccurate to say that democracy is the mean or balance somewhere between the extremes of autocracy and anarchy. Democracy is clearly different from both autocracy and anarchy; it does not lie in a middle position that partakes, if only in a limited way, of certain qualities of each extreme position. For example, democracy has qualities of freedom and control distinctly different from those exhibited by either autocracy or anarchy. Rather than lying on a scale somewhere between autocracy and anarchy, democracy might more accurately be thought of as being clearly distinct from and equidistant from both autocracy and anarchy.

SOME FURTHER CONSIDERATIONS

The boundaries between the various governing processes are shadowy areas, not clear-cut lines. One of these areas is the place at which democratic limitations on the basic freedoms of speech, press, and assembly become so restrictive that they become autocratic limitations on the freedom of individuals to participate in the democratic process. Another shadowy area encompasses the problem of which specific groups, if any, are deemed incompetent to participate in the democratic process. Present practices in the United States do not allow the feebleminded, the insane, criminals, and the chronologically "immature" to participate in local, state, and federal elections. A valid question could be raised as to whether or not "immature" junior high school and senior high school students are as competent as their elders to participate in making governmental decisions. Disenfranchisement on the basis of presumed incompetency is a potentially dangerous area since democratically-made decisions may designate other groups, such as those who do not own property, to be incompetent to participate in the democratic process.

Another danger area is the relationship of economic power to the democratic process. In America, certain economic interests tend to control many communications media. Influential newspapers, magazines, and radio and television networks tend to be controlled by powerful economic groups who, quite naturally, desire to preserve their dominant positions. Such groups can and often do control and limit the types of information disseminated to the general public. Insofar as these limitations prevent the adequate or full understanding of issues by a people as a whole, they tend to be autocratic limitations on equality of opportunity to participate in the democratic process of lawmaking.

Assumptions Underlying Democracy

Democracy is bolstered by the assumption that conditions may change and unforeseen circumstances may develop, thereby necessitating altered socio-governmental decisions. Democracy represents the assumption that no group has a monopoly on truth. No person or group is taken to be in possession of infallible wisdom. There is a non-dogmatic and tolerant attitude toward diverse beliefs which involves an awareness of the possible imperfection in any individual's outlook and standard of values. Minority groups who obey democratic decisions, yet disagree with these decisions, are not looked upon as dangers to be exterminated. Democratic groups need to "listen to eccentrics and suffer with fools." All opinions are entitled to a hearing, but it is not required that the opinions presented be valued or accepted.

There is no fixed or final determination of the validity of values; no changeless formula for judging them. It is not assumed that there is an all-wise and all-powerful force or moral law over and above a people which determines what is right or wrong, wise or foolish. A people determines those values to be accepted and leaves the way open for new groups to determine what values, in the light of changing circumstances, will be accepted in the future. Since absolute truth, if there be such, is not assumed to be yet known, reasonable men differ as to the wisdom of particular decisions, and all decisions are assumed to be tentative and changeable.

Is our society based on these assumptions? Are we living in a democracy?

SELECTED REFERENCES

Arendt, Hannah, *The Origins of Totalitarianism.* New York: Harcourt, Brace & Company, 1951. An examination of the social and psychological bases of totalitarianism.

Barbu, Zevedei, *Democracy and Dictatorship.* New York: Grove Press, 1956. Sociological and psychological patterns of life in democratic and dictatorial countries are analyzed.

Bayles, Ernest E., *Democratic Educational Theory.* New York: Harper & Row, Publishers, 1960, Chap. 10. Bayles presents a brief and lucid analysis of the inadequacies of many popular definitions of democracy and then gives what he believes is a more adequate definition of democracy.

————, *Pragmatism in Education.* New York: Harper & Row, Publishers, 1966, Chap. 4. A precise analysis of democracy.

Dewey, John, *Democracy and Education.* New York: The Macmillan Company, 1916, Chap. 7. The most acclaimed American philosopher describes his democratic ideal of associated living.

Jent, H. Clay, "A Study of the Meaning of Democracy and of Its Salient Implications for Teaching." Unpublished doctoral dissertation, School of Education, University of Kansas, 1951. A comprehensive study of conflicting historical and contemporary meanings of democracy.

Orwell, George, *1984.* New York: Harcourt, Brace & Company, 1949. (Available in paperback from New American Library, 1954.) This novel is a terrifying account of a totalitarian state of the future.

Redden, John D., and Francis A. Ryan, *A Catholic Philosophy of Education.* Milwaukee: The Bruce Publishing Company, 1956, Chap. 18. Also note the scholastic definition of democracy on page 523. An excellent presentation of a definition of democracy which is in conflict with those presented by Bayles and Jent.

Sayers, Ephraim Vern, and Ward Madden, *Education and the Democratic Faith.* New York: Appleton-Century-Crofts, 1959, Chap. 2. A discussion of various historical interpretations of democracy.

Smith, T. V., and Edward C. Lindeman, *The Democratic Way of Life.* New York: New American Library, 1951. A classic description of democracy as a way of life.

THOUGHT AIDS

1. Examine the definitions of dictatorship, totalitarianism, authoritarianism, despotism, tyranny, monarchy, theocracy, plutocracy, oligarchy, aristoc-

racy, democracy, and anarchy in various encyclopedias. If available, use the *Encyclopedia of the Social Studies.* Also check the definition of democracy in Good's *Dictionary of Education.* Contrast these definitions with the definitions of autocracy, democracy and anarchy presented in this chapter.

2. Some Americans are surprised to learn that Russia has a federal constitution. Study the Soviet Constitution, giving particular attention to Chapter 10—Fundamental Rights and Duties of Citizens. Contrast Chapter 10 with the Bill of Rights in the United States Constitution. Sometimes the Soviet Constitution may be found as an appendix in comparative government and comparative economics texts.

3. Collect newspaper articles, pamphlets, and other statements illustrating the various definitions of democracy analyzed in this chapter. For example, some statements foster the equating of democracy and freedom. Others equate democracy with "The American Way of Life."

4. It may be argued that there are no societies or countries that are either completely democratic, completely autocratic, or completely anarchistic. Therefore, to make precise definitions of democracy, autocracy, and anarchy is a waste of time. What do you think of such an argument?

5. View the film, "Defining Democracy." Contrast the definitions of democracy and despotism presented in the film with the definitions of democracy and autocracy presented in this chapter.

6. Plato apparently argued against democracy and in favor of philosopher-kings by indicating it would be foolish, when setting out on a perilous voyage, to elect the pilot of the ship. Since the "pilot" of most ships of state has an even more perilous and difficult task, it is even more foolish to elect him. What to you are the possible strengths and weaknesses of Plato's argument?

7. Contrast Roman Catholic concepts of democracy with the concept presented in this chapter. Besides the Redden and Ryan book, excellent brief but adequate sources are the following Knights of Columbus pamphlets: Number 21—"Is the Catholic Church a Menace to Democracy?" Number 35—"Let's Test Catholic Loyalty," and Number 49—"Is the Catholic Church Out of Place Here?"

8. The writer has indicated that equating democracy with capitalism is illogical since democracy, to him, is a decision-making process and capitalism is only one of several possible economic products of democratic or autocratic decision-making processes. Although the equating of democracy and capitalism may be illogical, might such inconsistent thinking be wise? Why?

9. To you, is our society basically democratic? Why?

5

Are Our Schools Democratic?

While traveling in the Colorado mountains, a driver failed to observe carefully the highway markers, with the result that, when he finally realized he was going in the wrong direction, irretrievable travel time had been lost. It often appears that teachers are lost and unaware that they are going in the wrong direction, losing irretrievable time. Why do so many teachers seem to be going astray?

Teachers generally tend to teach in the way in which their teachers taught them. Those teachers apparently believed that there are only two alternatives: To teach, or not to teach. To them, "to teach" meant to transmit the facts and concepts of a given discipline, whereas "not to teach," which they held to be an abhorrent alternative, meant to leave students to their own chaotic devices. Consequently, to those teachers, there was only one valid alternative—to transmit accepted facts and concepts.

Today's teachers, of course, possess varying degrees of competence or effectiveness in teaching. Some may know very little about their subject-matter fields and others may be top flight scholars. Some may have uninteresting and uninspiring personalities, whereas others are pleasing and exciting. Some are concerned about the personal needs of each student, dealing with individual differences. Others are not.

Some make effective use of recently developed media, such as over-head projectors, classroom television systems, and programmed instruction. Others cling to the traditional lecture method and belittle modern media.

However, all of these conventional teachers have one thing in common; they believe that teaching is a transmissive process. They emphasize what should be learned, not how to learn. Their students are expected to accumulate and retain known truths. These teachers give out correct answers and keep at them until their students can show, usually on closed-book tests, that the answers have been firmly established. These teachers value the "tell 'em" method.

> We tell 'em what we are going to tell 'em; then we tell it to 'em; then we tell 'em what we have told 'em. Afterwards we give examinations in order to find whether they can tell us what we have told them.[1]

How can the assertion be made that this transmissive or "tell 'em" way of teaching and testing is a wrong road? What makes it a wrong road? This transmissive concept encourages developing the ability of the student to be a dependent follower who accepts and values what his teachers accept and value. Instead of promoting critical inquiry in the minds of students, transmissive teachers encourage students to develop passive, credulous, unquestioning, and reproducing minds. As Harry A. Overstreet noted in his book, *The Mature Mind,* ". . . students are insidiously led to believe that the mature art of thinking for themselves is 'dangerous.'"[2] Another statement has been attributed to Bertrand Russell: "Some people are born with the ability to think; a major teaching task is to eliminate that ability." Many students subjected to a steady diet of authoritarian-transmissive teaching learn to play the rote-memorization or "tell 'em" game, but quickly learn that this game has little relevance to outside-of-school living. In school, irrelevant facts are committed to memory because teachers reward those students who most rapidly do so. Two unrelated worlds are formed. Outside of class, things are true because they make sense. Inside class, things are true because the authority (the teacher) says they are true.

The ability to be an unquestioning follower probably is useful in a totalitarian society, yet the very same teachers who indulge in

---

[1] Ernest E. Bayles, "Democratic Education and Philosophic Theory," *Educational Administration and Supervision* 36, no. 4 (April, 1950): p. 217.

[2] Harry A. Overstreet, *The Mature Mind* (New York: W. W. Norton and Company, 1959), p. 249.

transmissive teaching often profess to believe that democracy, not totalitarianism, should be fostered. They ostensibly believe in encouraging students to become effective participants in a democratic society, yet their actions belie what appear to be their beliefs. How, then, can democracy be manifested in the classroom?

THE JURISDICTION PROBLEM

Some educators have held that our nation and its schools should be democratic "as far as possible." Such beliefs seem to be based on the assumption that teachers should allow student freedom "as far as is possible" and then, when such freedom becomes intolerable, the resultant laying down of coercive rules and regulations is autocratic. From this point of view, democracy in the classroom means that the students run the class, making their own rules and regulations, regardless of the rules and regulations prescribed by school boards and school administrators. On the basis of the previously presented definition of democracy, the allowing students to do as they please "as far as is possible" seems to be a confusion of democracy with anarchy. Since democracy involves limitations on personal freedom, the laws and regulations of society as a whole are binding also on students. Democratic schools are not "jungles" outside the jurisdiction and control of authorities empowered by a people.

Actions of subordinate groups in a democracy must conform to decisions made by more encompassing jurisdictional groups. Student groups may not make decisions in areas in which larger jurisdictional groups such as school boards and their administrative representatives have jurisdiction. As the authorized representative of a higher jurisdictional group, a teacher's power is greater than that of all the students in his class. To draw an example from a different area, let us assume that a small group of citizens in a particular state vote to increase the speed limit in their state to 100 mph. Despite their decision, if apprehended while driving at such speed they will be arrested by the highway patrolman, since he is serving as a representative of a higher jurisdictional group, the state. Students also have jurisdiction only in areas in which higher jurisdictional groups allow their decisions to prevail. Students should be allowed to make decisions only in areas in which the results are allowed to stand, no matter what the results may be. Areas traditionally reserved for student decisions include election of class officers and student council members, choice of elective courses, and choice of individual classroom projects, but recent developments may alter this tradition. Students in some colleges and universities now have an influential voice in determining the curriculum and in evaluating teachers and administrators.

Subordinate individuals and groups in a democracy are not required to agree with or like the regulations made by higher jurisdictional groups. However, students and others should accept the fact that democratic regulations must be obeyed, regardless of how distasteful the regulations may be. Students and other groups, however, have in recent years brought about some changes in those areas distasteful to them. They have discovered that minority group pressures can influence majority group decisions and bring about changes that otherwise would never have been effected. In an autocracy, students are required to obey the laws and regulations established by the ruling clique. If students and others are not members of the ruling group, their protests usually will be silenced. Even if the expression of dissent is allowed in an autocracy, dissenting opinions do not have to be reckoned with when decisions are made.

THE INDOCTRINATION PROBLEM

In a democracy, persons are required to act in harmony with regulations and laws, but they may think as they please, and express their thoughts in legally authorized ways. Convictions are held to be personal and private until an individual wills to make them public.

However, democratic schools are based on the assumption that student thoughts and actions do not measure up to adult standards. Students are assumed to be not yet competent to participate in the democratic process; their thoughts and actions must be guided and improved. Through a teacher's influence, errors in student thinking should be corrected. However, if a teacher guides or controls student thinking, is he not acting in a dictatorial way? Can a teacher criticize, guide, or control student thoughts in a democratic way? Is indoctrinative thought-control consistent with democracy?

If a teacher guides and controls student thoughts by promotionally leading them to acceptance of his own convictions—what he takes to be important—totalitarian indoctrination of specially privileged beliefs is fostered. The teacher's beliefs have a specially privileged position in the classroom. In such a dictatorial educational system, the students are expected to accept the concepts, values, and conclusions that the teacher propounds. Student thinking must be in agreement with the teacher's thinking. Only ideas and attitudes which are "correct," which conform to the teacher's ideas and attitudes, are to be accepted and habituated in the students. Specially privileged ideas held by specially privileged ruling cliques are to be stamped into students. This is indoctrination—autocratic thought-guidance or control.

A teacher fostering autocratic thought-control may be very kind and loving in his insistence that students conform to and accept "the truth." He may allow students to make their own decisions, but only as long as the decisions do not deny his own system. Since his ends justify the use of any means to attain them, the methods he uses may be kindly suggestive or forcefully harsh, depending upon what methods used in specific situations will most effectively foster his attempts to indoctrinate "correct" thoughts and values.

On the other hand, letting students think as they please, without thoughtful evaluation, is anarchy. In an anarchy, each student accepts only the conclusions, concepts, and values that he individually likes. However, democratic education implies avoidance of both anarchy, letting students arrive at their own conclusions, and autocracy, requiring that students accept specially privileged, teacher-valued conclusions.

Although democracy implies that there should be no specially-privileged ideas held by specially-privileged ruling cliques, it also implies that student thinking should be guided and improved. Can a teacher avoid forcing students to agree with his own beliefs and also avoid letting each student think as he pleases? Can both autocratic guidance and anarchistic student freedom be avoided? Can there really be an educational process of thought guidance that is democratic?

For purposes of illustration, the dilemma of teacher dictation versus anarchistic student freedom will be shifted to a basketball court. Does the referee require that the players must accept and value *what he believes* about basketball? Must they accept the rules he likes and reject those he rejects? On the other hand, does he allow the players to play the game in any manner they please? Most basketball enthusiasts would answer these questions in the negative. Both the referee and the players are expected to abide by "the rules of the game." The rightness or wrongness of player actions is determined, not by whether their actions agree with the referee's personal beliefs, but by whether the actions conform to the rules of the game.

Similarly, in a democratic classroom, the students and teacher set up criteria, standards, or rules by which both student and teacher thinking may be analyzed and guided. Democratic education avoids the dilemma of either accepting autocratic indoctrination or accepting anarchistic permissivism by adopting a third alternative: *critical analysis of teacher and pupil thought processes on the basis of tentative criteria adopted for the present purpose.* All proposals, including the teacher's, are to be judged on the basis of the presently adopted criteria. Neither teacher nor students are free to arrive at whatever conclusions they please. They are bound by the criteria and, in reaching a given conclusion, must accept the conclusion most in harmony with the criteria. Teacher guidance and criticism on the basis of overtly recognized criteria eliminates pupil permissiveness. Teacher indoctrination is prevented by the principle of pupil analysis of teacher-presented viewpoints on the basis of adopted criteria. A teacher's point of view does not receive preferential status since the teacher is required, equally with the students, to abide by the relevant criteria.

Democratic education does not require, in order to avoid indoctrination, that a teacher be neutral in expressing his likes or dislikes. A basketball referee is not required to believe that both teams are equal; he may have personal convictions about the comparative skill of the teams. However, his only task is to see that each player obeys pertinent rules, to maintain a "fair field." He is not even required to like the rules. Similarly, a democratic teacher is not required to believe that all thought processes are equally valid. His task is to see that all points of view have equal opportunity to be proven, or fail to be proven, on the basis of their own merit when tested against established criteria. It is to be expected that examination will indicate that certain concepts are less convincing than others. Similarly, a referee's foul calls may hinder one team more than the other. A democratic teacher's task is to see that a "fair field" is maintained when conflicting concepts are presented and analyzed in the classroom.

Certain teachers and students believe that the only acceptable criteria under which democratically-oriented classes may operate must be group-adopted, through class vote. But criteria often (perhaps usually) are a matter of curriculum choice and are, therefore, determined by higher jurisdictional groups, not by the personal likes or dislikes of particular teachers or students. However, reflective teachers do have the responsibility to make students aware that, since conclusions basically are determined by the criteria used, criteria should be carefully scrutinized and consciously adopted. Students should be encouraged to ask, "What do these particular criteria require as conclusions to our study?" Reflective criteria are not assumed to be fixed and final. Criteria, although serving as clear and definite points of relative stability, may be examined and changed. Conclusions to a given study must be seen as, "Using the criteria presently in force, the conclusion appears to be thus and so." For example, a class dealing with the question, "Which is better, classical or rock-and-roll music?" may first use pay of performers as the criterion; then, in turn, they may try other criteria to see what the various criteria require in terms of conclusions. In this way, students get experience with the vital role that criteria play in reflective thought, and come to appreciate the value of trying out various ones before settling upon one as their own. They also come to see that certain criteria are desirable or applicable at one time and others at other times.

On the basis of defining democracy as equality of opportunity to participate in making group decisions and mandatory responsibility to abide by decisions, indoctrination is ruled out if it means "... the attempt to fix in the learning mind any doctrine ... to the exclusion of all contrary doctrines, and in a manner preventing serious comparison and evaluation." [3] Indoctrination is undemocratic because it provides special privileges for certain persons and ideas. Thus, the presently accepted definition of democracy should not be indoctrinated in democratic schools, since indoctrination would put the definition in a specially privileged position.

In an autocratic school, the students are expected to value what the teacher values—think "correct" thoughts after the teacher. In anarchistic classrooms, the students may believe and do as they please. There is no attempt to guide student thinking. Anarchistic permissiveness is undemocratic because it eliminates group guidance based on recognized criteria—rules and regulations. Student thinking in democratic schools is guided by the teacher through the process of requiring that the relevant concepts of both teacher and pupils must be subjected to recognized criteria for judging the validity of the concepts.

METHOD-CURRICULUM ALTERNATIVES

Democracy and autocracy logically point to conflicting method-curriculums. The compound word, method-curriculum, is introduced to emphasize the close relationship between methodological and cur-

---

[3] *Dictionary of Education,* Carter V. Good, ed. (New York: McGraw-Hill Book Company, 1959), p. 285.

ricular assumptions. Autocracy implies an indoctrinative method of presenting the curriculum. In contrast, democracy involves a reflective or critical-analysis method of studying problem situations.

Dewey defined a problem as a "forked-road" situation. A traveler is thrust into an unresolved or unclear situation. Which road leads to his goal? He must pause to analyze alternatives, formulate hypothetical (possible) solutions, then test these solutions, possibly by driving down one of the forks to see whether this hypothetical solution is verified. As this illustrates, the reflective, problem-solving method has two phases: (1) formulation of hypotheses and (2) verification of hypotheses.

In school situations, problems are raised and then solved. Possible problem-solutions are accepted or rejected on the basis of how well they fit criteria or goals functioning at the time. In terms of the above illustration, the acceptable fork in the road is the one that leads the traveler to his goal. The hypothesis that pointed to that road is valid because it fit the criterion of accuracy of prediction.

In a democratic classroom the conclusion of a problem-solving process must conform to criteria; the scientific-method criterion of accuracy of predictability of hypotheses *may* be adopted since it is consistent with the democratic process. But it doesn't have to be; democratic groups are free to choose their own criteria.

Referring again to our coined word, method-curriculum, it can be seen that, reflectively, it would be difficult to present curriculum materials organized to present the "right" answers; conversely, it would be difficult to use the method of indoctrination when the curriculum is composed of competing alternatives, fairly evaluated.[4]

Rather than merely storing up transmitted knowledge, students in democratic-reflective schools are to develop thoughtful abilities to raise and resolve significant problems which cannot be immediately answered, yet which they feel a need to deal with. When a student chooses to grapple intellectually with a given matter, he feels an intrinsic need for the matter to be resolved. It becomes a *problem,* and cannot be dealt with in utter objectivity; it makes a difference to the learner and, psychologically, virtually forces him to reflect on it. The probabilities are that students cannot help but reflect on problems which involve sharp discrepancies in beliefs *held by them.* Thoughtful decision-making tends to occur most frequently when

---

[4] For a further discussion of the inseparability of method and content, see Maurice P. Hunt and Lawrence E. Metcalf, *Teaching High School Social Studies* (New York: Harper & Row, Publishers, 1955), Chap. 10, pp. 214–32.

students feel a need to deal with inconsistencies and self-contradictions which they recognize as existing within their own belief patterns.

A recent "tri-university project" was centered on identifying inconsistencies that would effectively provoke reflective thought by elementary school students. A number of such mutual contradictions were suggested by elementary school students themselves. Examples presented in the project report included:

1. Bars of soap are yellow, green, blue, lavender, and pink. Since they are different colors, why do they all make white soap suds?
2. If the United States is the richest country in the world, why do we have so many poor people?
3. We say that all men are created equal. Why then do some men live in big houses and other men live in little houses?
4. Our school is made of brick. Bricks cannot burn. Why should we have fire drills in our school?
5. Some people are born with yellow, brown, or black skin. Other people find it desirable or fashionable to acquire a darker skin tone by lying in the sun for hours or by using a sun lamp. Why do many of these same people have feelings of prejudice toward the people who were born with a darker skin color? [5]
6. If warm air rises, why is air on mountain tops cold? [6]

In their book, *Teaching High School Social Studies,* Maurice Hunt and Lawrence Metcalf present a number of mutually contradictory cultural beliefs which they believe illustrate what should be the curriculum in problem-centered social studies classes. The following are representative of the inconsistent beliefs which they suggest high-school students should investigate.

1. It is believed that ours is a society of law and that law protects the weak against the strong; but it is also believed that many laws favor the rich and powerful and act to keep the common man in his place. [7]
2. It is believed that spending by government is a burden on the economy which must be borne by taxpayers; but it is also believed that spending by private corporations is not a burden and that private corporations never tax the public. [8]

---

[5] Grant Bateman, William Lieurance, Agnes Manney, and Curtis Osburn, *Helping Children Think* (New York: New York University, Tri-University Project in Elementary Education, 1968), p. 40.

[6] Bateman, Lieurance, Manney, and Osburn, *Helping Children Think*, p. 42.

[7] Maurice P. Hunt and Lawrence E. Metcalf, *Teaching High School Social Studies* (New York: Harper & Row, 1968), p. 318.

[8] Hunt and Metcalf, *Teaching High School Social Studies*, pp. 337–38.

3. It is widely believed that patriotism consists of serving government wishes, whether right or wrong, in time of emergency; but it is believed also that the best kind of patriotism is constructive criticism of one's government.[9]

4. It is believed that persons should take their religion seriously and try to understand and believe its teachings in order to practice them in daily living; but it is also believed that anyone who tried seriously to practice the philosophy of Jesus would not get very far in today's world, and besides, extremely pious individuals are usually somewhat "nutty." [10]

In summary, reflective learning is based on exploration rather than explanation.

A SEMANTIC PROBLEM

Words such as "totalitarian," "autocratic," and "indoctrination" often are considered to have negative connotations, and words such as "democracy," "reflective," and "problem solving" are accepted as having positive connotations. However, instead of attaching negative or positive judgments to these words, as used here they are assumed to be operational and non-judgmental. That is, they have been used to represent operational principles rather than to indicate whether the principles and actions are judged to be "good" or "bad."

CONFLICTING CLASSROOM CLIMATES

The conflicting governmental alternatives of democracy, autocracy, and anarchy may foster the following tendencies or emphases in classroom atmosphere or climate:

A. Democracy

1. In areas of group (students and teacher) jurisdiction, group policies may be arrived at through group discussions and decisions.

2. The teacher is a participant and technical advisor.

3. Available alternative solutions to problems are analyzed and

---

9 Hunt and Metcalf, *Teaching High School Social Studies*, p. 361.
10 Hunt and Metcalf, *Teaching High School Social Studies*, p. 394.

contrasted, decisions being based on supportable criteria and presently available facts.

4. The teacher communicates the criteria for his praise and criticism of individual and group activities and encourages student analyses of criteria.
5. Balance between student dependence and independence is emphasized.
6. Group decisions are held to be tentative and changeable. Decisions are not necessarily constantly changing.
7. There is a tendency toward cooperation between students and students, and students and teachers.

B. Autocracy

1. All decisions and policies are determined by the teacher, or higher jurisdictional authorities.
2. The teacher is an authoritarian director, dictator or teller of the truth.
3. The teacher's truths are presented as being self-evidently right.
4. In evaluating individual and group activities, the teacher keeps his standards of praise and criticism to himself.
5. Since the teacher is the giver of rewards and criticisms, student dependence on the teacher is fostered.
6. All decisions and right answers are permanent, except when the teacher or higher authorities want them changed.
7. There is a tendency toward student rivalry in gaining favors from the teacher. Antagonisms may be released in the harassing of scapegoats.

C. Anarchy

1. All persons are completely free from group policies and decisions. Students may make group decisions which are in conflict with the decisions of higher jurisdictional groups. Thus, the students, both as individuals and as a group, may do entirely as they please. There may be student rivalry to organize unstructured situations.
2. The teacher suggests projects and activities which the students may carry out, if they desire.
3. It is not necessary that alternatives be presented or that decisions be made.
4. The teacher does not make any attempt to evaluate the behavior or learnings of individuals or the group.
5. Students are completely independent of the teacher.

6. It is not required that group decisions be made.
7. Students may do as they please, cooperate if so inclined or fight like cats and dogs.[11]

WISDOM AND DEMOCRATIC EDUCATION

Since the persons making decisions in a democracy must abide by and live with their decisions, it would be to their own self-interest to be as wise as possible in the making of decisions. Another factor which may foster wisdom is that, when democratic decisions prove to be unwise, a people as a whole may make other decisions. The opportunity for self-repair and change, implemented in the democratic process, seems likely to foster the adoption of wiser decisions.

Democracy does not require any fixed amount of popular education. Conceivably, a democratic people might decide not to support any system of education whatever. However, in terms of how much education is valuable and wise, a democratic people need as much as they can afford. Since democratic decisions are only as wise and discerning as the persons making them, democratic groups must provide an optimal degree of reflective education. It is hoped that enhanced wisdom, fostered by enhanced educational opportunities, will lead to a wiser and more humane future. Although democracy does not guarantee achievement of such a future, the democratic process, when contrasted with autocracy and anarchy, is more likely than the others to provide opportunities to promote group wisdom and increase the quality of human living.

Are our schools democratic? Are most teachers confused?

SELECTED REFERENCES

Arnstine, Donald, *Philosophy of Education—Learning and Schooling.* New York: Harper & Row, 1967, Chap. 5. A major portion of this chapter is

---

[11] For studies in this area see Ronald Lippitt and Ralph K. White, "An Experimental Study of Leadership and Group Life" in *Readings in Social Psychology.* Theodore M. Newcomb and Eugene L. Hartley, eds. (New York: Henry Holt and Company, 1947), pp. 315–30. *Also see* Kurt Lewin, *Resolving Social Conflicts* (New York: Harper & Row, 1948), pp. 71–83.

devoted to a perceptive examination of difficulties and limitations involved in the reflective approach to learning.

Bateman, Grant, William Lieurance, Agnes Manney, and Curtis Osburn, *Helping Children Think.* Tri-University Project in Elementary Education, New York University, 1968. A report of the implementation of the reflective teaching strategy in elementary schools.

Bayles, Ernest E., *Democratic Educational Theory.* New York: Harper & Row, Publishers, 1960, Chap. 11. An excellent analysis of the educational implications of democracy.

————, *Pragmatism in Education.* New York: Harper & Row, Publishers, 1966, Chap. 4. A democratic educational program is presented.

Glasser, William, *Schools Without Failure.* New York: Harper & Row, Publishers, 1969. Dr. Glasser presents a challenging program based on increased involvement, relevance, and thinking, as opposed to mere memory drill.

Hunt, Maurice P., and Lawrence E. Metcalf, *Teaching High School Social Studies—Problems in Reflective Thinking and Social Understanding.* New York: Harper & Row, Publishers, 1968, Chap. 9. A challenging analysis of relationships between democracy and reflective learning. Also examine the chapters dealing with problematic areas of culture.

Jent, H. Clay, "Student Attitudes May Have Undemocratic Roots," *Educational Forum* 30, no. 2 (January, 1966): 197–204. Confusions in defining democracy and the educational implications of these confusions are examined. *Also see* Jent's "Watchwords and Catchwords of Democracy," *Phi Delta Kappan* 48, no. 1 (September, 1966): 36–40.

Leonard, George B., *Education and Ecstasy.* New York: Delacorte Press, 1968. A devastating criticism of current educational practices and a creative vision of possible learning ecstasies in 2001 A.D.

Postman, Neil, and Charles Weingartner, *Teaching as a Subversive Activity.* New York: Delacorte Press, 1969. Assaults on popular teaching methods are coupled with thought-provoking proposals for future-centered learning.

Raths, Louis E., Selma Wasserman, Arthur Jonas, and Arnold M. Rothstein, *Teaching for Thinking—Theory and Application.* Columbus, Ohio: Charles E. Merrill Publishing Company, 1967. Provided are specific techniques to help develop thinking in the classroom.

Rogers, Carl R., *Freedom to Learn.* Columbus, Ohio: Charles E. Merrill Publishing Company, 1969. A long-awaited systematic presentation of the Rogerian approach to education.

Wynne, John P., *Philosophies of Education.* New York: Prentice-Hall, 1947, Chap. 19. A basic analysis of many important educational principles from three viewpoints: Educational Authoritarianism, Educational Laissez Faire, and Educational Experimentalism. In certain aspects, these points of view are similar to the autocratic, anarchistic, and democratic positions delineated by the present writer.

THOUGHT AIDS

1. Are most textbooks autocratic? Explain.
2. Many public school teachers appear to teach in autocratic ways. What reasons might be given for the dominance of this type of teaching?
3. To you, what are the strengths and weaknesses of democratic, autocratic, and anarchistic education?
4. Would you recommend that first year teachers basically utilize autocratic teaching procedures? Why or why not?
5. Select a subject matter area and present specific examples of the implications of democratic, autocratic, and anarchistic education in that area.
6. Some educators may argue that since no known teacher consistently follows completely democratic, autocratic, or anarchistic educational procedures, it is a waste of time to learn about the educational implications of precise definitions of democracy, autocracy, and anarchy. Indicate strengths and weaknesses of this argument.
7. The writer has assumed that indoctrinative educational procedures, of necessity, are fostered by totalitarian governments. Present arguments for and against this assumption.
8. Read George Orwell's *1984* and then contrast his description of the educative devices of the totalitarian nation-state of the future with present American and Soviet educative devices.
9. Is it necessary that some subject matter areas, because of their inherent nature, be taught in a totalitarian way? Defend your answer.
10. What inconsistencies and self-contradictions can you formulate?
11. Do you agree with the contention that most teachers are confused? Why or why not?
12. Give examples of teaching procedures which emphasize exploration rather than explanation.

6

Can Autocratic Testing Be Avoided?

"I want my students to be able to think," is a typical response when teachers are asked to describe the abilities they want their students to develop. However, when their students are interviewed, a different picture often emerges. As one noted bitterly, "Sure, they all say that they want us to think, but if I dare to use my brain on tests, I will flunk. They really don't want us to think; they just want us to memorize and then hand back to them what they hand out to us. They want us to parrot-back memorized information." This may not necessarily be a typical student response, but it may be a discerning one and it serves to pinpoint a problem. Although many teachers claim to value thinking things through, they are often viewed by their students as voicing empty platitudes. Some students reason that, if teachers really want thoughtful students, they should give tests that require demonstration of thoughtfulness. Most tests do not require such.

LEVELS OF THINKING

A way to examine testing practices is to note their relationships to three levels of thinking: (1) memory, (2) understanding, and (3) reflection.

Memory-level thinking involves recollection or remembering. It is sheer recall. It involves exact reappearance of previous experience. Facts or answers are restated exactly as they were memorized. Recall of memorized information is fostered.

Understanding-level thinking involves recognition of the meaning of a situation, often immediate. Seeing or sensing means understanding how a situation relates to other situations; how it may be generalized. Through the use of such generalizable insights, a person may successfully apply previously grasped principles to situations that are similar but not identical to previously experienced ones. Understanding-level thinking involves awareness of what must be done to handle a novel situation.

Reflection-level thinking involves an attempt to resolve a problem situation for which the meaning must be reasoned out or thought over. The person attempts to ascertain what to do in an "I-don't-know" situation; it is unclear; it must be studied; various meanings are sought and pondered. Possible solutions must be weighed and examined. Reflective thinking takes time; alternative meanings of unclear situations must be explored. Thus, reflection-level thinking is a process of formulating and testing meanings in situations wherein meanings are not immediately clear.

AUTOCRATIC TESTING

The basic goal of autocratic teaching is to indoctrinate or inculcate specially privileged truths. Autocratic tests are designed to determine the degree of absorption and retention of such truths. Students are tested on their abilities to retain and understand the "correct" truths that have been transmitted to them. They are to demonstrate that they can hand back the specially-privileged facts and principles which were handed to them. Such tests require memory-level and understanding-level thinking.

DEMOCRATIC TESTING

Effective participation in a democratic society involves being able to weigh alternatives and to make choices based thereon. Education in such decision-making is precisely what the method of reflective study is about. Rather than merely storing up transmitted knowledge, students in democratic-reflective schools are encouraged to develop abilities to raise and resolve problems they cannot immediately answer, yet which they feel a need to confront. Demonstration of student abilities to deal reflectively with problems is emphasized in democratic testing programs. The student must be put in a *novel* situation, one that is so problematic that he cannot quickly determine its meaning; he must cast about for possible solutions. He must work through to an understanding of the situation. Reflective testing is designed to determine how competent a student is in recognizing a problem, formulating possible hypotheses or solutions, establishing appropriate criteria, and testing the hypothetical solutions on the basis of those criteria. A reflective teacher should always be aware of the possibility that unanticipated problem-solutions may better satisfy recognized test-criteria than will the more conventional solutions the teacher may expect to receive.

Although emphasis in democratic testing programs is on demonstration of reflective abilities, memory-level as well as understanding-level testing can be democratically conducted, as long as both students and teacher understand the situation. For example, currently applicable criteria might involve using a memory-level test in order to ascertain how many rote items students can remember under a given set of circumstances. (For example, how many nonsense words can be memorized in a given period of time.) Also, if currently applicable criteria require determining whether a given principle is understood, an understanding-level set of novel situations in which students are to demonstrate their abilities to apply understandings should be designed and administered. Tests become autocratic only when one interpretation or principle is taken to be the *only* proper one, with the tacit assumption that any and all others are not to be tolerated. In contrast, ability to examine beliefs critically is of central concern in democratic testing.

Since reflective items take time, students probably will be able to deal, in a given period of time, with fewer reflective items than with understanding-level items. Also, test items that are on a reflective level for one student may be on understanding level for another, and those on understanding level for one may be on memory level for another.

OPEN-BOOK TESTING

Memory-level testing involves evaluation of student ability to recall information, perhaps correct, perhaps incorrect. In order to avoid testing for retention of memorized information, and to be assured that testing is on understanding or reflective levels, any information needed to deal effectively with test items should be freely available to students. They should have access to reference materials, textbooks, class notes, formulae, dictionaries, etc. It is fine if students can remember the necessary information, but if not, it should be readily accessible; tests for understanding should be "open-book."

If tests are given in order to ascertain a student's ability to apply general principles and/or solve problems, he should be free to utilize any materials needed for demonstrating *his* ability; of course, the test papers of his fellow students should be excepted. Understanding-level open-book tests require questions that involve handling or applying items of information in novel situations. Test-items must be new and unique since, if previously seen or thought through, they may be answered correctly on the basis of memory rather than through interpretation and application of principles.

OBJECTIVE VERSUS ESSAY TESTS

Debates over the relative merits of objective and essay tests have raged for many years. The writer has no desire to add more fuel to the fire. More relevant to this examination of testing procedures is the question of whether these types of tests *could* be used as reflective-testing instruments. Therefore, a brief analysis of possible uses of these two types of tests seems to be in order. The label, "controlled answer" test, seems to be a better description of the true-false, alternative-response, multiple-choice, matching, or completion-type tests than does the label, "objective," since such tests may not be free from subjectivity or bias. For example, how can test items be chosen, or stated, except in a subjective way? How can the decision on acceptable answers be other than the test maker's personal decision? And, does not personal bias also determine to what grade a given score will be assigned? Thus, the test maker's personal decisions, opinions, biases, or even prejudices cannot help but make a so-called "objective" test highly subjective. Conversely, an essay or "subjective" test may achieve a high degree of "objectivity," if scored on the basis of definite, clearly recognized criteria.

Whether it be objective or essay, in order to score a test in a generally impersonal and impartial manner, it would seem that some definite aspects of a student's test performance must be known. The first factor is the student's answer to an item; another involves his interpretation of the meaning of the item. As teachers know, many words normally have two or more meanings; how can one be sure exactly what certain key words mean to any particular student who takes the test? A third factor involves the extent of the body of information used by a student in arriving at his answer. More than a few may know even more than the test maker expected. And what about the degree of logic exhibited by a test-taker in organizing his information to arrive at his answer? Is the answer in harmony with the data or principles drawn upon?

In an objective test, usually only the student's answer is ascertained, and even in essay-type tests, clear criteria or standards usually are not made explicit. Thus, both types of tests may turn out to be vulnerable to the passing conviction or arbitrary whim of the examiner. However, through use of group review-and-analysis periods as well as of individual conferences, the factors involved in student responses to objective-test items may be fairly accurately and objectively ascertained. Through use of clearly stated and understood criteria, essay tests also may be made fairly objective. In summary, both types of tests tend to be both objective and subjective, the degree of each depending upon the test maker.

Both objective and essay-type tests may be used in evaluating progress toward either autocratic or democratic objectives. Both types may be constructed so as to measure student ability to memorize and recall presumed information (be it correct or not). Conversely, both types may be constructed and used to test student ability to apply principles or generalizations, or interpret "facts," in order to cope successfully with novel situations.

It should be noted that evaluation of pupil progress may be based on many factors other than performance on formal objective or essay tests. For example, evaluation may also be based on written and oral reports; on teacher observation of study skills, and of leadership and initiative shown in discussion groups; on projects such as scrapbooks, notebooks, and displays; on participation in group activities; and on teacher conferences with individual students.

ANARCHISTIC TESTING

The basic objective of anarchistic education is presumably to allow each student to grow to his fullest capacity by freeing him to follow his own self-directed interests. Each student may follow his own desires as to whether or not he will judge his own activities. If he chooses to judge them, he alone determines how they will be judged.

He may ask teachers and/or fellow students to suggest possible ways to judge his accomplishments, but he alone determines which judgment, if any, he will use. He may even choose to take a standardized achievement test, but he alone determines whether or not he will accept the test results as indicative of his progress.

CONCLUSION

Many teachers claim that they want their students to think; but also require their students, under fear of receiving lower grades, to demonstrate conformity to predetermined standards by responding "correctly" on tests. They indicate that they want their students to develop skills in thinking things through, yet test on abilities to retain and recognize right information. For grading purposes, students are compared to others in terms of how many "facts" they are able to remember. Such widespread inconsistencies between commonly stated teacher beliefs and actual testing and grading practices may be a potent factor contributing to current student frustration and unrest. If teachers really desire to teach and test democratically, reflective teaching and testing procedures may be effective ways to achieve these objectives.

SELECTED REFERENCES

Bayles, Ernest E., *Democratic Educational Theory*. New York: Harper & Row, Publishers, 1960, Chap. 14. A lucid analysis of memory, understanding, and reflection-level testing. Also see his *The Theory and Practice of Teaching*. New York: Harper & Row, Publishers, 1950, Chap. 15.

Bigge, Morris L., *Learning Theories for Teachers*. New York: Harper & Row, Publishers, 1964, Chap. 11. Bigge examines memory, understanding, and reflection-level learning and teaching, and then relates these to conflicting types of testing.

Englehart, Max D., *Improving Classroom Testing* ("What Research Says to the Teacher" Series, No. 31). Washington, D.C.: Department of Classroom Teachers, National Education Association, 1964. A good brief introduction to problems involved in testing.

Glasser, William, *Schools Without Failure.* New York: Harper & Row, Publishers, 1969. In chapters 6 and 7 Dr. Glasser suggests some perceptive ways to improve current testing practices.

Gronlund, Norman E., *Measurement and Evaluation in Teaching.* New York: The Macmillan Company, 1965, Chap. 9. Samples of interpretive test items are presented.

Hunt, Maurice, and Lawrence Metcalf, *Teaching High School Social Studies.* New York: Harper & Row, Publishers, 1968, Chap. 11. A presentation of ways to test for understanding, for attitudes, and for thinking.

Stanley, Julian C., *Measurement in Today's Schools.* Englewood Cliffs, New Jersey: Prentice-Hall, Inc., 1964. A basic text. Particularly note Chapter 8.

THOUGHT AIDS

1. Contrast the assumptions underlying democratic, autocratic, and anarchistic types of testing.
2. Would an autocratic teacher be acting in harmony with his basic assumptions if his teaching and testing program was consistently on an understanding level? Defend your answer.
3. Debate the issue: Resolved, that testing should be abolished.
4. Some educators believe that slow students make better scores on memory-level tests than on reflection-level tests. Thus, it is believed that democratic tests discriminate against slow learners. Indicate possible arguments for and against this belief.
5. In this chapter, the idea was advanced that open-book tests are democratic. Could a consistently autocratic teacher also utilize open-book tests? Defend your answer.
6. Read Ernest E. Bayles, *Democratic Educational Theory,* Chapter 14—Appraisal of Pupil Progress. On page 227, Bayles implies that objective-type examinations and reflective testing are incompatible. Contrast Bayles' viewpoint with that of the present writer in the chapter section entitled, "Objective Versus Essay Tests." Which viewpoint, to you, is more adequate? Why?
7. What is your reaction to the following situation? A teacher tells his students that he wants them to learn to think, but if they dare to present thoughts which are at variance with those held by the teacher, they are penalized by the teacher.
8. Prepare sample test items in your major subject area. Ask your fellow students to evaluate the validity of the items on the basis of the three testing levels discussed in this chapter.

7

What Does Cheating Show?

When test time arrives, many students use ingenious ways to smuggle and use basic information. "Cheat sheets" have been secreted in wrist watch cases, dummy pens and pencils, match covers, and cigarette packs and lighters. Students have written information on sticks of gum and then chewed up the incriminating evidence. Data have been written in strategic locations on clothing and skin. Shirt cuffs and sleeves have been most popular with male students. Women have found the skin inside the leg above the knee to be an area not closely inspected by discreet male teachers.

In this transistorized age, some students turn to tape recorders camouflaged as hearing aids. This cheating technique requires foresight, since the fake hearing aid must be worn to class throughout the term. Students who are not so persevering can use special pencils to write invisible basic information on notebooks or test papers. Such information becames visible only through special glasses prepared for dishonest gamblers.

The popularity of student use of unauthorized information has been interpreted by many teachers as indicative of a moral decline in education. Although such speculations about student morality are often fascinating, this chapter deals with a different aspect of the cheating problem: What does cheating show about teachers? When teachers prohibit student use of information during tests, what is revealed about these teachers?

THE CHEATING "PYRAMID"

As illustrated in the following "pyramid," types of cheating are based on types of testing which are based on types of teaching which are, in turn, based on types of thinking which are valued in certain types of societies.

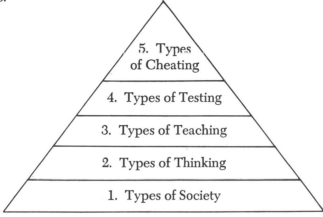

1. *Types of Society.* Societies generally may be classified as tending to be either totalitarian or democratic. Totalitarian societies tend to emphasize unquestioning acceptance of "The Truth." In contrast, since democratic societies assume that the masses should be able to govern themselves, the ability to question, examine, and evaluate alternative courses of action is of central value.

2. *Types of Thinking.* Since acceptance of The Truth is valued in totalitarian countries, emphasis is given to memory and understanding-level thinking. In contrast, the reflective thought process of weighing alternatives and making decisions is a basic ability needed in democracies.

3. *Types of Teaching.* The role of the teacher in a totalitarian society is to induce students to memorize The Truth, as it is defined by the ruling clique. Specially privileged right answers are indoctrinated or inculcated. Students are conditioned to value what the rulers value. In contrast, democratic teachers stimulate student abilities to analyze alternatives by involving the students in meaningful problems

which they proceed to examine and resolve. Students are placed in problem situations which are so novel that they must pause and "think it over" in order to work their way to a solution.

4. *Types of Testing.*   Since totalitarian testing emphasizes checking to see whether the students really know the right answers, student use of various sources of information during test periods is strictly taboo. In contrast, democratic-type testing involves confronting students with problem situations which are so novel that they must determine and evaluate alternatives. Democratic teachers then check the effectiveness of the students' attempts to solve the problems. Since students are to be tested not on their abilities to accept right answers, but rather on their abilities to solve problems, they should be free to use any materials in their open-book exams except the test papers of fellow students.

5. *Types of Cheating.*   The opening discussion of common cheating techniques showed that these techniques involve secreting, in various ingenious ways, such things as notes, important formulae, and other types of information. What kinds of teachers would classify the use of basic information as cheating? It appears that only those teachers who emphasize memory-level thinking, who use right-answer handout teaching procedures, and who test for recall of right answers would consistently define such student activities as cheating.

In contrast, open-book reflective testing by democratic teachers probably would eliminate much of the present cheating, since most of the activities now classified by totalitarian teachers as cheating would be accepted as legitimate student use of information in demonstrating problem solving abilities. Cheating on reflective tests would not only involve obtaining the answers of fellow students, but also would involve noting how they arrive at their answers. Such cheating may be hindered through student awareness that copying another student's answer does not necessarily provide, for the copyist, an adequate reason or justification for his answer. However, few educators would be so naive as to claim that open-book testing will eliminate cheating. Reflective-testing probably would challenge students to rise to new levels of creative ingenuity in devising ways to cheat.

CONCLUSION

The use of notes, formulae, and other information can be branded as cheating only when memorization of right answers is being tested. Cheating practices reveal that many teachers apparently are indulging in totalitarian teaching and testing procedures and, therefore, are thwarting the reflective abilities needed in a democratic society.

SELECTED REFERENCES

"A Startling Survey on College Cribbing," *Life* 58, no. 5 (February 5, 1965): 84. A study by the Bureau of Applied Research at Columbia University shows that students who cheat are under great parental pressure.

Coppola, August F., "B.A. in Cheating," *Life* 50, no. 25 (June 23, 1961): 13–14. An entertaining account of ingenious cheating techniques.

Ellison, Jerome, "American Disgrace: College Cheating," *The Saturday Evening Post* 232, no. 28 (January 9, 1960): 13, 58–59. Note the type of cheating which is examined in this article.

Laurita, Raymond, Robert Grinder, W. C. Becker, C. H. Madsen, Jr., and Roger Burton, "How We Encourage Cheating—A Forum-in-Print." *The PTA Magazine* 60, no. 6 (February, 1966): 21–23. Home and teacher pressures are presented as encouraging cheating.

"The Amount of Cheating on U.S. Campuses," *U.S. News and World Report* 58, no. 6 (February 8, 1965): 10. Studies indicate that cheating is more widespread than officials realize.

Weldon, John Carter, "Cheating." *NEA Journal* 50, no. 2 (February, 1961): 43–44. Lack of confidence is suggested as a basic cause of cheating.

THOUGHT AIDS

1. Look under "Cheating" in *The Education Index* for current articles on cheating. Do the articles deal only with totalitarian types of cheating? Why do you think this is so?
2. Do you think that student use of unauthorized information is evidence of a moral decline among students? Why or why not?
3. Do you agree with the contention that certain types of cheating practices are based on certain types of teaching and testing? Why or why not?
4. Do you believe that many teachers force their students to cheat? Why or why not?

5. A cartoon in the *Rocky Mountain News,* Denver, Colorado, February 17, 1960, p. 41, portrays a father standing at the door of his children's play room. His two pre-school age children are playing a card game. The father is saying to an onlooking visitor, "It's a very educational game. Already the kids have learned how to cheat." What do you think this cartoon says about our way of life?

6. Analyze the film, "Cheating," on the basis of the major concepts presented in this chapter.

7. Some writers believe that cheating tends to occur when students are pressured to obtain high grades. Do you agree? Are grades valid indicators of student achievement? If you do not agree with present systems of grading, what type of evaluative system would you set up? Why?

8

How Should Students
Be Disciplined?

Whether a teacher is an effective disciplinarian has been credited with being the most important factor in predicting teacher success. However, at least three major approaches to discipline are discernible: (1) authoritarian, (2) permissive, and (3) developmental. What are strengths and weaknesses of each type?

AUTHORITARIAN DISCIPLINE

Authoritarian discipline or classroom control will be presented first because it has been widely accepted by the public as what discipline means and because it has been used by many teachers. In this concept of classroom control, the teacher is the superior authority who dominates his inferiors, the students. Responsibility for control of the classroom resides in the teacher. The extreme of this concept was described by a student who said that his teacher tells the students exactly what to do, how to do it, when to do it, and with whom it is to be done. Responsibility for student conduct in the classroom rests squarely on the shoulders of the teacher, the adult authority figure.

The teacher compels conformity to rules and regulations by force, if necessary. Responsibility for determining acceptable behavior lies outside the student. His task is to submit to order and control and obey regulations.

Classroom emphasis is on quiet, order, passivity, and subjection to rule. The teacher sets firm limits through emphasizing strict teacher-established rules and regulations. Student behavior is controlled through teacher approval of good behavior and prompt teacher punishment of bad. Misbehavior is penalized and good behavior rewarded. Students are "kept in line" by external strictures and formal rules. This form of discipline is not new. It has its American roots in the early schools of this country and it is interesting to note that in modified form it still exists 300 years later.

Criticisms of Authoritarian Discipline

Granting that the authoritarian type of control may be efficient, what are the students learning? They appear to be learning to respond out of fear of punishment, rather than out of an understanding of appropriate behavior. Students tend to become robots, and compliance with orders is automatic. Students cannot respond freely. They are so tightly controlled in mental strait jackets that they cannot outwardly express their own thoughts and feelings. Healthy personality growth is inhibited, since free expression and autonomy are not allowed to develop. They are not allowed to build personal integrity, since so rigid a conformity is enforced on them that they lack the opportunity to test and try themselves. They feel no need to think, since they know the teacher will do it for them. Besides, if they do think, they may think incorrectly and be punished for it. The effects of authoritarian group controls were studied by Kurt Lewin, Ronald Lippitt, and Ralph K. White. They concluded that, under authoritarian leadership, students lack self-reliance; they are dependent, leaning heavily on directions by the authority. There is no group initiative. Students exhibit apathy and hopeless submission to the powerful leader. They tend to make demands for attention, to be discontent, to be unfriendly, and to take little pride in their work. In such a punitive setting, student frustrations result in aggressive, destructive, and hostile behavior. Hostility within authoritarian groups leads to specific individuals being singled out as "scapegoats" for persecution. When left alone for any length of time, the classroom atmosphere tends to degenerate into noisy disorganization. To its critics, this type of discipline is in itself a principal cause of discipline problems. Teacher domination piles frustration on frustration and results in disorder and student rebellion.

PERMISSIVE DISCIPLINE

Although the permissive or anarchistic concept of discipline has ancient roots going back long before Jean Jacques Rousseau, it has been championed in this century by William H. Kilpatrick's progressive-education movement and by certain mental hygienists. The teacher's task is to permit the felt needs of students to be satisfied. The teacher is to foster a warm, permissive, accepting, and non-directive atmosphere. The student's inner self-direction is respected and encouraged in an informal climate. Free expression and lack of pressure are emphasized. There are no restraints or external controls placed on the students.

Discipline in the permissive classroom is individual self-discipline. Intrinsic student interests and motivations cause the students to discipline or control their own actions in order to achieve their own purposes. In order to pursue activities having a purpose to the student himself, he must discipline or govern his own actions from within. When a student is not free to meet his own needs, he is frustrated, thwarted, and warped psychologically. In contrast, in a permissive atmosphere of self-discipline, students tend to be highly creative, spontaneous, and original. Since each student has the freedom to make his own decisions, his own experiences, not autocratic teachers, direct him toward what works out well and he consciously avoids what does not. Students from such non-directive classrooms tend to be the most socialized, cooperative, and best accepted students because they have been free to develop self-respect.

Criticisms of Permissive Discipline

Permissive self-discipline is unrealistic because under such a system students do not achieve knowledge of the limitations which society demands of them. In such a program of sheer indulgence, students are never made aware of the realistic societal limitations to which they must eventually adjust. The student who has not learned to control his feelings is in for a rude shock whenever he enters life situations which demand conformity to the established rules of society.

The effects of anarchistic self-control were also studied by Kurt Lewin, Ronald Lippitt, and Ralph White. In a laissez-faize atmosphere, students played around and were unproductive, dissatisfied, and bored with their lack of accomplishment. They demonstrated a high degree of discontent and aggressiveness.

Indulgence and frustration, not true mastery and control of oneself, are encouraged by permissiveness. The laissez-faire attitude toward discipline is likely to produce a confused and disorganized person who continually tests the situations which confront him in a frantic effort to see if any rules exist.

DEVELOPMENTAL DISCIPLINE

Students are given the opportunity to develop within recognized and changeable rules and regulations. The student is not made into a robot, nor is he placed entirely on his own. His growth toward self-discipline is guided by rules which he understands and which he may criticize and may help to change to more acceptable rules. The teacher helps students to grow toward self-guidance and self-control by helping them acquire the ability to make decisions intelligently, with skill, promptness, and finesse. Students are taught to think their way through discipline problems. As students share in responsibility for group behavior, they learn to control problem situations by thinking of possible alternative solutions, by weighing each in terms of its probable effects, and by choosing the most adequate one. If students are confounded by problems, the teacher is ready to suggest alternatives. There are reasoned discussions of rules, with the focus on their causes and consequences.

In order that students gradually may learn to direct their actions toward socially acceptable behavior, school situations must allow them to make mistakes and suffer the consequences. For the effects of actions to be real, students must make choices and then live with the bitter or sweet fruits their actions produce. Developmental discipline involves guided growth to self-discipline.

Criticisms of Developmental Discipline

It is apparent that many students do not have the maturity needed in order to participate successfully in making decisions about their own behavior. Students simply cannot be allowed to participate in making decisions about questions which must be decided on the basis of professional competence and administrative responsibility. Attempts to introduce student participation in decision making into these areas lead only to aimless activity, disunity, disrespect, and insecurity. If students are allowed to make mistakes, will they be allowed to make mistakes which are irreparable? If not, it is apparent that the advocates of developmental discipline are simply sugar-coating authoritarian discipline since, when the chips are down, school personnel are imposing their own rules on the students.

CONCLUSION

Authoritarian types of discipline have been criticized as fostering dependent robots, not mature, self-directive persons. Permissive discipline has been attacked for being unrealistic, since indulged students are not prepared to cope with the societal limitations they must accept and adjust to when they enter adulthood. Developmental discipline seems to be weak in that many students do not have the maturity needed to participate successfully in developmental disciplinary situations.

What is the best type of discipline?

WHAT ARE THE MOST SERIOUS
TYPES OF DISCIPLINE PROBLEMS?

Research indicates that there are a number of notable discrepancies between the discipline problems teachers believe are the most serious and those which mental hygienists believe are the most serious. These differences of opinion were investigated a number of years ago by E. K. Wickman, and several additional studies have been made since that time.[1] The following is a list of 36 traits which teachers and mental hygienists were asked to rank in order of their seriousness: [2]

---

[1] *See* E. K. Wickman, *Children's Behavior and Teachers' Attitudes* (New York: Commonwealth Fund, 1928); Elmer Henry Garinger, *The Administration of Discipline in the High School* (New York: Teachers College, Columbia University, 1936), pp. 81–83; and George A. W. Stouffer, Jr., "Behavior Problems of Children as Viewed by Teachers and Mental Hygienists," *Mental Hygiene* (April, 1952), pp. 271–85.

[2] Lee J. Cronbach, *Educational Psychology* (New York: Harcourt, Brace and Company, 1954), pp. 557–59.

Carelessness	Inquisitiveness	Sullenness
Cheating	Interrupting	Suspiciousness
Cruelty, bullying	Masturbation	Tardiness
Destroying materials	Profanity	Tattling
Disobedience	Obscene notes, talk	Temper tantrums
Domineering	Restlessness	Thoughtlessness
Dreaminess	Shyness	Truancy
Enuresis	Silly, smartness	Unhappiness
Fearfulness	Smoking	Unreliable
Heterosexual activity	Stealing	Unsocial withdrawing
Imaginative lying	Stubbornness	Untruthfulness
Impertinence	Suggestible	Whispering

The mental-health clinicians disagreed with the teachers in regard to the relative seriousness of many of the disciplinary problems. For example, heterosexual activity and masturbation were considered by teachers to be among the most serious offenses, whereas the hygienists rated them among the least serious. Shyness was rated by the mental hygienists as being among the most serious discipline problems, whereas teachers rated shyness as almost the least serious. Why are there such differences of opinion between teachers and mental health authorities?

Mental hygienists apparently emphasize attitudes rather than overt behavior. They believe that shyness, unsociability, and other recessive traits are more serious than the manifest problems of classroom control that have traditionally disturbed teachers. They are more concerned with behavior that indicates social and emotional maladjustment and tensions, rather than with superficial behavior, such as profanity, which may disrupt the learning environment of a classroom. Mental health experts are not concerned about smoking, profanity, whispering, and sexual experimentation because, no matter how irritating they may be to a teacher, they are all actions that most normal students will try at one time or another. These actions may get the pupil in trouble, but they do not indicate personality disturbances. These acts may cause inconvenience, and they are signs of immaturity, but they are not signs that something is basically wrong with the student. Both mental health clinicians and teachers placed cruelty and bullying as serious discipline problems. However, instead of rating these activities in terms of their disruption of the classroom, the hygienists evaluated the seriousness of any student offense in terms of carry-over into later life. The hygienists gave emphasis to general attitudes rather than to specific disruptive classroom acts.

In contrast, the types of behavior that teachers believe are serious discipline problems are those which violate the teachers' standards of morality, their authority, and classroom order. Disobedient, disorderly, irresponsible, and untruthful types of behavior concern them. Since school routine is of primary concern to teachers, offenses against the established order and routines of the school are taken to be serious discipline problems. Teachers are more concerned about their own welfare, in terms of classroom order, than with the emotional maladjustments of students, which might lead to disabling habits and attitudes.

Who is right, the mental hygienists or the teachers? What are the most serious types of discipline problems?

DO COMPETENT TEACHERS SUCCESSFULLY HANDLE DISCIPLINE PROBLEMS?

Many school administrators and some teachers appear to believe that the important causes, and cures, of discipline problems lie within the teachers' power. They tend to believe that if a teacher cannot control a student or a class, it is the teacher's fault. To them, if a teacher is competent, he should be able to handle any discipline problem that may arise.

On the other hand, mental-health authorities believe that there are many discipline problems that are beyond a teacher's control. For example, even the best teacher cannot maintain an adequate learning-atmosphere in a classroom where there are students with pathological personality disorders. There also are many home-caused problems as well as intrinsic, personality and group problems that require psychiatric and social-welfare skills that are outside the competency areas of most classroom teachers.

Do competent teachers successfully handle all types of discipline problems? May a good teacher fail, in certain classroom situations, to be a successful disciplinarian?

What Is the Major Cause of Teacher Failure?

The traditional liberal arts position has been that if a teacher knows the subject matter of his field, he will be a successful teacher. Content knowledge, not methodological ability, is the determinative factor in teacher success. The major cause of teacher failure is inadequate subject matter preparation. The educationists are to blame for this state of affairs since they require students to take psychology and education courses when the students should be taking valuable content courses.

In contrast, most of the studies of unsuccessful teachers indicate that inability to handle discipline problems is the major cause of teacher failure, particularly for the inexperienced teacher. Knowledge of subject matter, on the other hand, appears to be a relatively unimportant factor in terms of teacher failure. Poor maintenance of discipline ranks near the top in all surveys of teachers' difficulties.

What is the major cause of teacher failure? Is lack of knowledge of effective disciplinary procedures the most important factor, or are the liberal arts professors right in their belief that lack of subject matter knowledge is the major cause of this problem?

ARE DISCIPLINE AND PUNISHMENT THE SAME THING?

To most students and adults, discipline is a nasty and unpleasant word. For most people, it is synonymous with punishment; and school discipline is equated with the idea of corporal punishment. Punishment is often automatically taken to be the immediate and effective remedy for most discipline problems.

On the other hand, it is claimed that if punishment does not get to the root of a discipline problem, it may only shut a student up for a while, without ever touching on his real trouble. He may be mixed up, or determined to hurt people in reprisal. Punishment may be necessary in certain disciplinary situations, but the creatively effective teacher will seek ways of dealing constructively with individual students. Consideration, the feeling of success, and friendship may be more effective than punishment in most problem situations. Discipline is training, but not all training involves punishment. The imparting of an orderly, purposeful, skillful and responsible method of meeting life's problems does not necessarily involve punishment. From this viewpoint, training toward right conduct and prompt and effective action may involve punishment, but it is not synonymous with punishment.

Are discipline and punishment the same thing?

DO GUIDANCE AND DISCIPLINE MIX?

Does discipline enhance or interfere with the counselor-student relationship in the classroom? Those who believe that discipline enhances the counselor-student relationship point out that both have always been present in the parent-child relationship. Does disciplining students hurt a teacher's counseling relationships with his students? Parents, clergymen, and good teachers have long demonstrated that good discipline does not diminish one's ability to establish effective counseling relationships. Without assuming both guidance and disciplinary functions, the teacher is dealing with something less than the whole student in the school setting, and the teacher's total effectiveness with all his students is limited to that extent.

On the other hand, some educators believe that discipline interferes with the warm and permissive relationship guidance authorities claim is necessary in order for adequate counseling to occur. To them, guidance requires an accepting and non-punitive climate. The teacher, however, must enforce classroom discipline and carry out punishment. Since the teacher's disciplinary functions often represent a threat to students, few of them will be willing to freely share with him in a guidance relationship. From this viewpoint, it is difficult, if not impossible, to mix guidance and discipline.

Can guidance and discipline be mixed in the classroom?

SELECTED REFERENCES

Blount, Nathan S., and Herbert J. Klausmeier, *Teaching in the Secondary School.* New York: Harper & Row, Publishers, 1968, Chap. 15. Note particularly the analysis of types of classroom climates.

Glasser, William, *Schools Without Failure.* New York: Harper & Row, Publishers, 1969. Dr. Glasser presents a very thought-provoking and challenging concept of discipline.

Gray, Jenny, *The Teacher's Survival Guide.* Palo Alto, Calif.: Fearon Publishers, 1967. A guide to help the new teacher deal more effectively with discipline problems.

Holt, John, *How Children Fail.* New York: Pitman Publishing Corporation, 1964. A disquieting dissection of why schools often fail to meet the needs of students. *Also see* Holt's *How Children Learn.*

La Mancousa, Katherine C., *We Do Not Throw Rocks at the Teacher.* Scranton, Pennsylvania: International Textbook Company, 1966. A stimulating excursion into problems of classroom control.

McDonald, Blanche, and Leslie Nelson, *Successful Classroom Control*. Dubuque, Iowa: Wm. C. Brown Company, Publishers, 1959. Practical techniques for improving classroom control.

Muuss, Rolf, *First-Aid for Classroom Discipline Problems*. New York: Holt, Rinehart and Winston, 1962. Causes and cures of various types of discipline problems are suggested.

Nordberg, H. Orville, James M. Bradfield, and William C. Odell, *Secondary School Teaching*. New York: The Macmillan Company, 1962, Chap. 10. Autocratic and democratic attitudes toward discipline are contrasted.

Schain, Robert L., *Discipline—How to Establish and Maintain It*. Englewood Cliffs, New Jersey: Teachers Practical Press, distributed by Atherton Press, Inc., 1961. A practical guide to effective disciplinary techniques.

Steeves, Frank, *Fundamentals of Teaching in Secondary Schools*. New York: Odyssey Press, 1962, Chap. 16. Note the suggestions for maintaining adequate classroom control.

THOUGHT AIDS

1. Is it proper for students to be required to carry out learning activities as punishment? Why? For example, should students be required to write term papers when they have committed some infraction of classroom regulations?
2. How might teachers cause discipline problems?
3. What discipline problems, if any, probably are beyond the ability of the good teacher to cope with? Why?
4. See the film, "Maintaining Classroom Discipline." Do you agree with the beliefs expressed in the film? Why?
5. Analyze possible educational implications of the following quote: "A hundred years ago persons who were ill were bled to cure their ailments. Modern medicine recognizes the futility of this procedure. But children are beaten and scolded even today because parents are still in the dark ages of mental hygiene conduct." L. F. Schaffer. *The Psychology of Adjustment* (Boston: Houghton Mifflin Company, 1936), p. 500.
6. What is the most important cause of discipline problems? Why?
7. Evaluate the discipline implications of the following quote: "I have taught in high school for ten years. During that time I have given assignments among others to a murderer, an evangelist, a pugilist, a thief, and an imbecile. The murderer was a quiet little boy who sat on the

front seat and regarded me with pale blue eyes; the evangelist, easily the most popular boy in school, had the lead in the junior play; the pugilist lounged by the window and let loose at intervals with a raucous laugh that startled even the geraniums; the thief was a gay-hearted Lothario with a song on his lips; and the imbecile, a soft-eyed little animal seeking the shadows. The murderer awaits death in the state penitentiary; the evangelist has lain a year now in the village churchyard; the pugilist lost an eye in a brawl in Hong Kong; the thief, by standing on tiptoe, can see the windows of my room from the county jail; the once-gentle-eyed little moron beats his head against a padded cell in the state asylum. All of these pupils once sat in my room, sat and looked gravely across worn, brown desks. I must have been a great help to these pupils—I taught them the rhyming scheme of the Elizabethan sonnet and how to diagram a complex sentence." N. J. W. "I Taught Them All," *The Clearing House* 12, no. 3 (November, 1937), pp. 151, 192.

8. Which is the more serious discipline problem, an unruly student who is disrupting the class or a shy and retiring student in the same class? Why?

9. Listen to the record by Myron S. Olson, "Developing Classroom Discipline," produced by Educational Recording Services, Los Angeles, California. Particularly note Dr. Olson's ten rules.

10. R. M. is 16 years old and is in the 10th grade in an average size high school. He has become unruly and surly in his English and history classes. He is one of the better students in physical education and industrial arts. What types of discipline might his teachers use? What type or types would you recommend? Why?

11. J. D. is an average student in his 11th grade class. He is inattentive at times. He is painfully shy and often appears to be daydreaming. What should be done, if anything, to correct his behavior? Why?

12. Read William Glasser's *Schools Without Failure*. Do you agree with his concept of discipline? Why or why not?

9

Is Teaching a Good Career?

On the one hand, many educators claim that teaching is advancing toward new and challenging opportunities. It is an exciting and exacting profession with almost unlimited opportunities. Teaching requires "topnotch" ability, real scholarship, and long, careful preparation. Teaching is a satisfying career for those who have ability and drive. Obviously, for those who can measure up to the high standards, teaching is a good career.

On the other hand, critics blast teaching as a degrading condition from which self-respecting persons flee. The average person going into teaching is mediocre because the pay is sickeningly low, advancement is practically nonexistent, and teachers are very low in the status-and-prestige pecking order. Teachers experience public disparagement and exist in "genteel poverty." Obviously, to these critics, teaching is not a good career.

Is teaching a good career?

FINANCIAL STATUS OF TEACHERS

As one wag said, "Money isn't everything, but it's way ahead of whatever's in second place." Money usually is the major gauge of success

82

in our materialistically-centered culture. Although many other factors are important in teaching, such as the joy of seeing students "blossom," the one factor that usually overshadows all others is financial status. In most communities the most popular measure of prestige is income. In order to draw highly competent persons, an occupation in our society usually must provide monetary remuneration markedly above average. What are the present financial conditions in teaching?

Before examining such conditions, a note of caution should be sounded. Teacher compensation involves many complex factors, the most important being salary. However, other forms of compensation, such as medical services and retirement allowances, are often significant factors in the economic status of teachers. Also, although there are marked differentials between college and public school teachers' salaries, between rural and urban salaries, and between salaries in rich and poor states; for the sake of brevity, these will all be lumped together in the statistics presented. Since certain of the references at the end of this chapter go into the details of the economic status of teachers, it is recommended that the reader check the sweeping generalizations presented in this chapter against the facts presented in the references.

What is the status of teachers' salaries when compared with the earnings of other occupational groups? Those who entered business, sales, accounting, and engineering in 1951 had an average annual salary close to $10,000 in 1961. What about the person who entered teaching in 1951? His annual salary in 1960 was less than $5,500. What starts out as an unfavorable situation becomes acute for the person dedicated to a teaching career. In 1954, when the average salary of teachers was $3,815, estimates for budgets required for a family of four at the non-professional wage earner level ranged from $4,285 to $5,500. The average compensation of the *total* instructional staff in the public schools for the school year 1959–60 was about $300 less than the *beginning* salary paid 1960 graduates recruited by business and industry. In 1961, when the average beginning salary for teachers with a bachelor's degree was about $4,100, a general business trainee would start at about $5,200, a salesman at $5,400, an accountant at $5,500, and an engineer at $6,200.

In spite of large increases in teacher salaries, the teacher's relative economic position has continued to deteriorate. In 1967, the average salary of *all* classroom teachers was $6,830. In contrast, the median income of all employed men over 25 years old with no post-high school education was $7,244. In 1968, the average salary of classroom teachers was $7,423. In contrast, the National Science Foundation found that the median salary of scientists with only a bachelor's degree was $12,000 in 1968. Starting salaries in 1968 for male teachers with the bachelor's degree in larger school systems, those with enrollments of 6,000 or more, averaged $5,941. In contrast, the average 1968 starting salary for bachelor's degree holders in accounting was about $8,300, $9,200 for engineers at that level, $8,400 for chemists, and $9,000 for physicists. Average incomes of employees in manufacturing and civilian employees of the federal government are substantially higher than those of teachers. Salary ceilings for teachers are much lower than those in comparable occupations. Teacher salaries are near the national average for all employed persons. It is fairly apparent that the NEA has made little, if any, progress toward its major goal of raising the comparative financial status of teachers.

In his article entitled, "How We Drive Teachers to Quit," Richard Meryman says:

> A Harvard University report described one inevitable result of the relatively poor pay levels in the teaching profession with these words: "They (teachers) live on the fringes of the middle class. But they cannot afford to indulge in the tastes of their peers. . . . They—and their wives and children—make admirable sacrifices. But in doing so, they confirm society's impressions of a lowly group, not quite first-class and deserving of no better than the hand-me-downs of our civilization." [1]

To reduce their sacrifices, many teachers have turned to "moonlighting," a second occupation, to supplement their meager income. As one teacher noted bitterly, "Teaching is an occupation where two have to live as cheap as one." A teacher recently said to the writer, "My daughter, with just a high school education, is making more today than I am with my college degree and twenty-two years experience teaching. She has worked in her position five years and climbed gradually, financially, faster than I." In brief, teaching has been described as "essentially a poor man's profession."

Another way to examine the economic status of teachers in the United States is to compare it with that of teachers in other countries. Teachers in the United States earn more than the teachers in almost all other countries, but this is true for practically every occupation in the United States. When the relative income of American teachers is compared with that of teachers in other countries, a very different picture appears. The ratio in the United States of the teacher's average

---

[1] Richard Meryman, "How We Drive Teachers to Quit," *Life* 53, no. 20 (November 16, 1962): 110.

salary to per capita income is about 1:9. In Belgium it is 4:5; in Denmark it is 3:2; in England it is 2:5; in France it is 5:1; in Germany it is 4:7; and in Israel it is 5:8. It is apparent that the relative economic position of teachers in the United States is much poorer than that of teachers in most of the above countries. This becomes even more significant when it is noted that economists indicate that the average income of employed persons usually is two or three times greater than the national per capita income, and that the remuneration of professional persons usually is five or six times the national per capita income.

Can teaching in the United States attract the kind of people who should be attracted to teaching, and hold them, with the kind of salaries now being paid? Many of the competent students who become teachers are forced out by the insufficient pay in public schools. Those who do go into teaching often leave for more lucrative positions. For approximately one out of every twelve teachers in the public schools this will be his last year in teaching. After five years only one-half of the original number who enter teaching remain in it. After ten years, only ten to fifteen percent of the people prepared for teaching are still in it. The vast majority of "dropouts" from teaching liked to teach, but left because of the poor pay and lack of advancement opportunities. Can competent persons be blamed for shifting to occupations which provide adequate remuneration for their competencies and which satisfy their ambitions and self-respect?

Some have argued that it is in the nature of things for American teachers to be poorly compensated, since teacher salaries come from tax funds and the public is not willing to pay for adequate teacher salaries. Therefore, teachers will always lack fair compensation for their services. However, in rebuttal, it may be noted that the salaries of physicians on the staffs of state medical schools also come from public tax funds. Allowing for differences in years of professional training, the teacher is still paid proportionately far less than the staff physician. Why?

Has teacher income always been substandard? Most of the colonial school teachers were poor in worldly goods. Many supplemented their meager incomes by "moonlighting" as tailors, blacksmiths, and church janitors. Many of the schoolmasters in the middle and southern colonies were indentured servants. One comment on teachers being advertised for sale in the latter part of the seventeenth century was that the only difference between teachers and other tradesmen was that they did not "usually fetch so good a price." In 1843, Horace Mann surveyed a town and found that shoemakers, carpenters, painters, blacksmiths, harness makers, and cabinet makers were receiving fifty to one hundred percent more than the district school teachers. In 1863, the average annual salary of teachers in California was $387, while that of a servant girl was $300, plus board. At the turn of the century, the teachers' salary status was still that of a semiskilled person.

Why has teacher remuneration remained low, lagging far behind occupations requiring equivalent periods of training? Why must college graduates be financially penalized for going into teaching? Why should their income be approximately half of that enjoyed by workers in other occupations which require equivalent training? Why, in relation to other workers, have teachers made so little significant economic progress in the last thirty years? Why has the National Education Association failed markedly to advance the comparative financial welfare of teachers, when one of its avowed major purposes is to do just that? Why has the NEA's program for promoting the relative financial status of teachers been basically ineffective for decades?

SOCIAL STATUS OF TEACHERS

As could be expected, there appears to be a close relationship between economic and social status of teachers, since teacher status seems to be a reflection of the value, or lack of it, placed upon teaching. A person's social status may be defined as his place in the prestige system of society. The most popular measure of prestige is income. Therefore, it might be assumed that the image, recognition, rank, or power position given to teachers would be about average, since that is where teacher income falls.

Before moving into a discussion of the social status of teachers, some reasons for caution should be noted. This will be a cursory presentation of a highly complex area. Also, acceptable research studies have been difficult to set up. Most of the studies have for various reasons been suspect on the basis of bias and unrepresentative sampling. Many of the studies have been based on ratings or rankings of occupations. However, not all participants in an occupation have equal social status. For example, the social status of teachers tends to rise as the grade level taught becomes higher. Also, many of the studies are based on social classes, yet these are on a continuum, merging into each other. Therefore, any breaking up of this continuum into discrete divisions is rather arbitrary. Recognizing these and other limitations, some tentative generalizations will be presented.

Social status studies generally indicate that public school teachers are given an average ranking in extensive lists of representative occupations. Public school teachers are most commonly identified with the lower-middle class. Their origins in the social classification are usually somewhat lower than middle class. Many are recruited from the top of the lower half of the population. Approximately seventy percent attain middle-class social standing. Thus, the average teacher is in the lower fringes of the middle class.

Traditionally, teaching has been considered by many to be an inexpensive avenue of advancement to the middle class. Myron Lieberman has noted in his book, *Education As a Profession*, that not only does a majority of teachers come from homes that are "culturally unpromising if not impoverished," but in their aspiring to middle-class status they tend to overemphasize the values and customs of the middle class. As documented by August B. Hollingshead in his book, *Elmtown's Youth*, this overemphasis has resulted in preferential treatment of upper-class students and discrimination against students from the lower classes.

Some persons claim that teachers tend to have the image of not being very much different from the "run of the mill" and therefore not worth emulating. Other, less charitable, evaluators of teacher status indicate that many Americans take teachers to be fools for working for such deplorable wages when their talents and training should entitle them to a much larger portion of the American economic profit. There is a general consensus that, to most Americans, the image of the teacher is far from a highly favorable one. Becoming a teacher is not generally considered to be a very high ambition or a very laudable goal. Teaching is not looked upon as being a source of influence and excitement. Businessmen, politicians, athletes, entertainers, scientists, and physicians seem to draw much more favorable reactions from the public.

As former United States Commissioner of Education, Sterling McMurrin, said, "Many first-rate individuals go into teaching, but they aren't treated as people with enormous talent, great skill, training and education." [2] Traditionally, teachers have been deprived of the full rights of citizens, their activities circumscribed by the public and by school boards. Richard Meryman noted, "Today the community provides the teacher with very little prestige and sometimes actually

---

[2] Meryman, "How We Drive Teachers to Quit," p. 105.

goes out of its way to make him feel hapless." He presents a Harvard University report that society's impression of teachers is of "a lowly group, not quite first-class and deserving of no better than the hand-me-downs of our civilization." [3]

Public school teachers have a significantly lower social status than the average practitioner in many other professions. Patrick Groff points up the somewhat pathetic status of teachers: ". . . teachers might best be classified as 'middle-class professionals.' This term, while retaining for them the distinction of having had professional-type education and of subscribing to professional-type purposes and ethics, takes a realistic view of their comparative social status with the other professionals and the propertied class which appear truly to constitute the upper social class." [4]

The public image of teaching has tended to be essentially feminine. Teachers are often expected to be gentle, benevolent, passive, submissive, yielding, bland, non-combative, and fussy about insignificant things. Like Casper Milquetoast, they are pictured as acceptant, retiring, timid, reticent, self-effacing, long-suffering, patient, and pitiably inept and defenseless.

What is even more distressing is that the National Education Association itself, claiming to champion the interests of teachers, has projected the image of teachers as being weak, ineffectual, and powerless, having to trust in the possible benevolence of those in power over them. A clear example of the NEA's traditional position is the NEA-sponsored film, "Freedom to Learn," which may be obtained from most major audio-visual centers and from NEA-affiliated state education associations. In the film, a teacher is called before her local lay school board to answer the charge that she has been teaching communism. She is put on trial before the wielders of power in education. She humbly accepts the bullying and inquisitional questions of some of the board members. The impression is given in the film that perhaps some of the teacher's former students, now on the board, will charitably come to her rescue. The image of teachers presented by this NEA film is of a powerless group basically defenseless before the educational decision-making power exercised by persons either not trained or not functioning as teachers, persons such as lay school board members and their administrative representatives.

In defense of the NEA, and its state and local affiliated organiza-

---

[3] Meryman, "How We Drive Teachers to Quit," p. 110.
[4] Patrick J. Groff, "The Social Status of Teachers," *The Journal of Educational Sociology* 36, no. 1 (September, 1962): 24.

tions, it should be noted that the NEA, in recent years, has been pushed by the American Federation of Teachers into a more militant stance. The NEA's growing programs in "professional negotiations" and "professional sanctions" are evidence of the NEA's shift, particularly in urban areas, away from its traditional passive and conservative role in American education.

Does the public hold an adequate image of teachers? Are teachers pictured as courageous and intelligent community leaders, as responsible persons competent to be entrusted with the welfare of our nation? Are they seen as being assertive and confident, or are they pictured as "Our Miss Brooks," good-intentioned but scatterbrained? Teachers bear the stereotype of being feminine, not being vigorously masculine. In brief, it appears that public school teachers basically are in the backwash of American society, far from the vibrant and flowing mainstream of important decision-making power.

MENTAL ABILITY OF TEACHERS

The mental competency of teachers is most easily determined by examining the abilities of students majoring in education. A number of studies indicate that students majoring in education compare unfavorably with students majoring in other areas. This is true for those graduating with the bachelor's degree and also true for those enrolled in graduate school. A summary of statistics on the Selective Service College Qualification Tests given in 1951 indicated that at all undergraduate levels the percentage of education majors equaling or exceeding the critical score on the test was lower than the percentage of majors in all the other areas examined. Even the students in teacher education colleges or divisions who had not designated themselves as majoring in education or planning to teach were found to be substantially below the averages for their respective major fields. As Richard Meryman said in his previously noted *Life* article, "Unfortunately, colleges of education tend to become havens for students who are well down in the academic barrel." [5]

Why are education students inferior to students pursuing work in other areas? Why does teaching fail to get its proper share of the most able, energetic, and aggressive college and university graduates? Can it compete with occupations which offer satisfactory prestige and economic rewards? The loss of educational leadership and the

---

[5] Meryman, "How We Drive Teachers to Quit," p. 112.

reduced adequacy and effectiveness of the entire American educational system, which an apparent lack of competitive ability of teaching signifies, is staggering.

This lack of competitive ability is based on the image of teaching and teacher training institutions. Teachers colleges, many of them being former normal schools, have the image of inferiority and low standards. It is common knowledge on many campuses that education courses are farcical and beneath the dignity of scholars. Standards in "Mickey Mouse" education courses are so low that practically anyone can slide through them. It is rumored that the poorer students in the various content fields are often counseled to go into teaching. For many of the education students, teaching is merely something to fall back on if they fail in more adequate occupations.

The generally accepted concept of teacher competency, or incompetency, was succinctly stated by Bernard Shaw, "Those who can, do; those who can't, teach." Critics of teacher education programs have gone Shaw one better by adding, "Those who can't teach, teach teachers."

PERSONALITY TRAITS OF TEACHERS

The personality traits ascribed to teachers by the public were briefly noted in the section on social status. The image of teachers as being dependent and subservient is particularly important to the degree that people tend to act as they are expected to act. Teachers tend to be labeled as troublemakers and insubordinate upstarts if they violate the public image of teachers by being aggressively militant. Perhaps one of the reasons that teachers have been called apathetic is that they are inhibited by the "professional status" of teaching which requires that the power tactics used by other professions be looked upon as undignified and unethical.

Many of the persons who reject teaching as a career have aspirations for prestige, income, and professional recognition. They have been frustrated by the subordinate and feeble status of teachers. As Meryman noted in his *Life* article, a study of teacher personality traits was conducted in Ohio by a psychologist, Dr. Salomon Rettig. He found that the teachers had a sense of restriction and had no freedom of expression. "They are a highly selected kind of person, compared to other professional people: a highly intelligent person on the one hand, and on the other hand one who doesn't mind being told by rules, parents, and supervisors what he or she can and can't do." Meryman also noted that a group of women teachers with an average of 10 years' experience were examined at the University of Chicago. "The group showed no drives at all to accomplish demanding tasks, to do things better than other people, to analyze themselves and others, or to show sympathy toward any person in trouble." ". . . colleges of education throughout the U.S. attract a kind of person psychologically precast to fit the mold—undemanding and non-competitive." Another study indicated that teachers tend to be less curious and slower in making decisions than practitioners in comparable occupations.[6] It is fairly apparent that in order for a person to be content with the subordinate position of teachers, he probably would need to have a low level of personal aspiration.

Some observers have concluded that many teachers work in a restrictive climate dominated by fear of administrative authority, since administrators are perceived by many teachers as wielding oppressive power over them. Personality traits of fear and insecurity tend to flourish in such a climate. The effects of these teacher personality traits on the students in the teachers' classrooms are predictable. When teachers are dominated by fearful submission to authority, they tend in turn to dominate their students. They tend to project and transfer their own feelings about authority onto their students. They tend to thwart creativity and freedom of thought. They teach their students not to strike out against authority, not to be different, and to think as they are told to think.

CONCLUSION

Certain educators contend that the studies cited in this chapter give a highly misleading and inaccurately negative picture of teachers and teaching conditions, particularly in regard to social status and intellectual capacity of teachers, because the studies deal only with comparisons in a small segment of the United States population. These educators hold that comparisons taking in the population as a whole yield more positive conclusions.

Various writers contend that teachers are well-situated. For example, not only do teachers have unequaled job security granted to them as a result of tenure laws, their annual salaries compare favor-

---

[6] Meryman, "How We Drive Teachers to Quit," p. 112.

ably with other occupations on an "hours-worked" basis when the teachers' summer vacations are taken into account.

Is teaching a good career?

SELECTED REFERENCES

Blumberg, Arthur, "Are Teachers Doormats?" *Educational Administration and Supervision* 45, no. 4 (July, 1959): 215–19. A thoughtful analysis of possible effects of teacher personalities on their students.

Clark, David L., and Arvid J. Burke, "Economic, Legal, and Social Status of Teachers," *Review of Educational Research* 25, no. 3 (June, 1955): 239–51. A dated but useful guide to research in teacher status.

Grambs, Jean Dresden, *Schools, Scholars, and Society*. Englewood Cliffs, N.J.: Prentice-Hall, Inc., 1965, pp. 134–40. A thought-provoking examination of conditions in teaching.

Groff, Patrick J., "The Social Status of Teachers," *The Journal of Educational Sociology* 36, no. 1 (September, 1962): 20–25. Note the extensive references.

Hollingshead, August B., *Elmtown's Youth*. New York: John Wiley and Sons, 1949. A basic sociological study of the effect of social classes on the behavior of young people, particularly in schools.

Lieberman, Myron, *Education As a Profession*. Englewood Cliffs, N.J. Prentice-Hall, Inc., 1956, Chap. 8. Note his discussion of the feminization of teaching. Also note the chapters dealing with the economic and social status of teachers.

Meryman, Richard, "How We Drive Teachers to Quit." *Life* 53, no. 5 (November 16, 1962): 104–106, 109–12, and 114. An excellent introduction to the problems teachers face under the present educational power structure. However, the solutions offered to the problems appear to be unrelated to the problems.

Miller, Herman P., "Annual and Lifetime Income in Relation to Education: 1939–1959." *American Economic Review* 50, no. 5 (December, 1960): 962–86. A study based on Bureau of the Census data.

NEA Research Bulletin. Washington, D.C.: Research Division of the National Education Association. The issues of this bulletin contain a number of timely and authoritative reports on conditions in teaching.

Ruml, Beardsley, and Sidney G. Dickton, *Teaching Salaries Then and Now*. New York: Fund for the Advancement of Education, 1955. A comparison of the economic status of teachers, from 1904 to 1953.

The Yearbook of Education—1953. Yonkers-on-Hudson, New York: World Book Company, 1953, Chaps. 1 and 6. Indicates traditional conditions in teaching. Note the table on page 108 which compares the average salaries of teachers in a number of countries to the per capita incomes in those countries.

Westby-Gibson, Dorothy, *Social Perspectives on Education.* New York: John Wiley and Sons, 1965, Chap. 19. A good introduction to existing conditions in the teaching area.

THOUGHT AIDS

1. Analyze the educational problems and the solutions to those problems presented in the Meryman article, "How We Drive Teachers to Quit." What must be done to correct the conditions described in the article? Why?

2. Do you agree with the belief that those who remain in teaching are either dedicated competent persons or those who are not able to achieve a better occupation? Why?

3. By its charter, the National Education Association aims to elevate the character and advance the interests of the profession of teaching and to promote the cause of education in the United States. Is it adequately doing this? Why?

4. Do you disagree with the concepts expressed in this chapter? Why?

5. Do you agree with the belief that there is little respect shown by pupils for teachers? Why?

6. Some educators have argued that the salaries of all teachers should be raised to a professional level. Other educators have argued that this is unrealistic, since it would more than double the cost of education. What could be done to improve the financial status of teachers? Why?

7. Evaluate the following statement: "The average person going into education today is mediocre because of the salary situation, the lack of advancement and the lack of prestige." Harold Taussig, President, Society of Academic Teachers, *The Denver Post,* Bonus Section, October 19, 1965, p. 8.

8. Indicate possible weaknesses of this chapter. How might they be corrected?

9. View the NEA-sponsored film, "Freedom to Learn." Was the status of teachers exemplified in the film accurately described in this chapter? Why?

10. Look in *The Education Index* for current articles dealing with present conditions in teaching.

11. Analyze the following statement: "The emerging picture is of a vocation which is perceived to be of relatively low social status, as compared with other professions, followed by poorly compensated persons, mostly women, who probably could not compete too successfully in other occupations." Jean Dresden Grambs. *Schools, Scholars, and Society.* Englewood Cliffs, New Jersey: Prentice-Hall, 1965, p. 140.

12. Approximately 30 percent of those trained to teach never teach and about 60 percent of those who do go into teaching leave during the first five years. Why do you think these conditions exist?

13. Look for current salaries in teaching and comparable occupations in the latest editions of the U.S. Department of Commerce's *Statistical Abstract of the United States* and the U.S. Department of Labor's *Occupational Outlook Handbook.*

10

Is Teaching a Profession?

Although many teachers, particularly those in the National Education Association, apparently believe that teaching is a profession, some teachers are uncertain as to the basic traits of a profession. Teachers regularly tolerate invasions of professional decision-making areas, such as lay school board invasions in determining teacher competency and remuneration, which would be intolerable to generally recognized professional groups such as physicians or lawyers. Teachers are far from the professional income level enjoyed by physicians, lawyers, and dentists. These conditions logically lead to this question: Is teaching a profession? To answer this question, the characteristics of a profession must be ascertained. For the purpose of this study, seven of the basic characteristics of two occupations generally accepted by teachers and by the public as being professions, those of medicine and law, will be enumerated and used as standards for a profession. Present practices in teaching will be analyzed on the basis of how adequately they conform to the seven characteristics of medicine and law.

AN ANALYSIS OF THE CHARACTERISTICS OF TEACHING

A note of caution should be sounded. Due to the broad range of complex functions grouped within the area of teaching, only generalizations can be presented in this brief discussion. Such generalizations may not fit certain unique specific situations. With this limitation in mind, teaching will be evaluated on the basis of seven hallmarks of medicine and law.

1. *A high level of competency based on an extended period of specialized training.* In professional occupations such as medicine and law, three to five years of graduate occupational training are required. Most physicians have a total of at least nine years of preparation: four years of undergraduate liberal arts with a biological sciences major and five years of graduate occupational training. In contrast, on the basis of state certification requirements, a person may become an elementary teacher in most states with a combined liberal arts and occupational training program totaling only four years. Although *total* requirements for secondary teachers are consistently higher than for elementary teachers, they rarely exceed the average elementary teacher's training by a full year. The average period of occupational training of both elementary and secondary teachers falls far below the length of occupational training required in professional occupations. In addition, temporary or substandard certification is common in teaching, yet is practically nonexistent in the generally recognized professions.

2. *All practitioners are required to have equivalent training and competencies.* In the graduate occupational training programs for recognized professions, such as medicine and law, all students must develop basically equivalent competencies. Practitioner administered state examinations determine whether or not the would-be practitioners have achieved the requisite occupational competencies. After satisfying these basic occupational requirements, practitioners may go on to specialize in certain phases of their occupations. A physician may remain as a general practitioner or he may specialize in surgery, pediatrics, obstetrics, internal medicine, pathology, neurology, psychiatry, etc. However, all physicians must have basically equivalent competencies in all the major ability areas in their professional occupation.

Must all teachers have basically equivalent occupational training and competencies? Does a social studies teacher's training make him competent to teach reading readiness skills to first graders? Is a science teacher trained to teach English? Does an industrial arts teacher have the ability to direct a choir? Is it even remotely possible for all teachers to have basically equivalent competencies? Could it be that medicine is an occupational field, whereas teaching is an area encompassing a number of occupational fields?

3. *Control of training for, entrance into, and expulsion from the occupation vested in the practitioners.* Professions involve practitioner control of training for the professions. Control of training usually is achieved through accreditation or approval of training institutions which comply with the standards or requirements established by the professional practitioners' association. Training institutions are also influenced to conduct their programs in a manner which will enable graduates to satisfy the certification requirements established by professional associations. The licensing authority in most professions is a state board composed of members of the profession. For example, legal and medical examinations administered by state boards in those professions serve as controls on training for and entrance into law and medicine.

Practitioner control over training for, entrance into, and expulsion from the various teaching fields is practically nonexistent. For example, practitioners in social-studies teaching are not even organized to accredit training programs for their field. They, and the practitioners in the various other teaching areas, exhibit almost no interest in taking over control of training for and entrance into their fields. Perhaps part of this disinterest is derived from the NEA's position that strong occupational organizations, which are essential in professional occupations, are "divisive." In contrast, clear delineation of the areas of jurisdiction of each occupation in the teaching area probably would result in much more cooperation between occupations than now exists.

Practitioners in the various teaching occupations also take little interest in and exercise very little, if any, control even over accreditation of existing generalized teacher education programs. Accreditation of institutions for teacher education basically is carried out by the National Council for Accreditation of Teacher Education, which is usually abbreviated to NCATE. It appears that administrative personnel, not teachers, have held most of the positions on this council. Even the National School Boards Association has been represented on NCATE.

Most teacher education institutions are not encouraging teacher control of training programs. Strong teacher organizations, if they existed, might tend to set more exacting standards than do teacher education schools, since the schools often need the income from higher enrollments. More exacting standards might eliminate part of the present turnover in teacher personnel, with a reduced need for students in teacher education programs being a probable direct result.

The various teaching occupations have practically no control over the licensing of practitioners. The authority to issue teaching certificates usually is vested in non-teacher state boards, commissioners, or training institutions. Even in the rare instances in which certification requirements are set by "educators," it is administrators, not teachers, who usually set the requirements. There is a continuing trend, encouraged by educators, away from teacher representation on the state boards which control certification standards for the various teaching occupations. Paradoxically, the NEA, which labels itself as a professional organization, has traditionally supported lay board control over certification. In contrast, every state medical licensing board is controlled by the medical occupation.

4. *Clear delineation of competencies expected of practitioners.* Society determines the broad objectives for each profession, and the occupational practitioners determine how the broad objectives will be implemented. In brief, society determines the general ends of the profession, and the profession determines the means to achieve those ends. For example, our society has indicated that physicians should attempt to prolong life and alleviate suffering. The profession delineates the competencies and procedures for implementing the general objectives. The profession clearly differentiates the implemental competencies expected of a physician from those to be possessed by nurses, laboratory technicians, hospital administrators, and other personnel.

The public seems to be generally in agreement that the practitioners in the various teaching fields should foster the development in students of attitudes, knowledge, and skills which will cause the students to become competent citizens in our society. However, the implemental competencies expected of practitioners in the various teaching fields basically are determined by powers outside those fields. Also, the competencies often are non-professional in nature. For example, in some communities teachers are expected to take tickets at athletic contests and perform other menial tasks. In contrast, physicians are not expected to perform menial tasks such as making the beds of hospital patients. This is not to say that menial tasks are unimportant, but it does indicate that the medical profession has delineated the expert skills needed by practitioners while relegating to other medical occupations the tasks that do not require such an extended period of intensive training. In contrast, such professional delineation of implemental competencies has not, as yet, occurred in the educational occupations area.

5. *Practitioners have the power to make decisions within the area of assumed professional competence.* Professional autonomy is the power to make professional decisions in regard to the training and qualifications needed for entrance into the profession, and the conduct which may be considered grounds for expulsion from practice by members of the profession. Physicians control training and certification standards and also control decisions in other professional areas, such as choice of surgical procedures.

In contrast, the public and many teachers take it for granted that non-practitioners should make decisions in areas that are considered to require professional competency in professional occupations. For example, choices of textbooks and subjects to be studied are regularly made by non-professional lay boards or their non-teaching school administrator representatives. Many teachers even approve of the anti-professional practice of inviting the public to determine what courses and materials should be used in the public schools. Would physicians approve inviting the public to determine what surgical techniques and materials should be used?

A strong case can be made for the argument that teachers are giving away more professional autonomy than is being taken away from them. It is apparent that many teachers are not even aware of the characteristics of a profession, particularly in regard to the autonomy of occupational practitioners to make professional decisions, since teachers readily acquiesce in allowing school boards and their administrators to make decisions in various teaching fields. In contrast, it would be publicly recognized as a flagrant violation of professional autonomy for a hospital board or non-physician administrator to decide which surgical procedures are to be carried out by physicians.

6. *Actions of practitioners controlled by the professional group through the enforcement of a clear and definite code of ethics.* The American Bar Association adopted a code of ethics in 1908 and the American Medical Association adopted a code in 1912. Most law schools have courses in legal ethics. Professions have been active in clarifying and enforcing codes of ethics on national, state, and local levels. For example, from 1928 to 1948 the state bar association of California conducted over 9,000 investigations of purported unprofessional conduct, which resulted in disbarment in over 140 cases. Violation of medical codes can also result in suspension or expulsion. One state medical association threatened to expel all physicians who would not allow examination of their financial records to ascertain if they accepted unethical compensations.

To the writer's knowledge, not one teaching occupation has developed a code of ethics. The NEA has had a "unified teaching profession" code of ethics for many years. The NEA code was last revised in 1968. The code appears to the writer to have a highly anti-professional effect since the code seems to equate "professionalism" with administrator and lay board control over the various teaching fields. The NEA code of ethics will be carefully examined in a later chapter.

7. *Remuneration consistent with the expected level of professional competency.* Some economists have defined a professional level of compensation as being at least two or three times the national average earnings of all employed persons. The average income of physicians and lawyers exceeds this level, but teachers' salaries consistently have remained far below this level. Teacher income has remained near the national average for all employed persons. The dismal financial position of teachers is highlighted by the fact that the average employed person has not even graduated from high school. Also, the average number of hours worked by teachers has actually increased since the turn of the century, whereas the number worked in industry had decreased significantly.

Another factor involved in the melancholy financial picture of teaching is that in order to approach even partially what is commonly considered to be a professional level of remuneration, a teacher usually must leave his particular teaching field and go either into school administration or leave education entirely. The very negative effect of such a financial dead end on the morale of those in the various teaching fields is evident. In addition, many teachers are moonlighting, holding down other jobs. Such conditions are not tolerated by recognized professions.

SOME TENTATIVE CONCLUSIONS

1. *A person may become a teacher with much less training than is generally required in medicine and law.* The greater the professional status generally accorded an occupation, the more its requirements exceed those in the teaching occupations.

2. *It does not appear to be even remotely possible for all teachers to be expected to possess equivalent training and competencies.* Perhaps teaching is not an occupation, but rather an area encompassing many teaching fields.

3. *Control of training for and entrance into the various teaching fields is almost universally vested in authorities outside those fields.* Expulsion from an occupation by practitioners is nonexistent. The major educational association, the NEA, apparently continues to foster the anti-professional policy of lay board and administrator control over the various teaching fields.

4. *The competencies expected of practitioners in the various teaching occupations are, at best, hazy and ill-defined.* In contrast, physicians have clearly defined and established their areas of professional competency.

5. *Teachers are rarely free to make basic decisions within their areas of presumed competency.* The decision-making autonomy of teachers is regularly and massively invaded by legislatures, by lay boards and, particularly, by school administrators.

6. *No teaching occupation has a code of ethics.* The NEA's code appears to foster anti-professional school administrator and lay board controls over the various teaching fields.

7. *Remuneration for teaching has consistently remained near the national average for all employed persons.* This has been far less than half the average income of physicians and lawyers.

Can teaching validly be called a profession?

SELECTED REFERENCES

Bestor, Arthur, *The Restoration of Learning—A Program for Redeeming the Unfulfilled Promise of American Education.* New York: Alfred A. Knopf, 1955. An historian presents his program for American education. Particularly note Chapter 18, pp. 269–82.

Gross, Neal, *Who Runs Our Schools?* New York: John Wiley and Sons, 1958. A report of educational problems found through interviews of school superintendents and their school board members.

Huggett, Albert J., and T. M. Stinnett, *Professional Problems of Teachers.* New York: The Macmillan Company, 1956. A comprehensive survey of many important aspects of professionalism in teaching.

Lieberman, Myron, *The Future of Public Education.* Chicago: University of Chicago Press, 1960. A thought-provoking analysis of the future of professionalism in teaching.

————, *Education as a Profession*. Englewood Cliffs, New Jersey: Prentice-Hall, Inc., 1956. Although dated, this remains the most comprehensive and authoritative volume presently available in the area of professionalism in education.

Orlich, Donald C., and S. Samuel Shermis, "Teaching as a Profession, in *The Pursuit of Excellence: Introductory Readings in Education*. New York: American Book Company, 1965, pp. 288–314. An excellent analysis of various professional problems.

Stanley, William O., B. Othanel Smith, Kenneth D. Benne, and Archibald W. Anderson, *Social Foundations of Education*. New York: The Dryden Press, 1956, Part 5. A compilation of articles on various aspects of professionalism in teaching.

Westby-Gibson, Dorothy, *Social Perspectives on Education*. New York: John Wiley & Sons, 1965, Chap. 18. An introduction to professional problems.

THOUGHT AIDS

1. Present possible arguments for and against the belief that the various teaching occupations should be professionalized.
2. Evaluate the professional characteristics presented in this chapter on the basis of the characteristics presented by Myron Lieberman in the first chapter of his book, *Education As a Profession*.
3. Indicate possible standards for a profession which would be consistent with calling teaching a profession at the present time.
4. What, to you, is the most important problem or issue in the area of professionalization of teaching? Why?
5. Report on current trends in professionalism in teaching by summarizing recent articles on this topic which may be located through consulting the *Education Index*.
6. Analyze the discussions of professionalism in teaching to be found in many college education texts.
7. Examine various definitions of a profession.
8. Report on the professional status of teachers in other countries.
9. Should school administrators be paid more than teachers?
10. Indicate possible arguments for and against participation by non-professional groups in the making of decisions within assumed areas of professional teacher competence, such as selection of textbooks.
11. Is teaching a united profession, or should it be divided into separate

professions, as specified by present certification requirements in most states? Why?

12. Assuming that the NEA and AFT would disagree with parts, if not all, of this chapter, what valid arguments might each group use in criticizing this chapter? (Students might write to the state and national offices of these organizations for further information.)

11

Which Educational Power System Is Best?

The NEA champions one type of power structure in education; the AFT advocates a different one, and a number of school boards reject both the NEA and AFT systems and promote their own patterns of control. Could it be that all of these power systems have insurmountable flaws?

THE PRESENT UNILATERAL, CORPORATE POWER STRUCTURE

The present local school district educational power structure tends to be a corporate-type power system in which unilateral decision-making power is exercised in one direction—from top to bottom.

Until the last few years, this lay school board controlled system was supported by the National Education Association. Apparently this power system still is supported by most school board members, by many legislators, and by conservative members of the general public.

The charted pattern (p. 105) of lay or non-practitioner control over education has historical roots which reach back into the colonial

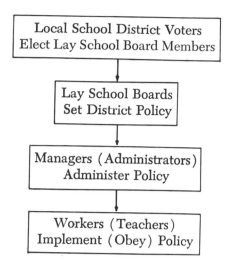

period. For example, the Puritan compulsory school support act of 1647, known as the "Old Deluder Satan Act," required every town of a hundred families to appoint a grammar master capable of preparing boys for the university. Generally, these Massachusetts Latin schools were controlled by the selectmen of the towns. During the nineteenth century expansion of education, local lay boards found it necessary to appoint head teachers or managers to administer school board policies. These school administrators eventually became subdivided into superintendents and principals.

What teaching conditions exist under the present generally accepted power system of lay or non-professional control over the schools? In such a brief presentation, only a few broad generalizations based on a number of research studies can be made:

1. Lifetime income for teachers is approximately half the income in other occupations, such as engineering, accounting, and chemistry, which also require four to five years of college or university training. Teachers' salaries remain near the national average of all employed persons.

2. Public school teachers tend to have lower middle class social status. They are "a lowly group, not quite first-class and deserving of no better than the hand-me-downs of civilization." [1]

3. These labels exemplify the public image of teachers: Feminine,

---

[1] Richard Meryman, "How We Drive Teachers to Quit," *Life* 53, no. 20 (Nov. 16, 1962): 110.

gentle, benevolent, passive, yielding, bland, non-combative, acceptant, retiring, timid, reticent, self-effacing, patient, long-suffering, pitiably inept, and fussy about insignificant things.

4. In their power and importance to society, public school teachers appear to be weak, ineffectual, submissive, defenseless, and powerless. They exist in the backwash of American society, far from the vibrant and flowing main stream of life. To illustrate this point, note that there are practically no nationally known Americans who have achieved prominence because they are teachers.

5. In regard to mental ability, the average public school teachers come from the lower third of their college or university classes.

6. Surveys of personality traits of teachers indicate that teachers do not mind being governed by rules, parents, non-professional school boards, and the boards' managers or administrators, being told what they can or cannot do. They tend to be undemanding and noncompetitive, and to have a low level of personal aspiration.

7. Only an unfortunately small minority of the men who enter public school teaching remain in it.

Are the above conditions really a result of the present educational power structure? One way to ascertain this would be to observe the conditions that might exist under some other type of educational power system. What other types of power systems have been proposed?

In the last few years the NEA has been attempting to shift to a "Professional Negotiations" power structure which is similar to the following labor union power model, except that the NEA would place school administrators with teachers on the right side of the chart.

The Labor Union Countervailing System of Power

The American Federation of Teachers, a labor union affiliated with AFL-CIO, supports a bilateral or countervailing system of power:

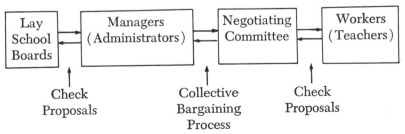

This AFT power structure proposal is based on the AFT's claim that, at the present time, teachers are poorly paid and overly restricted "factory" workers in "company unions." Therefore, according to the AFT, teachers are laborers who must unite in a workers' union in order to bargain collectively, from a position of group power, with lay school boards and the boards' administrative representatives. Through collective bargaining, contracts specifying working conditions would be negotiated.

Since most teachers, mistaken as they may be, appear to fancy themselves to be on a higher or more "independent" level than workers in labor unions, the AFT power structure proposal appears to have little appeal for most teachers. A comparison of the sizes of the NEA and AFT supports this conclusion, since the NEA has over a million members, but the AFT membership is only about one-tenth of that of the NEA. However, the AFT does appear to have a very valuable function in the present power structure, much like the "loyal opposition" in the British Parliament. It serves as a galling gadfly, biting at the exposed flanks of the NEA. It goads the NEA through serving as a trial balloon. When an AFT policy attracts teachers, the NEA is pressured either to counteract the policy or to adopt it. For example, in recent years the AFT has pressured the NEA to become more militant. The NEA has responded to the success of AFT-inspired strikes by fostering "no contract—no work" strikes which the NEA has euphemistically labeled as "professional sanctions."

PROFESSIONAL POWER SYSTEMS

Both the NEA and AFT label their conflicting power structures as professional. Since the generally accepted professional occupations of medicine and law also have power systems, one way to examine the conflicting NEA and AFT professional power systems is to compare them with the power traits of the medical and legal professions.

The power traits of the medical and legal professional occupations may be briefly summarized:

1. Through their occupational organization, association, or union, the members of each occupation control training for, entrance into, and expulsion from the occupation.
2. All members are required, by their occupational organization, to have equivalent minimal training and competencies.
3. The members' professional actions are controlled by their group through group enforcement of a definite code of ethics.

4. Within their general areas of professional occupational competence, as defined by society, the practitioners exercise decision-making power. For example, medical doctors, not lay boards or their administrative representatives, determine surgical procedures.

In summary, in the professions of medicine and law, the occupational practitioners, through their own organizations, control the management of their professional activities. What are the conditions which exist in these occupations?

1. Remuneration averages at least three to four times that of the average wage earner.
2. Practitioners tend to have upper class status.
3. The occupations have a sought-after public image.
4. The occupations are powerful groups to be reckoned with in our society.
5. The average mental ability of physicians and lawyers is in the upper portion of university graduates.
6. Their personality traits tend to be those of leaders and decision-makers.
7. Few practitioners ever voluntarily leave these occupations.

THE "UNITED TEACHING PROFESSION" BELIEF

When the traits of previously presented "professional" educational power structures are compared with those of the medical and legal professions, questions can be raised concerning the validity of a number of commonly held beliefs. One questionable belief is the "United Teaching Profession" belief. This also may be termed the "United Education Profession" belief, since the words teaching and education are commonly used interchangeably by many writers. This commonly held belief is that all educators, a category encompassing all teachers, supervisors, specialists, and administrators, should be and are in a "united profession."

In the previous chapter, teaching was compared with certain traits of the medical and legal professions. Some rather devastating, if valid, arguments against calling teaching a profession were noted. The belief that teaching is a profession also may be examined semantically. If a profession is defined as a professional occupation, a relevant question may be posed: "What is an occupation?" If an occupation is best defined as a job or vocation in which the practitioners have basically equivalent skills and abilities so that they are competent to interchange positions or roles, a series of questions may be posed: (1) Are teachers in interchangeable positions or roles? For example, are English teachers prepared to be competent art teachers, or physics teachers, or music teachers? (2) Are we forced logically to conclude that teaching is an area encompassing many non-interchangeable occupations, and is not itself an occupation? and (3) Must we therefore conclude that teaching is not a professional occupation because it is not an occupation?

THE "TEACHING IS LIKE MEDICINE" BELIEF

A number of educators defend calling teaching (education) a profession by saying, "The teaching profession, just like the medical profession, has many specialties." However, the "teaching is like medicine" belief also is questionable. Since a valid analogy must be based on similarities, the belief that teaching may be compared to medicine might be based on a false analogy. Is teaching like medicine? As has been previously noted, medicine appears to be an occupation requiring basically equivalent training and competencies of all practitioners. In contrast, if the previous questions were valid, it may be held that teaching is not an occupation, but a label for an area encompassing a number of occupations. If medicine is an occupation, and if teaching is not, then they are not comparable.

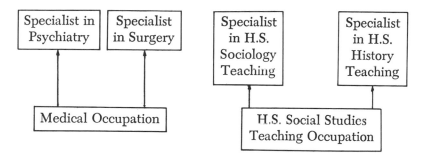

As the chart indicates, perhaps the medical occupation can be compared validly with various educational occupational specialties, such as the teaching of social studies. After medical practitioners have demonstrated they have basically equivalent training and competencies (often termed the "general practitioner" level), they may advance to specialized higher-level occupations such as psychiatry and surgery. Such specialized occupations beyond the medical occupation may be contrasted with specialized occupations beyond the social studies teaching occupation, such as the specialized occupation of teaching sociology courses.

It should be noted in passing that both the NEA and AFT seem to accept the "teaching is a profession" belief and the "teaching is like medicine" belief. Both organizations apparently would place all teachers in the same occupation. The NEA's traditional policy has been to place the school boards' managers, school administrators, in the same profession with the teachers they hire and fire. The NEA appears to be moving away from this policy.

THE "PUBLIC EMPLOYMENT" BELIEF

Another widely held belief is the "public employment—public control" belief. According to this belief, the education profession does not have the traits of the generally recognized professions because it is financed by the public, is responsible to the public, and serves a public clientele. Therefore, according to this line of thought, lay public school boards and their administrators should control the various teaching occupations because the boards pay for the teachers' services.

This belief that non-professional lay boards should control teachers because the boards pay for the teachers' services is open to devastating criticisms. Although some physicians, lawyers, and dentists in the United States are employed by public agencies, and although medical doctors who serve under the National Health Service program in England are remunerated from public funds, in neither country is it assumed that because the professional practitioners are remunerated from public funds their occupational decisions should be controlled by non-professional lay boards. Payment for medical services from public funds is not taken to be a valid reason for non-professional boards determining standards for medical licensure or determining what drugs physicians may use. With or without private fees, a physician controls his area of decision-making competency. The public pays members of professional occupations in order to receive services controlled by experts, not to control the experts.

THE "OCCUPATIONS ARE DIVISIVE" BELIEF

Another questionable belief is the assumption that "occupations are divisive." As expounded by some writers, this belief is that separating teachers from administrators, and separating teachers into their various occupations, is necessarily divisive and such divisiveness is harmful. This belief holds that since classroom teachers, administrators, and other educators have a common dedication and are engaged in pursuit of a common goal—the best possible education for all students —they should act in unity in the united and cooperative teaching profession under the direction of lay school boards and their administrative representatives. Therefore, any cleavage between teachers and administrators should be rejected automatically.

Possible inadequacies in this line of reasoning can be brought clearly into focus by drawing an analogy to professional occupations. Does the recognition that medicine and dentistry are distinct yet related and cooperative occupations cause harmful divisiveness between these occupations? The answer seems to be fairly obvious. Is it necessarily divisive to recognize that the administrator's present hiring and firing role differs from the teacher's role of being the one hired and sometimes fired? Is it necessarily divisive to recognize that the physical education occupation may have some objectives which differ from those of the English teaching occupation? It is the writer's guess that if the areas of each educational occupation were clearly defined and if each occupation were controlled by the practitioners in that occupation, there probably would be much greater cooperation and joint effort between the various educational occupations than now exists. Clear definition of roles possibly would reduce rather than increase friction.

THE "PUBLIC CONCERN—PUBLIC CONTROL" BELIEF

Another questionable argument for lay control over the various teaching occupations is based on the belief that education is too important to be left in the hands of educators. This argument holds that since education is an important area of public concern, the public must control it. This may be labeled as the "public concern—public control" belief. Possible inadequacies in this line of argument may be brought into bold relief by again making an analogy to professional occupations. For example, is medicine an area of public concern? The obvious answer is in the affirmative. Does this mean that the lay public should control the determination of correct medication dosages? Obviously not. What, then, are acceptable relationships between public concern and professional occupational control? Perhaps professionally acceptable relationships can best be described in terms of levels of control.

LEVELS OF CONTROL

Level 1—Public decision making power level (public determination of general occupational objectives)

Level 2—Professional occupational decision making power level (professional determination of occupational procedures to implement achievement of the publicly determined occupational objectives)

As an example of the levels of control indicated in the chart, public concern for and equity in the medical area is expressed through public control over medicine on Level 1—control over the general objectives of the medical occupation. The publicly determined objectives of medicine appear to be to prolong life, alleviate suffering, and increase physical and mental health. Similarly, if the various education occupations ever become professions, the public would set general occupational objectives and the practitioners themselves would determine how best to implement the objectives.

A PROFESSIONAL COUNTERVAILING POWER SYSTEM

Now that questions have been raised concerning a number of current beliefs about "professionalism," what might the writer suggest as a model for a professional power structure? The following chart indicates what the writer presently believes would be at least one possible type of professional power structure.

Like the AFT-advocated power structure, this would be a bilateral (countervailing) power system. However, in contrast to both of the previously presented power structures, this system would be based on professional occupations. Under this power system it is assumed that the various educational occupations may bargain either individually or collectively, through a joint occupations association, with the representatives of the federal government and of the local and state lay boards. This power system is based on the assumption that if the practitioners in the various educational occupations did take control of training for, entrance into, and expulsion from their occupations, the power struggle probably would escalate from present local and state lay board levels of decision-making to the national level. Local and state lay boards probably would be relegated to cere-

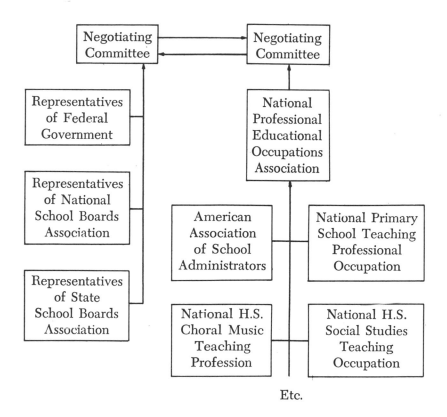

Etc.

monial functions. This is not to say that important negotiations will not occur on local and state levels, but only that the emphasis would shift from these to the national level. The federal government probably would become the most potent non-educator power group in this area since the dictum, "School funds should come from where the money is in order to serve the students where they are," probably would lead to the federal government shouldering the major portion of the financing of American education.

Only a few of the educational occupations have been noted on the chart. The number and boundaries of the educational occupations have, as yet, not been clearly established. It appears that such delineation of occupational areas is a requisite step toward professionalization of the various educational occupations. It is significant that neither the NEA nor the AFT appears to be eagerly fostering clear delineations of the various occupations.

How might practitioners in the various educational occupations take control of training for, entrance into, and expulsion from their particular occupations? A number of embryonic occupational organizations already exist in the NEA. For example, there is an organization for art teachers, one for mathematics teachers, one for administrators, one for social studies teachers, etc. However, the development of professional occupations probably would have to start at a more local level. For example, a social studies teacher who desires to transform the NEA's National Council for the Social Studies into a professional occupation might arrange statewide meetings of social studies teachers during the state conventions of the NEA-affiliated state education association. Then, over the years, he could foster statewide sharing of social studies curricular materials, job openings and, eventually, achieve group determination of training programs for social studies teaching. If successful, he could educate ultimately the social studies teachers in his state, and other states, to take professional control of their occupations. After a number of decades, his group of professionally-oriented teachers might be able to marshal enough strength to take control of the National Council for the Social Studies and convert it into a professional organization controlling training for, entrance into, and expulsion from the social studies teaching field.

If the practitioners in the various educational occupations did take control of their own occupations, they probably also would attempt to establish control, through national negotiations, over contractual conditions. Each occupational organization probably would set up an occupational contract, specifying occupational "academic freedom" conditions, to be signed by local school boards. If school boards refused to accept the professional autonomy which would be provided for in such contracts, the members of the occupation, like members of professional occupations such as medicine and law, could be obligated to go on strike, to withdraw their services. The medical and legal professions' codes of ethics obligate their practitioners to withdraw their services, to go on strike, when their professional decision-making areas are invaded by non-practitioner persons or groups. Physicians and lawyers are obligated to go on strike in such situations because they can not be professionally responsible for decisions which they do not control.

The long-held NEA belief that "Unions are antiprofessional" may also be questioned. In order to have a profession, it appears that there must be an occupational union, society, or organization which controls training for, entrance into, and expulsion from the occupation. Such unions, however, would be professional unions, perhaps like the American Medical Association, not like the AFT and its affiliated nonprofessional labor unions.

One additional area of contrast between nonprofessional and professional power systems should be noted. Under the generally accepted power system, school administrators are the managerial representatives of lay school boards and, therefore, play the role of educational leaders. They tend to be the leaders in hiring and firing teachers, and in determining the curriculum, teaching materials, and teaching practices. Administrators usually determine, with lay school board approval, what the overall school program will be.

What would be the role of the school administrator under a professional power system? A useful analogy may be made to the medical area. Who are the leaders in medicine, hospital administrators or the physicians themselves? Medical doctors usually are the leaders in medicine because basically they control medical decision-making power. Since medical doctors usually administer medical practices, with the assistance of hospital administrators, there appear to be at least two types of administration occurring in the medical area: Administration $_1$—hospital administration, and Administration $_2$—medical occupational administration. Similarly, if professional occupations ever did come into existence in the teaching area, such distinctions also probably would need to be made: Administration $_1$—school administration, and Administration $_2$—professional occupational administration. School administrators would be restricted to the occupation they usually are trained for—administration of the maintenance and other non-teaching but supportive functions of the schools. Practitioners in the various teaching occupations would administer their own occupational areas.

Most of the persons who function in the medical area are not in the medical profession. They serve as members of medical teams under the direction of medical doctors. The following chart shows the medical team concept and compares it to what might be a teaching team in a particular teaching area.

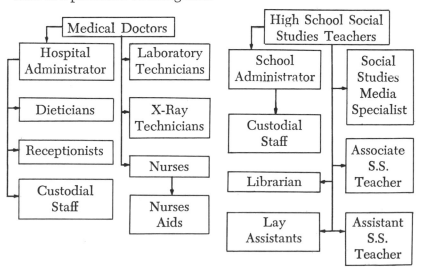

The following chart is a crystal ball gazing attempt to indicate possible team-teaching levels, in terms of years of training required and amount of remuneration, which might exist if the various educational occupations developed professional power structures similar to the one which exists in the medical area.

		Years of Training	Income	
LEVEL 1	American Medical Association Executive Director	12–14	$50,000	National H.S. S.S. Teaching Occupation Executive Director
LEVEL 2	Psychiatry	12–14	$40,000	Regional H.S. S.S. Teaching Director
LEVEL 3	Professional Medical Occupation	8–10	$30,000	H.S. S.S. Teaching Professional Occupation
LEVEL 4	Hospital Administrator	4–6	$15,000	H.S. S.S. Media Director
LEVEL 5	X-Ray and Laboratory Technicians	2–4	$6,000	Associate H.S. S.S. Teachers
LEVEL 6	Nurses	2–4	$5,000	Assistant H.S. S.S. Teachers
LEVEL 7	Nurses Aids	few weeks	$3,000	H.S. S.S. Lay Assistants

CONCLUSION

Although many questions can be raised about currently espoused educational power systems, the so-called professional occupations power system advocated by the writer has blatantly glaring weaknesses of its own. One of these is in the area of jurisdiction. What would prevent the interminable jurisdictional disputes, which have plagued labor union relations, from occurring endlessly between the various teaching occupations? A related weakness is the lack of any clear coordination between the occupations. What if a music teacher and a football coach both wanted the same students at the same hour? Who would make the final decision? Also, teachers characteristically have exhibited few abilities in the areas of initiative and leadership. How would these abilities be developed? If teachers did overcome these weaknesses, what guarantees are there that the teachers would not be duped out of their power, just as many labor union members seem to be mere pawns in the hands of union leaders?

Perhaps this chapter can be ended in a less pessimistic vein. The writer would prefer that teachers have the problems which attend being powerful, rather than the problems of being basically powerless. Also, surgeons in the Civil War were barbers, but the medical doctors raised their own occupation to a professional level. There is always the possibility that enlightened groups of practitioners in the various teaching occupations eventually will go beyond the present beliefs of the NEA and AFT and establish professional power systems in American education.

SELECTED REFERENCES

Campbell, Roald R., Luvern L. Cunningham, Roderick F. McPhee, and Raphael O. Nystrand, *The Organization and Control of American Schools*, 2nd ed. Columbus, Ohio: Charles E. Merrill Publishing Company, 1970. An extensive study of the present educational power system.

Chamberlain, Leo M., and Leslie W. Kindred, *The Teacher and School Organization*. Englewood Cliffs, New Jersey: Prentice-Hall, Inc., 1966, Chap. 18. An analytical introduction to the NEA versus AFT rivalry.

Full, Harold, *Controversy in American Education—An Anthology of Crucial Issues*, Part IV—The Profession: Authority and Autonomy. New York: The Macmillan Company, 1967. Articles range from local control through professionalism to merit rating.

Huggett, Albert J., and T. M. Stinnett, *Professional Problems of Teachers.* New York: The Macmillan Company, 1956, Chap. 14. An NEA-oriented presentation of the NEA and AFT power systems.

Lieberman, Myron, *Education As a Profession.* Englewood Cliffs, New Jersey: Prentice-Hall, Inc., 1956, Chaps. 9 and 10. An excellent introduction to the NEA and AFT power systems.

————, *The Future of Public Education.* Chicago, Illinois: University of Chicago Press, 1960, Chap. 9. An incisive examination of the NEA and AFT power systems.

Organizing the Teaching Profession. Glencoe, Illinois: The Free Press, 1955. The AFT presents its case for a union-oriented power structure.

THOUGHT AIDS

1. What, to you, are the strengths and weaknesses of the three educational power systems presented in this chapter?
2. Do you agree with the questions raised about various beliefs noted in this chapter? Why or why not?
3. Were the various power systems presented fairly? Why or why not?
4. What might be the traits of other possible educational power systems?
5. Some educators have suggested that the NEA and AFT should unite and stop their "unsightly squabbling." What do you think of this suggestion? Why?
6. Analyze Myron Lieberman's criticisms of the NEA and AFT in his book, *The Future of Public Education.*
7. Do you agree with the contention that both the NEA and AFT power systems are, at best, non-professional? Why?
8. Indicate possible weaknesses and dangers in the writer's suggested plan for teachers to take control of their own occupations.

12

Is Teacher Education an Illusion?

Beliefs about teacher education usually are divided into two opposing camps: (1) The liberal-arts professors' position that "Anyone who has mastered his subject-matter field can impart it," versus (2) The educators' position that prospective teachers must have a number of educational methods courses. Although not often clearly brought out in the open, this liberal arts versus education cleavage appears to exist on the campuses of most colleges and universities where there are teacher-education programs. The conflict often is manifested in a form of guerrilla warfare, in which each side ridicules the other before students.

THE LIBERAL ARTS VERSUS EDUCATION CONFLICT

Here are the most frequent liberal-arts criticisms of educators and their teacher-education programs:

1. Education courses only emphasize the how (techniques and methods), not the what (subject-matter content).
2. Teacher-certification requirements place emphasis on educational methods, thereby hindering subject-matter mastery.

3. Education is not a valid subject-matter field because it lacks a body of knowledge with form and tradition of its own.
4. Education professors and their courses are not on a scholarly level.
5. Education degrees are below the intellectual level of liberal-arts content degrees.
6. Education courses are unnecessary, since the only trait needed by a successful teacher that can be taught him is that of subject-matter mastery.

What causes a liberal-arts professor to make such devastating condemnations of the teacher-education programs established by education professors? Scholarship in a restricted academic field is the center of his life, and has been since his youth. In high school, the typical liberal-arts professor was an excellent student in the academic curriculum. In college, he took courses that immersed him deeply in his chosen academic field. He graduated with honors. He entered a university graduate school program in which he concentrated on scholarly research. His doctoral dissertation was the zenith of his analysis of restricted and minute details in his field. With his Ph.D. degree safely in hand, he moved into a college or university liberal-arts division. Then, in order to climb the ladder of academic success in his field, he continues to more specialized, content research.

To the typical liberal-arts professor, the aim of education is to acquire and transmit knowledge. The process of teaching is uncomplicated. It simply involves confronting budding scholars with the basic concepts and informational items involved in a liberal-arts field. Accordingly, there are two important factors in successful teaching: (1) advanced scholarship in a liberal-arts field, and (2) a pleasingly-enthusiastic teaching manner. The field of methods is a "bag of tricks," which can be quickly learned, if necessary, through apprenticeship under an advanced scholar in the field.[1] "Is it any wonder that, after worshipping at the shrine of the Goddess of Academic Scholarship for a period of at least a quarter century, he believes in her ritual with all his heart and looks upon any attack on her as intolerable blasphemy?" [2]

---

[1] For an excellent analysis of the foundations of the liberal-arts position, see Paul Woodring, *A Fourth of a Nation* (New York: McGraw-Hill Book Company, 1957), Chapter 2, pp. 31–53. For a presentation of liberal-arts criticisms of the educationists' position, see pp. 171–84.

[2] Edwin H. Reeder, "The Quarrel Between Professors of Academic Subjects and Professors of Education: An Analysis," *American Association of University Professors Bulletin* 37 (Autumn, 1951): 509.

Educators in turn have their reasons for reacting violently against the liberal-arts position:

1. Liberal-arts professors hold falsely narrow concepts of subject matter, since they value only "academic" learnings.
2. Liberal-arts professors believe, though not saying it in just so many words, that the anti-democratic indoctrination of "right" answers is the only teaching method.
3. Liberal-arts professors fail to realize that teaching competencies involve much more than just knowing the facts and concepts of a liberal-arts subject matter field.
4. Liberal-arts professors fight against the professionalization of the teaching profession.
5. Liberal-arts professors believe, mistakenly, that education courses emphasize methods to the almost total exclusion of content.
6. Liberal-arts professors hold unfounded, prejudiced, inaccurate, and inadequate concepts of education degree requirements, since they believe, mistakenly, that these degrees are inferior and easier to attain than liberal-arts degrees.
7. Instead of fostering student recognition of prejudices and provincialisms, liberal-arts professors violate the liberalizing ideal of the liberal arts by encouraging narrow, mutually exclusive subject-matter specialization, and irrational prejudices against education courses and educationists.

Educationists believe that the crowning scholarly achievements of the past are of value only if they prove to be functional in the flux of present social institutions and problems. Rather than centering education on knowledge of specific information and concepts, usually divorced from present institutional problems, educators center their attention on the problems of a presently burgeoning cultural institution—public education. In striving to satisfy the continually increasing demands for adequate teachers, educators are immersed in the pressures of the present. The kaleidoscopic present cannot be dealt with satisfactorily on the basis of the traditional liberal-arts concentration on training the minds of brighter students. Educators must develop teacher-education programs which will result in teachers who are competent to deal with a vast variety of student abilities and interests. Teachers must not only be academic scholars training student minds; they must understand how each student learns and develops in his own cultural environment. Scholarly knowledge of the cultural heritage is not taken to be an educational end in itself, but as a means to be used in guiding individuals toward their optimum development. Developing the mind, the traditional liberal arts objective, is only one of many equally important aspects of the development of whole persons. In summary, functional or operational modern sociological and psychological concepts, not medieval traditions, are the foundations of the educators' position.[3]

PERSPECTIVES ON THE CONFLICT

In attempting to gain perspective in examining the liberal arts versus education conflict, it first should be noted that the conflict has been going on for a long time. Contemporary liberal-arts supporters, such as Arthur Bestor, Mortimer Smith, John Keats, and Hyman Rickover, reiterate the accusations that were made at the turn of the century. Both groups tend to talk in vague generalities, failing to specify the educational levels and areas they mean to be talking about. Most of the bitter name calling and caustic assertions apparently are not supported by scholarly evidence on either side.

Through their failure to recognize teaching as a respectable area, the liberal-arts professors apparently defaulted and lost the initiative in teacher education to the educators. The liberal-arts group has counterattacked vigorously in the last two decades. So far, the educators' lines basically have held, possibly because a large segment of the public appears to agree with their emphasis on functionalism. Some classroom teachers have questioned whether either group has basic knowledge of what is going on in today's schools or knows what problems classroom teachers commonly face.

In his *A Fourth of a Nation*, Paul Woodring eloquently argues for a synthesis of the classicist liberal-arts position and the pragmatic educator position. Apparently, he would seek a "golden mean" between the extremes. However, the liberal arts versus education dualism, and Woodring's middle-of-the-road synthesis of the dualistic extremes, are based on the assumption that education is something different from liberal arts.

THE CONFLICT ANALYZED

Is it valid to assume that education is something quite different from the liberal arts, or may education be a liberal-arts field? Since, for

---

[3] See Woodring, *A Fourth of a Nation*, Chapter 3—The Growth of the Whole Child: The Pragmatic Antithesis, pp. 54–90.

example, study of the economic facets of our society is the liberal-arts field of economics, the study of the educational aspects of our society seemingly qualifies as the liberal-arts field of education. Since education thus appears to be a liberal-arts field, it would thereby become a part of a liberally educated person's competency. If education is recognized as a liberal-arts field, the liberal arts versus education dualism is invalidated, since education could not logically be placed in a dualistic position in opposition to the liberal arts; nor could there be a position midway between the extremes because there are no extreme positions.

Since liberal arts versus education does not provide a valid contrast, are there any distinctions that can be made? Traditionally, there has been a distinction made between the liberal-arts studies which, hopefully, develop a broadly cultured person, and occupational training programs which prepare a person for a particular vocation.

As indicated by the following chart, biology is a necessary foundation for medicine, just as social studies education is based on social studies and art education is based on art.

Liberal Arts	*Occupational*
Subject-Matter Fields	Subject-Matter Fields
1. Biology ———————→	1. Medicine
2. Social Studies ——————→	2. Social Studies Education
3. Art ————————→	3. Art Education

Many writers fail to note that there are significant differences between liberal arts and occupational content-fields. They recognize only the existence of the liberal arts as subject-matter fields.

Consider the case of a physician who went through a four-year, biology curriculum, took a "methods" course in medicine, interned in a hospital for a semester, then was licensed to practice medicine. Could it be said that he had been through a valid medical-preparatory program? Obviously not. Similarly, is a person who completes a major in social studies, takes a "methods" course in teaching social studies, then student teaches for a term, qualified as a social studies teacher? Has he been through a valid preparatory program for social studies teaching? Again, obviously not.

What, then, is "teacher education"? Teacher education programs presently involve a number of liberal-arts content courses, some liberal-arts-education courses (such as Introduction to Education and

Philosophy of Education), and one or two occupationally-oriented methods courses. The previous comparison of medicine and social studies education illustrates the inadequacy of such teacher education programs.

GRADUATE, OCCUPATIONAL EDUCATION

Perhaps a more tenable pattern of beliefs in regard to preparatory programs for occupations in the teaching area can be built on the premises that: (1) there are a number of occupations in the teaching area; (2) each should require separate graduate study, similar to medical school; and (3) each graduate program should be based on relevant, undergraduate, liberal-arts studies.

The following chart compares the present medical education program with a projected similar program in social studies education.

Years		Years	
9.	Internship	9.	Internship
	M.D. Degree		S.S. Education Doctorate
8.	Occupational	8.	Graduate
7.	Graduate	7.	School of
6.	School of	6.	Social Studies
5.	Medicine	5.	Education
4.	Undergraduate	4.	Undergraduate
3.	Liberal Arts	3.	Liberal Arts
2.	Program in	2.	Program in
1.	Biology	1.	Social Studies

The shaded sections of the chart indicate that, just as contact with patients tends to increase gradually as students move through a medical school program, a similar increase would be appropriate in a social studies education program.

The generally accepted traditional assumption that all "teachers" are on the same role level can be questioned. A very small percentage of those working in medicine are at the physician level, the others being persons in paraprofessional jobs such as nurses, laboratory technicians, dietitians, nurses aids, etc., who function in medical teams under the direction of physicians. Similarly, only a very small number of participants in the social-studies teaching area would be graduates with degrees comparable to the M.D. level. The rest would be in paraprofessional roles, such as social studies media laboratory technicians, social studies field trip assistants, etc., functioning as team members under the direction of social studies "master teachers."

Very little work, if any, has been done about extremely basic things, such as determining how many educational occupational areas there are and what competencies should be involved in each one. Even less work has been done, if this is possible, in projecting and defining competencies to be required in para-occupations in the various areas, such as in the social-studies teaching area.

Another question is, what would happen to present education professors if existing teacher education programs were replaced by occupational programs? Obviously, a number would be needed to teach undergraduate liberal arts education courses and a number would be needed in graduate schools where education teachers would be trained. It also is fairly obvious that various occupational graduate schools would need to be staffed. Education professors thus inclined probably could prepare themselves to help to staff such programs.

TRANSCENDING THE LIBERAL ARTS VERSUS EDUCATION DUALISM

Replacing teacher education programs with graduate occupational programs probably would transcend, not synthesize, the liberal arts versus education dualism. Such occupational programs might satisfy the liberal arts professors' desires for scholarly liberal-arts subject-matter knowledge, but would transcend the liberal-arts professors' nonawareness of or lack of interest in the existence of occupational subject-matter content. Graduate occupational programs might satisfy the educators' desires for student knowledge of "education," but would transcend their nonawareness or ignoring of occupational competencies.

The chances for a shift from present teacher education programs to graduate occupational programs are problematical, due to the apparent lack of awareness by many public school teachers, by most education professors, and by other educational leaders, that teacher preparation programs are based on questionable premises. Will teacher education be replaced?

Is teacher education an illusion?

SELECTED REFERENCES

Combs, Arthur W., *The Professional Education of Teachers*. Boston: Allyn and Bacon, Inc., 1965. A challenging study of teacher education from the perceptual-existential approach.

Conant, James B., *The Education of American Teachers*. New York: McGraw-Hill Book Company, 1963. An introductory study of teacher education.

Education for the Professions. The Sixty-first Yearbook of the National Society for the Study of Education, Part II, Nelson B. Henry, ed. Chicago, Illinois: University of Chicago Press, 1962. A comparative study of professional education. Particularly note the chapters on Medicine, The Teaching Profession, and The University and Professional Education.

Koerner, James D., *The Miseducation of American Teachers*. Boston: Houghton Mifflin Company, 1963. A slashing attack on educationists and their teacher education programs.

Lieberman, Myron, *The Future of Public Education*. Chicago, Illinois: University of Chicago Press, 1960, Chaps. 6 and 7. A stimulating analysis of teacher education.

McGrath, Earl J., and Charles H. Russell, *Are School Teachers Illiberally Educated?* New York: Teachers College, Columbia University, 1961. A defense of the educationist position. Also see McGrath's *Liberal Education in the Professions*.

Schwartz, Lita Linzer, *American Education—A Problem-Centered Approach*. Boston, Mass.: Holbrook Press, 1969, Chap. 10. Provocative reactions to teacher education are presented.

Sources for Intellectual Foundations of Modern Education, William E. Drake, ed. Columbus, Ohio: Charles E. Merrill Books, 1967. Thoughtful articles on teacher education.

Stinnett, T. M., *Professional Problems of Teachers*. New York: The Macmillan Company, 1968. A basic teacher education text.

THOUGHT AIDS

1. How valid, to you, are the liberal-arts advocates' criticisms of teacher education programs? Why?
2. How valid, to you, are the educators' criticisms of liberal arts professors? Why?
3. Obtain the forty-minute tape recording "How Should America's Teachers

Be Educated?" from the National Tape Repository, Bureau of A-V Instruction, University of Colorado, Boulder, Colorado. The two opposing speakers are Arthur Bestor and Karl Bigelow. How valid to you are their positions? Why?

4. Do you agree with the contention that education is a liberal-arts field? Why or why not?
5. Do you agree that there should be occupational content-fields which would be distinct from liberal-arts content-fields? Why or why not?
6. What are possible arguments for and against the "graduate occupational education" concept? How valid to you are these arguments?
7. Do you believe that the "graduate occupation education" concept successfully transcends the liberal arts versus education dualism? Why or why not?
8. Do you agree with the contention that "teacher education" is an illusion? Why or why not?
9. "There is a principle which is a bar against all information, which is proof against all argument, and which cannot fail to keep a man in everlasting ignorance. That principle is condemnation before investigation." (Herbert Spencer) Relate Spencer's statement to the teacher education conflict.

13

Which Type of Academic Freedom Is Best?

The post-World War II period has been turbulent in the area of freedom of thought. The McCarthy-type investigation has come and, many hope, gone. Loyalty oaths have been prescribed by possibly insecure legislators who believed that public educational institutions were hotbeds of subversion. The practice of determining disloyalty to "Americanism" by association rather than by individual action has cast a mantle of caution and fear over many teachers, particularly in the social studies area. Association with alleged "communists" has been a basis for ejection from teaching. Conformity, rather than creativity, seemingly has been the basic intellectual climate fostered by the uncertainties of a protracted cold war. To many Americans, national survival requires a completely united front against the enemy. Dissent and subversion become blurred together. In such a climate, the freedom of teachers to reach scholarly and intellectually defensible conclusions, regardless of commonly accepted beliefs, has been questioned by many groups.

In this time of turmoil, several conflicting types of academic freedom have been advocated. One type of academic freedom which has been long practiced and which finds strong support, particularly among many conservative groups, is autocratic or totalitarian. In totalitarian academic freedom, teachers have complete freedom only to indoctrinate students with self-evident specially-privileged conclusions, beliefs, or "right" answers. Since many local lay school boards appear to be dominated by conservative community groups, teachers are allowed only to foster student acceptance of present economic and political institutions. Teachers usually are expected to ". . . stress the soundness of the principles on which our nation was founded . . ." [1]

A second type of academic freedom, apparently advocated by some college and university teachers, is "total freedom and liberty," or anarchism. Advocates of this permissive academic freedom appear to believe that teachers should be completely free to teach whatever they please in any way they please. This anarchistic freedom apparently also would be accorded to students. They would be free to learn, if they please, what they please, and when they please.

A third type of academic freedom, reflective academic freedom, also has been advocated. Under this system, students and teachers are free only to carry out the reflective investigative method of modern science. Instead of being free only to inculcate conformity to "self-evident" conclusions, or being free to do as they please, teachers are free only to foster student abilities to carry out the reflective method of raising and solving problems. Teachers are free only to develop student abilities to weigh conflicting alternatives on the basis of clearly recognized standards.

Under the totalitarian type of academic freedom, teachers are free only to cause students to develop the abilities to revere, respect, accept, value, acquiesce in, and conform to "The Truth." Such abilities are appropriate in totalitarian societies where unquestioning obedience to authority and acceptance of established institutions and values is the only acceptable course. In contrast, under the anarchistic type of academic freedom, teachers and students may do as they individually please. Student abilities to do as they please, abilities appropriate in anarchistic societies where total autonomy reigns supreme, are fostered. In further contrast, under the reflective type of academic freedom, teachers are free to foster only the analytical abilities needed in democratic societies, the abilities to evaluate alternatives and to participate in the democratic decision-making governmental processes. Which is the best type of academic freedom?

---

[1] *Report of the Committee on Tenure and Academic Freedom* (Washington, D.C.: National Education Association, 1950).

TOTALITARIAN ACADEMIC FREEDOM

Under the totalitarian type of academic freedom in which teachers are free only to indoctrinate right answers, the major considerations are what are the right answers and who determines that they are right? As might be expected, there are a number of conflicting answers to these questions. They range from the classicist's insistence that classical truths are the right answers, through the American conservative's patriotic assertion that capitalistic free enterprise and rugged individualism are immutable truths, to the collectivist's "unquestionable" knowledge that collectivism is clearly right and that capitalism is antiquated and evil. All of these types of totalitarian academic freedom have had their followers on the American education scene. However, since most public school teachers appear to be controlled by local lay school boards who are generally conservatively oriented, our attention here will be given to the conservative type.

The totalitarian belief that teachers should be allowed only to transmit "The Truth" is based on the assertion that teachers are governmental employees. Lay school boards, representatives of the public, have the responsibility to see that students are taught to be good Americans and are not exposed to insidious un-American influences. The privilege to teach what the community wants taught is a reward bestowed on teachers who conform to accepted institutions, beliefs, and values; and they are allowed to do only this. They are not allowed to teach anything subversive to the fundamental principles and ideals of the United States.[2] In essence, supporters of totalitarian academic freedom believe that the schools should be loyal agencies for support and preservation of the present form of society and government.

One of the most effective groups apparently fostering totalitarian academic freedom is the public school teachers themselves. Many teachers tend to hold, unquestioningly, the values and beliefs held by the conservative power groups who usually control local lay boards of education.[3] Therefore, these teachers are not aware of their freedom being restricted to transmitting the status quo because they unknowingly restrict themselves to it. They sense no infringements upon their teaching since they believe in and impose on their students their

---

[2] Elizabeth Staples, "Academic Freedom," *American Mercury* 90, no. 434 (March, 1960): 69.

[3] Howard K. Beale, *Are American Teachers Free?* (New York: Charles Scribner's Sons, 1936), pp. x–xi and 634–39.

own conventional and orthodox beliefs. Teachers who foster totalitarian academic freedom are not concerned with whether or not they have the freedom to express unorthodox ideas because they do not have them. They tend unquestioningly to accept and use the totalitarian teaching procedures most of their own college and public school teachers used.

Since totalitarian teachers tend to be unaware of the conventional values they have absorbed, they usually have not even thought about the possibility of being free to differ from or disagree with conventional community opinion. They do not feel a need to protect their freedom of expression since they are free to express the conventional cultural beliefs to which they are accustomed. Their background has conditioned them to accept automatically the conservative American value system, and it would not occur to most of them even to question whether or not accepted "facts" and values could be open to controversy. Instead of thoughtfully analyzing current prejudices, such totalitarian-oriented teachers often unknowingly share them.[4]

Totalitarian academic freedom appears to be actively fostered by many school administrators. They are interested in running school systems which foster the conservative beliefs of their employers—lay school boards. They value a peaceful and smoothly functioning school system, one that is acceptable to the conservative groups who tend to lead and control the community. The successful administrator often is the one who is skilled in avoiding "scenes." In such situations, the "uncooperative" teacher who questions generally accepted values or institutions can rarely be tolerated because he has an unsettling effect on the status quo.

As may be expected, conservative lay school boards tend to be powerful forces aligned with totalitarian academic freedom, since they tend to have a fairly free hand in their schools. Through their power over the hiring and firing of teachers, they can encourage the teacher who indoctrinates the status quo and discourage the "subversive" teacher who would cast doubt on the accepted order of things.

The conservatism that is a dominant element in the American social structure also strengthens totalitarian academic freedom. Although Americans have been inventive and original in technical areas,

---

[4] *See* Maurice Hunt and Lawrence Metcalf, *Teaching High School Social Studies* (New York: Harper & Brothers, 1955), pp. 434–36. Hunt and Metcalf claim that any individual who has never doubted or questioned what he has absorbed from his environment is an unreflective victim of cultural conditioning and is imprisoned by the dictates of cultural determinism.

they have tended to be extremely cautious and conservative in the areas of ideas and institutions. America's prosperity has resulted in worship of rugged individualism, property rights, and nationalism. The public tends to be openly opposed to radical social and economic changes. The authoritative pronouncements of the past, many of which are enshrined in the Constitution, tend to foster immutable values and institutions. In such a conservative climate, teachers and students tend to be so inculcated with traditional folkways that they are practically immune to the disturbing influence of unique ideas.

Totalitarian academic freedom is encouraged by certain pressure groups. Patriotic organizations working in conjunction with the conservative press develop highly effective restraints on teachers who would criticize the status quo. For example, patriotic organizations, including women's clubs, have spearheaded the drives for loyalty oath legislation in some states. Such loyalty oaths usually obligate teachers to support the Constitution and other conservative institutions. Various religious, labor, business, racial, and fraternal groups also have fostered allowing teachers to be free only to teach the "right" things. Each group, of course, would insist that their beliefs are the "right" ones.

Some persons have contended that teacher beliefs are not restricted as much now to totalitarian academic freedom procedures as they were in the past. For example, science teachers generally are free to teach about evolution; religious restrictions are almost anachronisms. However, it can be contended that the reason teachers are no longer restricted to totalitarian academic freedom in these areas is that such areas no longer are matters which are of vital concern to the general public. Colonial restrictions on religious teachings and the allowing of teachers to express only sectionally popular viewpoints (for example, either supporting or opposing slavery during the pre-Civil War period), are now viewed by many as amusing examples of the narrow-mindedness of our ancestors. Perhaps these are amusing only because they are no longer matters of vital interest to the public.

It validly may be asked, "Has the totalitarian academic freedom principle—denial of intellectual freedom to analyze unorthodox ideas in the classroom—been rejected? Or, are teachers restricted now to teaching only orthodox ideas in presently vital areas, just as teachers were restricted to approved beliefs in the past vital areas of religion and slavery?" It may be argued that today's teachers are no more free to analyze capitalism and nationalism than were the nineteenth century teachers in the South free to criticize slavery. Just as the slaveholder restricted abolitionistic teachings because they threatened to destroy a way of life on which he depended, so the dominant business interests of today appear to restrict criticism of the capitalistic way of life on which they depend. As Howard Beale has noted, intellectual suppression wears different garbs in different periods; therefore, a change of dress should not be confused with a change of heart.[5] Intolerance toward "communist" teachers and the denial of adequately unbiased analyses of the segregation-integration problem are cases in point in a long history of the acceptance of totalitarian academic freedom in areas of vital public concern.

ANARCHISTIC ACADEMIC FREEDOM

Anarchistic academic freedom also has a long and distinguished history, with the belief that teachers should be free to teach the truth as they see it receiving strong impetus in German universities. Over the centuries, these universities developed the tradition that the professors should be free from the requirement of conformity to accepted beliefs. This freedom of expression was particularly emphasized in the area of political beliefs. In the last century, this German tradition of intellectual freedom has found fertile ground in American colleges and universities. Most college and university professors appear to accept the belief that teachers should have the privilege of being free to teach what they accept as the truth; the scholar should be intellectually free to express his beliefs, no matter how currently unpopular they may be.

The belief in anarchistic student freedom has historical roots in the practices and writings of Jean Jacques Rousseau, Johann Heinrich Pestalozzi, and Friedrich Wilhelm Froebel. Student liberty received tremendous impetus in the student-centered progressive education movement under the guiding genius of William H. Kilpatrick. Students were encouraged to arrive at and express whatever beliefs or "project" conclusions they desired.

A difficulty with many of the writings in the area of academic freedom is that the writers often seem to fail to indicate clearly what type of academic freedom they are talking about. Although they usually do not offer clear definitions of academic freedom, most of them do appear to be fostering anarchistic freedom because they appear to favor allowing teachers to be free to teach as they please.

---

[5] Howard K. Beale, *A History of Freedom of Teaching in American Schools* (New York: Charles Scribner's Sons, 1941), pp. xii–xiii, 263. *See also* Robert M. MacIver, *Academic Freedom in Our Times* (New York: Columbia University Press, 1955).

REFLECTIVE ACADEMIC FREEDOM

In contrast, reflective academic freedom allows teachers to foster only the abilities needed in democratic societies, the abilities to evaluate conflicting alternatives and participate in decision-making processes. Under reflective academic freedom, a teacher is not free to be anarchistic, to teach as he pleases. Conversely, he also is not free to indoctrinate the students, to condition them to accept certain "self-evident" conclusions or beliefs. The teacher has only the freedom to use the reflective problem-solving process, the method of modern science which provokes analytical thought and encourages reflective inquiry. Teachers and students only have academic freedom to: (1) Raise conflicts; (2) Formulate hypothetical solutions for the conflicts; (3) Formulate standards or criteria for evaluating the adequacy of the solutions; (4) Carry out activities judging the solutions on the bases of the criteria; and (5) Arrive at only the solution or solutions which most adequately satisfy the criteria.

Reflective academic freedom involves the freedom to analyze critically teacher and pupil conclusions on the basis of tentative standards or "rules" adopted by the classroom group. There are no specially-privileged viewpoints. All viewpoints, including the teachers', are to be judged on the bases of the accepted criteria. All beliefs must stand or fall on the basis of thoughtful examination. Neither teachers nor students are free to do as they please; they are bound by tentative criteria and must arrive at the problem solutions most in harmony with the criteria. Anarchistic academic freedom of teachers and students to do as they please is eliminated by teacher guidance and criticism of students on the basis of the criteria, and by student guidance and criticism of teachers on the same basis. Totalitarian academic freedom to indoctrinate the students is eliminated since teacher-presented viewpoints do not receive preferential status.

Teachers and learners have the freedom to doubt, question, discuss, criticize, and reflectively examine any institutions and beliefs, no matter how self-evidently sacred they may be to certain groups. Student freedom to express, and to defend, their beliefs and to question and doubt accepted beliefs without repression or scholastic penalization must be encouraged and safeguarded. There must be liberty to dissent, to doubt, and to stir up controversy. If, in contrast, a teacher imposes his beliefs and conclusions on his students, he is violating their reflective freedom, which is a right of both teacher and students.

Teachers who foster reflective academic freedom are loyal to the problem-solving thought process rather than to particular conclusions which may be arrived at either through it or through non-reflective thought processes. Reflective teachers are loyal to analytical thought rather than to capitalism, socialism, individualism, collectivism, naturalism, supernaturalism, nationalism, or internationalism. They are not reactionaries, conservatives, or compulsive radicals. They hold the basic concept that any belief deserves reflective examination if circumstances seem to indicate such examination is warranted. Recognizing that today's patriotic orthodoxy probably was yesterday's disloyal heresy, reflective teachers do not emphasize placing labels, such as orthodox and loyal or heretical and subversive, on ideas, institutions, and beliefs.

A basic argument for totalitarian academic freedom is that, since teachers are public servants, it is proper for them to be told what to teach. This concept is in conflict with the functions of teachers in reflective or scientific societies. Their basic task is to foster reflective thinking, which may involve critical analyses of existing policies and which may result in recommendations for change. In contrast, the public official or public "servant" swears to perpetuate certain policies and institutions.

In totalitarian countries, schools are loyal agencies for the support and perpetuation of existing institutions, including the current form of government. Under totalitarian academic freedom, teachers must renounce criticism of the status quo, and only teachers who loyally support the ruling group are allowed to teach. In contrast, reflective schools stress thoughtful examination of presently accepted institutions, the status quo, in order to ascertain whether or not improved forms can be devised. Some conservatives, with the most to lose if the status quo were replaced, object to reflective academic freedom because there is no guarantee as to precisely where reflective thinking will lead, what sacred idols might be displaced. In classrooms where reflective thinking is promoted, there are no foregone or self-evident conclusions, and such uncertainty can put the status quo in peril. But such uncertainty also provides the opportunity for growth beyond present concepts of the "American Way of Life." Some who advocate totalitarian academic freedom seem to equate reflective doubting and examining of existing things with subversion and disloyalty. They fail to recognize that doubting things as they are is a necessary ingredient in a democratically-oriented society.

The disloyal teacher in a democratic society is the one who either attempts to inculcate specially privileged unquestionable facts and beliefs, or attempts to teach what he pleases and attempts to let students believe as they please. Totalitarian teachers who condition their students to accept the status quo are undermining student ability to weigh alternatives, a basic competency needed for participation in democratic societies. The disloyal teacher in a democratic society is the one who fails to foster reflection.

It is sometimes believed that in order to avoid personal indoctrination, the teacher must be neutral when the class is dealing with controversial issues. This belief seems to be based upon inadequate concepts regarding the function of a reflective teacher. The neutrality belief seems to assume that any positive guiding of student beliefs in controversial areas involves indoctrination. However, student learning may be guided in both totalitarian and democratic ways. Democratic thought-guidance involves analysis of both student-held and teacher-held beliefs on the basis of acceptable criteria. In order for students to have adequate experiences with evaluation of beliefs on the basis of evidence or merit, rather than on the basis of the source of the beliefs, students must be given opportunities to examine reflectively all relevant beliefs, regardless of source. The teacher's beliefs, along with those held by students and other groups, should serve as raw material for reflective analyses by the class group. In order to avoid surreptitiously indoctrinating the students with his beliefs, a teacher should attempt to indicate his position, and warn the students to be on their guard against his biases. The ability to be critical of beliefs, including those held by the teacher, should be encouraged in reflectively-oriented classrooms.

It becomes fairly apparent that a reflective teacher is not neutral. He demonstrates a belief in the value of the reflective process. He values doubt, questioning, controversy, and the inclination to base conclusions on adequate evidence. He values reflective examination of his beliefs. In order to foster student academic freedom to develop reflective abilities, teachers should attempt clearly to indicate their beliefs so students may examine such beliefs on the basis of evidence. The democratic teacher does not pretend to be isolated and detached from significant issues, but will attempt to understand his biases and assume responsibility for them.[6]

The neutrality concept also finds expression in textbooks which are designed to be as innocuous or harmless as possible. In harmony with the neutrality concept, textbooks should not stir up conflicts or foster reflective thinking. Textbooks should present accepted facts and concepts in a clear, well-organized and interesting manner. It

---

[6] For an excellent presentation of criticisms of the neutrality concept, see Hunt and Metcalf, *Teaching High School Social Studies*, pp. 439–42.

is assumed "apparently" that if the textbook writer takes a stand in a controversial area, the students will be indoctrinated with his viewpoint. This is based on the totalitarian assumption that the text should convey the absolute truth. In contrast, from a reflective viewpoint, a text should be a resource for conflicting or controversial materials which will foster reflection.

Since reflective academic freedom seems to be the only type of academic freedom that clearly is compatible with democratic goals, why do few teachers understand and use it? One answer is that most teachers appear not to have been made aware that there even is a reflective type of teaching, let alone how to acquire the competencies for using it. They have unquestioningly accepted the "right answer handout" system as the only way. They take for granted the totalitarian or transmissive teaching procedures which have been passed on to them by their own teachers.

Freedom of teachers and students to follow the reflective thought process wherever it may lead seemingly never has been generally accepted as a basic principle in American education either by the general public, by school boards, by administrative representatives of the boards, or by teachers. Even in higher education, which is the usual source of discussions about academic freedom, such freedom has not usually been taken by administrators and governing boards to be indispensable. Historically speaking, reflective academic freedom has never been securely rooted in the American culture, even though it has found support in the rise of the modern scientific method and in the teachings of John Dewey and some of his followers.

ACADEMIC FREEDOM AND PROFESSIONALISM

As was noted in the section on totalitarian academic freedom, the present educational power structure directed by lay boards of education apparently tends to support totalitarian academic freedom. What type of education power structure would support and effectively protect reflective academic freedom? Other than the writings of Myron Lieberman and Howard Beale, there is almost a total lack of clear and effective suggestions as to how the present basically anti-reflective conditions could be alleviated. In fact, most writers seemingly favoring the reflective type of academic freedom fail to indicate that they are even aware that the power to make most of the significant decisions about freedoms in the teaching occupations lies with persons who are not teaching practitioners. Under the present structure, lay school boards or their administrators are able to invade or destroy reflective academic freedom at will, since there is no countervailing power with which they must reckon.

It should be made clear: there is no implication made here that board members or school administrators are sinister, vicious, or unprincipled. Like most teachers, most board members and school administrators appear to be normal, intelligent, well-meaning, and often self-sacrificing individuals. However, the present educational power structure seemingly tends to provide for the fostering of interests other than reflective academic freedom when conflicts between such freedom and other interests occur.

What type of power structure could effectively implement and protect reflective academic freedom? If teachers were united in professional organizations which effectively controlled training for, entrance into, and expulsion from the various teaching occupations, reflective academic freedom probably could be effectively protected. Without group control by occupational practitioners, there are no teaching professions, and without teaching professions there appear to be no consistently adequate safeguards for reflective academic freedom. Certain writers who praise this freedom seem to be confused; they would leave decision-making powers and responsibility for implementation of reflective academic freedom in the hands of lay boards and their administrative representatives who have tended, traditionally, to support totalitarian academic freedom. It is fairly apparent that, in order to foster reflective academic freedom, teachers themselves should control the making of significant decisions in their areas of teaching competency, including decisions about academic freedom.

Most of the writers on this subject avoid any discussion of possible relationships between professional power and academic freedom. One of the basic traits of a profession is that practitioners are free to make decisions about occupational objectives within their professional areas of competency. For example, within the general objectives of medicine, which are established by society, medical doctors are only free to act and make decisions which are designed to foster those objectives. They are not free to act contrary to stipulated goals. Similarly, in accordance with the commonly expressed democratic national goals of the United States, teachers should have the professional autonomy to develop the reflective abilities needed in democratic societies.

Are the various types of academic freedom compatible with professional autonomy? Anarchistic academic freedom appears to conflict with professional autonomy, since anarchistic teachers would be free to teach as they please. In contrast, professional autonomy requires that teachers be free to foster national democratic goals. Totalitarian academic freedom also appears to be in conflict with professional autonomy since it not only rejects democratic professional objectives, but also rejects teacher freedom to determine how the objectives will be implemented. In contrast, professional autonomy is compatible with reflective academic freedom. Reflective teachers would be free to operate within the limitations of general objectives requiring them to develop students competent to participate in a democratic society. They would be free to choose subjects, concepts to be emphasized, and curricular materials, such as textbooks, which would best foster student reflective abilities.

Reflective or democratic academic freedom does not occur in a vacuum. It is the result of a positive use of power by organizations within the various teaching occupations. Specifically, this would mean that the members of the social studies teaching occupation would organize to control the training, licensing, hiring, and firing procedures in their occupation. They would write contracts to be entered into with school boards, and the boards' administrative representatives. The contracts would require that the social studies organization's officials would determine, after receiving a complaint, whether or not a particular teacher's reflective academic freedom had been violated. The contract would stipulate that if they determine that occupational freedom had been violated, the social studies teachers in that district would continue to receive their pay; however, they would withdraw their services until such time as their occupational organization deems they are again free to be responsible for conditions in their schools. The contracts of the various other teaching occupations would stipulate that their teachers would also withdraw their services until academic freedom violations ceased in that school district. It is fairly apparent that if such power procedures were used by the various teaching occupations, few violations of reflective academic freedom would occur because most school boards, administrators, and pressure groups would be anxious to avoid the punitive results.

Therefore, if teachers desire to achieve reflective academic freedom, it appears that they should unite in aggressive and dynamic professional occupational associations. However, due to the absence of powerful teaching occupational organizations, it appears that lay boards, administrators, and other pressure groups generally are free to intimidate reflectively-oriented teachers. If forces against reflective academic freedom are not effectively opposed through use of professional power, reflective academic freedom may be almost totally extinguished, even though many eloquent individual voices may be raised high in its praise.

CONCLUSION

In many public schools totalitarian academic freedom, supported by conservative school boards and their administrators, appears to be prevalent. Anarchistic academic freedom is vigorously supported, at least verbally, by many college and university professors. There appears to be very little fostering of the reflective type of academic freedom which is most compatible with development of the democratic abilities popularly espoused in our society. Professional autonomy, necessarily involved in effective enhancement of reflective or democratic academic freedom, appears to be ignored by most writers in this area.

SELECTED REFERENCES

Beale, Howard K., *A History of Freedom of Teaching in American Schools.* Report of the Commission on the Social Studies of the American Historical Association, Part XVI. New York: Charles Scribner's Sons, 1941. A historical account of the restrictions on the freedom of American teachers in schools below the college level.

————, *Are American Teachers Free?* Report of the Commission on the Social Studies of the American Historical Association. New York: Charles Scribner's Sons, 1936, Part XII. A dated but basic analysis of many of the conflict areas in academic freedom.

Ehlers, Henry and Gordon C. Lee, *Crucial Issues in Education.* New York: Holt, Rinehart and Winston, 1964, Part I. Readings in the area of educational freedom and loyalty are presented.

Hofstadter, Richard and Walter P. Metzger, *The Development of Academic Freedom in the United States.* New York: Columbia University Press, 1955. A historical study of the rise, development and problems of academic freedom in the United States. It is a companion volume to Robert M. MacIver's *Academic Freedom in Our Time.*

Hunt, Maurice and Lawrence Metcalf, *Teaching High School Social Studies.* New York: Harper & Brothers, 1955, Chap. 20. An excellent introduction to problems in academic freedom.

Issues in Education—An Anthology of Controversy, Bernard Johnston, ed. Boston: Houghton Mifflin Company, 1964, Part Two. Articles on academic freedom range from Plato to testimony before the Jenner Committee.

Kerber, August and Wilfred R. Smith, *Educational Issues in a Changing Society.* Detroit, Mich.: Wayne State University Press, 1964, Chap. 9. A series of articles on academic freedom.

Lieberman, Myron, *The Future of Public Education.* Chicago: The University of Chicago Press, 1960. A recent study of relationships between professionalism and academic freedom.

MacIver, Robert M. *Academic Freedom in Our Time.* New York: Columbia University Press, 1955. An excellent exposition of many aspects of academic freedom. Although dated, the selected bibliography may be particularly useful in analyzing the status of academic freedom during the ten years immediately following World War II.

Schwartz, Lita Linzer, *American Education—A Problem-Centered Approach.* Boston, Mass.: Holbrook Press, 1969, Chap. 11. Article authors include Sterling M. McMurrin, Richard M. Nixon, and Henry Steele Commager.

THOUGHT AIDS

1. Indicate important topics in the area of academic freedom which were not presented in this chapter. Why are they important to you?
2. Read several of the references and report to the class on similarities and differences between the viewpoints on academic freedom as expressed in the references.
3. Evaluate the public myths about academic freedom which are noted by Hunt and Metcalf in their book, *Teaching High School Social Studies,* pp. 435–47 (1955 edition).
4. Analyze the definitions of academic freedom presented in various educational and general dictionaries and encyclopedias on the basis of concepts presented in this chapter.
5. Collect and evaluate examples of attacks on reflective academic freedom. Examples may be found in newspapers, magazines, books, and reports. Publications by certain conservative groups, such as the American Legion, sometimes are fruitful sources. Radio broadcasts also may contain criticisms of reflective academic freedom.
6. Do you agree with the contention that most teachers are not aware of reflective academic freedom? Why or why not?

7. Present to the class a comprehensive report on pressure groups who are attempting to undermine reflective academic freedom.
8. Analyze recent cases on alleged violations of academic freedom which are presented in recent issues of the *AAUP Bulletin.*
9. Study and report on the American Civil Liberties Union position on academic freedom. Compare the ACLU position with that held by the AAUP.
10. From a professional viewpoint, who should determine if academic freedom is being violated? Why?
11. Do you agree with the belief that the present educational power structure tends to support totalitarian academic freedom? Why or why not?
12. Are there any topics which teachers should not be allowed to present or discuss in their classes? If yes, which ones?

14

Which Is Better, the National Education Association or the American Federation of Teachers?

Education is one of the rare organizational areas in which there are two associations vying for acceptance. The National Education Association, about ten times the size of the American Federation of Teachers, traditionally has been conservative and rural-oriented. Conversely, the AFT has been militant, with its strength concentrated in the large cities. The NEA is an "umbrella" organization, covering all educational areas. The AFT claims to be the only organization which attempts to represent classroom teachers alone. The NEA claims that the AFT, a member of the AFL-CIO, is under the domination of the unions. Returning the "compliment," the AFT claims that teachers in the NEA are dominated by school administrators and the lay school boards the administrators represent. The NEA supports professional negotiations and endorses the use of sanctions if negotiations are unsuccessful. In contrast, the AFT supports collective bargaining and favors striking when bargaining fails.

Although both organizations unstintingly pat themselves on the back and heap scorn on the other organization, some thoughtful critics feel that both groups are dismal failures. In his thought-provoking book *The Future of Public Education,* Myron Lieberman is highly critical of both organizations.

> The foremost fact about teachers' organizations in the United
> States is their irrelevance to the national scene. Their futility in

protecting the public interest and the legitimate vocational aspirations of teachers is a national tragedy, much more dangerous to our democratic institutions than the excessive power wielded by such familiar bogeys as "Madison Avenue," "labor bosses," "captains of industry," "military high brass," and the like. Because their organizations are weak, teachers are without power; because they are without power, power is exercised upon them to weaken and corrupt public education.[1]

THE NEA AND AFT IN HISTORICAL PERSPECTIVE

The roots of the NEA go back to the organization of the National Teachers Association in 1857. In 1870 the NTA merged with the National Association of School Superintendents and the American Normal School Association to form the National Educational Association. When the NEA accepted a congressional charter in 1907, the name was changed to National Education Association of the United States. Prior to 1918, NEA enrollment apparently never exceeded 10,000, and most of this membership consisted of men in administrative positions. Many of these men believed that emphasizing teacher welfare was unprofessional and undignified. Such attitudes led certain teachers to set up organizations which would foster rather than stifle teacher welfare.

Local teachers' unions existed before 1900, but the American Federation of Teachers was organized in 1916 and affiliated with the American Federation of Labor the same year. After struggling to survive for the first two years, the AFT had more teacher members than the NEA by 1919. Some of the founders of the AFT believed that the two organizations should be complementary, not competitive. However, apparently frightened by the unexpected growth of the AFT, the NEA launched an anti-union campaign. Many superintendents forced teachers to join the NEA and its affiliated state and local associations, and forced them to sign non-union contracts. The campaign was so effective that the AFT has never again been a numerical threat to the NEA.

ORGANIZATIONAL STRUCTURES
AND ACTIVITIES OF THE NEA AND AFT

The NEA is like a giant circus with many rings under its big top. For example, in 1967, according to the 1967–68 NEA Handbook, the

---

[1] Myron Lieberman, *The Future of Public Education* (Chicago: University of Chicago Press, 1960), p. 179.

NEA had 1,028,456 individual members, with 59 state and 8,264 local affiliated associations. About 7,000 delegates gather annually for the Representative Assembly. A 94-member Board of Directors and an 11-member Executive Committee conduct Association business between the meetings of the Representative Assemblies. There are over 25 commissions and committees, 17 headquarters divisions, and 33 departments ranging from Art Education, through School Administrators, to Women Deans and Counselors. The Department of Classroom Teachers includes over 80 per cent of the entire NEA membership.

The NEA, one of the world's largest publishing houses, issues about 200 new publications annually. The National Council for Accreditation of Teacher Education fosters higher standards of teacher training. The NEA's research division is excellent. Its public relations program includes press releases, films, filmstrips, brochures, and conferences. The NEA has cooperative programs with the PTA, the American Legion, and the U.S. Office of Education. Its welfare consultants and investigating committees are very active.

The AFT operates with a fairly simple administrative structure. Between the meetings of the 500-member Annual Conventions, the 17-member Executive Council handles the Federation's affairs. The Executive Council is chosen directly by the Annual Convention every two years. Therefore, the AFT membership has more direct control over its executives than does the NEA's Representative Assembly.

The AFT has no occupationally-oriented departments and its research functions basically are restricted to salaries and working conditions. It lacks the manpower and other resources needed in order to compete with the services provided by the NEA. However, the AFT does not consider itself to be in competition with the NEA in the services area, since the AFT basically restricts its efforts to improving the working conditions of teachers. AFT leaders claim that the AFT does not dissipate its energy on numerous "peripheral" activities.

POWER SYSTEM MODELS

Apparently due to pressure from the AFT, the NEA in the last decade has moved from its traditional acceptance of the unilateral corporate power system model in which lay school boards set school district policies, the boards' managers (administrators) administered their policies, and the workers (teachers) unquestioningly carried out lay board policies. The NEA has developed a professional negotiations power system model in which teachers and school administrators in all-inclusive negotiating units work jointly with school boards to set up contractual agreements about conditions of employment.

When procedures for resolving impasses fail, or when lay boards refuse to negotiate, the NEA and its affiliated associations resort to the use of sanctions. Although sanctions may involve various types of censure, the emphasis seems to be on requesting administrators and teachers not to accept employment in school districts or states against which sanctions have been declared.

Instead of adopting the NEA-held assumption that teachers and administrators have an identity of interest when negotiating conditions of employment, the AFT adopts the conflict of interest or employer-employee (private industry) power system model. To the AFT, it is apparent that there is a basic conflict of interest between the administrator who hires and promotes teachers, and the teachers who are hired and promoted. Therefore, the AFT would exclude administrators from membership in classroom teacher organizations and from the teachers' collective bargaining units.

When collective bargaining procedures fail, the AFT seems to favor the strike. To the AFT, a one or two day strike is not a serious imposition on the public's health and welfare; such a brief withdrawal of services is a rapid and basically clean solution to bargaining impasses, whereas sanctions are slow, cumbersome, and messy, and may devastate a school district for an entire school year. Just to keep the record straight, the AFT claims that there have been many more strikes by non-union teachers than by union teachers.

Some thoughtful observers believe that there are only relatively unimportant differences between the NEA's professional negotiations and sanctions power system model and the AFT's collective bargaining and strikes model. For example, certain NEA affiliated local associations exclude management personnel and certain AFT locals welcome them. "Sanction" and "strike" are, to certain observers, merely different labels for the withdrawing of services. Regardless of labels, both the NEA and AFT have been criticized for being confused as to precisely what their "negotiating" or "bargaining" entails.

AFFILIATION PROBLEMS

The AFT's affiliation with organized labor has long been fair game for criticism by the NEA. To the NEA, since teachers work with all people, they should not give allegiance through their organizations to any particular social, economic, or religious group. Instead of gearing teaching to the dictates of the special interests of organized labor, the NEA holds that teachers must remain responsible, independent, self-directive, and free to teach. To the NEA, only the NEA and its affiliated associations are independent, voluntary professional associations. The NEA believes that education can be served best by teachers remaining independent of entangling alliances with any non-educational organizations.

The AFT defends its affiliation with the AFL-CIO by arguing that teachers rarely have the power to proceed alone against the entrenched "tax watchdog" forces. Therefore, since the labor movement is an effective power bloc in many states, virtually the only friendly organized force available to teachers, it is eminently wise for teachers to align themselves with such a powerful ally.

In response to NEA arguments that the AFT is hamstrung by union affiliation, AFT leaders insist that the AFT, like all other labor federations, is autonomous. It is free to follow its own policies, free to take any action it wishes on all specific issues, regardless of what action is taken by the other AFL-CIO federations. It may even leave the AFL-CIO if it desires. As critics of the AFT have noted, this argument appears to weaken decisively the argument for affiliation with the AFL-CIO, since if each labor federation is free to go its own way, each federation will support what it desires, regardless of affiliation. Also many groups outside the AFL-CIO support AFT goals, such as increased federal aid to education.

The NEA's much vaunted teacher independence has been branded as a "gross hypocrisy" by the AFT. To the AFT, the NEA historically has been a "company union," dominated and controlled by the school boards' administrative representatives. To the AFT, instead of teacher membership in the NEA being "voluntary," there traditionally has been a great deal of school administrator pressure on teachers to join the NEA. However, in the last few years the teachers in the NEA have become increasingly militant. Many school administrators have found themselves having to deal, across the bargaining table, with classroom teacher groups supported by the NEA. Therefore, some administrator groups already are withdrawing from NEA-affiliated state education associations.

Although the NEA has severely criticized the AFT for its affiliation with one segment of society (labor), critics of the NEA claim that the NEA traditionally has been allied with the conservative segment of society. To some critics, the NEA's partiality toward "big business" may be seen in its failure to take effective action to eliminate the extremely business-oriented programs of economic education conducted in many public schools. The NEA's joint programs with the American Legion have drawn many criticisms from liberals. Some observers find it difficult to distinguish between "cooperation" with conservative groups, which the NEA approves, and "affiliation" with labor organizations, which the NEA condemns.

Image Problems

The AFT's affiliation with the labor movement has given it a lower class, "blue-collar" worker image. Since many teachers come from upwardly mobile families seeking middle class status, they are almost morbidly fearful of being identified with blue-collar workers. As Jean Dresden Grambs has noted, "Having made the leap into respectability, often with great sacrifice and effort, the teacher is not likely to view with favor a call by organized labor that would jeopardize his job, or identify him with the lower-class elements of the community." [2]

Although most teachers appear to believe that they would lose their professional status if they joined a union, teaching conditions usually are better in the cities and suburbs where teachers' unions have their major strength. Also, some groups with much higher status than teachers, such as orchestra conductors and airline pilots, are unionized.

> The fact—sad from the AFT's viewpoint—is that teachers have descended from the "genteel" tradition. This means that teachers consider themselves to be thoroughly middle-class, "nice" people, and "nice" people do not affiliate with organized labor. Teachers wear white shirts or neat dresses, have regular hours, do not lift, tug, or pull, and in general comport themselves like professionals. When the subject of respectability and tactics was being discussed in a college class, one graduate student said, "I don't care if the AFT could get us higher wages, I still don't consider myself a union member." [3]

Since many teachers tend to be conservative, the AFT will have to lose its image as a dissident, noisy, gross, and overly-aggressive labor

---

[2] Jean Dresden Grambs, *Schools, Scholars, and Society* (Englewood Cliffs, New Jersey: Prentice-Hall, Inc., 1965), p. 154.

[3] Donald C. Orlich and S. Samuel Shermis, *The Pursuit of Excellence: Introductory Readings in Education* (New York: American Book Company, 1965), pp. 309–10.

union before it can ever expect to compete numerically with the NEA. As long as AFT leaders hold their labor affiliation to be almost holy, the AFT probably will remain merely a lobbying group for urban teachers.

Although the AFT has almost insurmountable image problems, the NEA is not totally immune from such difficulties. Traditionally, the NEA has had a conservative, rural, and anti-labor image. It has functioned on a "genteel" level by inoffensively and tactfully reminding the public that teachers are fine people who are valuable members of society. As certain critics have noted, such an approach has been "singularly unproductive."

To the NEA's credit, current NEA leaders are attempting to direct it away from this conservative, impotent, and do-nothing image. Its "Urban Project" and the professional negotiations and sanctions programs, even though they apparently have resulted from AFT pressure, are indications that the NEA is not as static and hidebound as some of its critics make it out to be.

Professional Problems

Critics of the NEA claim that it has fought against teacher control over admission to teaching, has accepted sub-standard programs of teacher education and low standards for teaching certificates, has not significantly raised the relative professional and economic status of teachers, has failed to foster professional autonomy, and has almost ignored professional ethics.

The AFT claims to be the only professional organization specifically devoted to the interests of classroom teachers. However, like the NEA, the AFT has apparently been content to leave control of various professional matters, such as control of admission to teaching, in the hands of lay boards and their administrative representatives. The AFT is virtually inactive in the areas of certification and accreditation.

It is interesting to note that both the NEA and the AFT accept the apparently fallacious concept that "teaching is a profession (occupation)." Both the NEA and AFT indulge in this fallacy by not making a distinction between "teachers" controlling "teaching," and practitioners in the various occupations in the teaching area controlling their own occupations. For both the NEA and AFT, teaching seems to be a nebulous term encompassing occupations ranging from, for example, high school band directing, through high school physics teaching, to elementary physical education teaching. The NEA and AFT apparently would have such teachers control entrance requirements into, for example, the social studies teaching occupation. In contrast, from a true professional viewpoint, the members of the social studies teaching occupation should control training and membership qualifications for their own occupation. Even Myron Lieberman appears to write vaguely about teachers controlling teaching, and fails to relate professionalism to the professionalizing of the various teaching occupations through their members controlling admission requirements for each occupation.

CONCLUSION

The long-time existence of two organizations competing to represent the practitioners in a field is rare. Although some have felt that the competition between the NEA and AFT has been stimulating and invigorating, most observers have concluded that a single organization would be better than two in competition.

Stanley Elam believes that "Too much money and energy are being wasted that might better be directed toward common goals, and bitterness is building up which can be exploited by the enemies of both groups for decades to come." [4] Myron Lieberman holds that the efforts of teachers are dispersed and that "attention is devoted to belittling the opposing organization instead of concentrating on the constructive work that needs to be done." [5]

The major barriers to a merger appear to be the NEA's insistence on all-inclusive negotiating units and the AFT's insistence on labor union affiliation. However, many of the local associations affiliated with the NEA already exclude administrative personnel, and the AFT's labor affiliation is being questioned by AFT members.

Although the stated positions of the NEA and AFT are in conflict, many observers claim that the practical effects of their programs are almost identical. "At the present time, the objectives of the AFT are practically indistinguishable from those of the NEA." [6] There appear to be few operational differences between the NEA's policy of

---

[4] Stanley Elam, "Teachers' Unions—Rift Without Differences," *The Nation* 201, no. 12 (October 18, 1965): 247.

[5] Lieberman, *The Future of Public Education*, p. 231.

[6] Lieberman, *Education as a Profession* (Englewood Cliffs, New Jersey: Prentice-Hall, 1956), p. 314.

professional negotiations backed by sanctions and the AFT's collective bargaining backed by strikes. Major differences seem to be based on semantic or verbal accusations, not operational descriptions, and it appears that the NEA and AFT are moving toward common programs.

What could the AFT bring to a merger that the NEA does not already have? As Elam has noted, the AFT's "caucus system" makes the organizational machinery of the AFT more responsive than that of the NEA to the desires of rank-and-file members. At AFT conventions, two parties present their programs and slates of officers to the delegates. This provides a "loyal opposition." No such mechanism exists in the NEA.[7]

Which is better, the NEA or the AFT, or should they both be replaced by professional organizations?

SELECTED REFERENCES

Elam, Stanley, "Teachers' Unions—Rift Without Differences," *The Nation* 201, no. 12 (October 18, 1965), pp. 247–49. An evaluation of the NEA versus AFT conflict. This article also is in Stanley Elam, Myron Lieberman, and Michael Moskow, *Readings on Collective Negotiations in Public Education.* Chicago: Rand McNally, 1967, pp. 269–73.

Lieberman, Myron, *Education As a Profession.* Englewood Cliffs, New Jersey: Prentice-Hall, Inc., 1956, Chaps. 9 and 10. Although a bit dated, this is still the most comprehensive study of the NEA and AFT.

————, *The Future of Public Education.* Chicago: University of Chicago Press, 1960, Chap. 9. A caustic and thought provoking analysis of the NEA and AFT.

Moskow, Michael H., "Teacher Organizations: An Analysis of the Issues," *Teachers College Record* 66, no. 5 (February, 1965): 453–63. An excellent brief analysis of the NEA-AFT competition. This article also is in Elam, Lieberman, and Moskow's *Readings on Collective Negotiations in Public Education,* pp. 234–47.

Orlich, Donald C. and S. Samuel Shermis, *The Pursuit of Excellence: Introductory Readings in Education.* New York: American Book Company, 1965, pp. 288–314. An excellent introduction to the NEA versus AFT problem.

---

[7] Elam, "Teachers' Unions—Rift Without Differences," p. 249.

THOUGHT AIDS

1. Analyze the following statement by an AFT member. "It seems obvious that the AFT can speak wholly on behalf of teachers, and the NEA position must be diluted by the interests of those who administer the schools, but do not teach the children." (Harvey Rudoff, Denver Public Schools, Denver, Colorado.)

2. Obtain a copy of the latest *NEA Handbook*. Note the many types of commissions, committees, divisions, and departments.

3. Evaluate the following criticism of the NEA. "But the NEA is incapable of moving with vigor and imagination, even when confronted by the most serious problems and challenging opportunities." (Myron Lieberman. *The Future of Public Education*, p. 189.)

4. Do you agree with the contention that the NEA and AFT both are basically "futile" organizations? Why or why not?

5. React to the following statement. "My own opinion is that anyone who claims that administrator coercion does not exist simply has not come in contact with classroom teachers." (Michael H. Moskow. "Teacher Organizations: An Analysis of the Issues," *Teachers College Record* 66, no. 5 (February, 1965): 456.)

6. Do you agree with the AFT's claim that the NEA dissipates much of its energy on "peripheral" activities? Why or why not?

7. Do you believe that the NEA has just as many affiliation problems as does the AFT? Why or why not?

8. What to you are the basic differences, if any, between the programs of the NEA and AFT?

9. Do you believe that the NEA and AFT will merge soon? Why or why not?

10. Do you agree with the contention that both the NEA and AFT are confused in the professionalism area? Why or why not?

15

Which Is Better, Collective Bargaining or Professional Negotiations?

The 1960's have been a decade characterized by increased teacher militancy. In some areas, notably certain urban locations, teachers are demanding opportunities to participate in the process of determining policies and working conditions in the schools. Is this drive for collective action to be molded to the American Federation of Teacher's labor union philosophy of collective bargaining, as developed in private industry, or is this drive for group action to take the form of "a new process designed to serve the unique needs of the teaching profession in the public service," the National Education Associations' professional negotiation process?

The AFT would exclude school administrators from membership in classroom teacher organizations and from the teachers' collective bargaining units. To the AFT, there is a basic conflict of interest between the school administrator who hires and fires the teachers and the teachers who are hired or fired. This AFT position is based on what is called the private industry or conflict-of-interest model of employer-employee relationships.

In contrast, the NEA would include school administrators in all-inclusive negotiation units. To the NEA, public school employees, both administrators and teachers, have a common interest and concern in providing the best possible education for students, and this mutual interest and concern overrides any differences between them. The NEA's professional negotiations position is based on the public service or identity-of-interest model. Which is best, the NEA model or the AFT model? Should administrative personnel be included in or excluded from the organizational unit which negotiates educational conditions with the school board?

PROFESSIONAL NEGOTIATIONS

The first edition of the NEA's *Guidelines for Professional Negotiation* (1963) suggested three types or levels of professional negotiation agreements. Level I is a recognition type agreement. It involves the school board of a given district recognizing a particular association as the spokesman and representative of the professional staff. This may merely be a statement in the school board's minutes. The board and administration agree to hear proposals from the recognized association and to discuss matters with the association—it is not a commitment to negotiate issues. Certain critics of the NEA say that although the NEA claims that many local affiliates engage in professional negotiations, most of these local groups are recognized by their boards merely as the representatives of the teachers in their districts. To the critics, this is a far cry from actual meaningful negotiations.

Level II includes an outline of procedures to be followed in negotiations. Sometimes a Level II agreement also will state the areas considered negotiable. As critics of the NEA note, there is no guarantee that adequate joint decision making is occurring under a Level II agreement. After the association expresses its opinions to the board, the board may continue its traditional policy of unilateral decision making.

Level III, in addition to what is included in Levels I and II, involves procedures for resolving impasses. Such written appeals procedures usually provide for impartial third-party mediation and fact finding in the event of persistent disagreement. The NEA supports turning to state departments of education for fact finding or third-party mediators. Since most state departments of education appear to be NEA oriented, the AFT has obvious objections to such "educational channels." Many administrators and school boards also appear to object to Level III impasse procedures as being impingements upon the legal authority of the boards. Nevertheless, the NEA is seeking only

Level III agreements. This is illustrated by the fact that the revised edition of the *Guidelines for Professional Negotiation* (1965) only include a discussion of the Level III type.

In extreme cases in which impasse procedures have failed to result in contractual agreements or where boards refuse to negotiate in good faith with their staffs, the NEA resorts to sanctions. Sanctions range from publicizing unfavorable teaching conditions in a state or particular school district to mass refusal to sign teaching contracts.

Stinnett, Kleinmann, and Ware register the NEA's new militant stance in favor of meaningful professional negotiations:

> Professional negotiation must mean something more than the right to be heard. Most teachers associations have had this right for years. The right only to be heard might be simply an annual supplicatory pilgrimage to the board of education, resulting only in warm expressions of gratitude and goodwill by both parties. This routine could consist of a polite presentation by the teachers, blank stares from the board, a polite "thank you." Then follows an interminable wait by the teachers; and finally reading of the board's action in the local newspaper or via the superintendent's bulletin with any connection between teachers' requests and board action strictly coincidental. This, of course, is not professional negotiation.[1]

The American Association of School Administrators, composed basically of school superintendents, has been an influential affiliate of the NEA. In its booklet *School Administrators View Professional Negotiation,* the AASA generally seems to be in agreement with the NEA's concept of professional negotiations. However, the AASA appears also to support certain beliefs which are in conflict with the NEA. For example, the AASA seems to believe that the school staff should have the right to discuss pros and cons and to participate in developing education programs, but not the right to make decisions. To the AASA, school boards must retain their traditional responsibilities and legal rights to make "administrative" decisions. Also, in its stand on grievance procedures, the AASA believes that after impartial third-party participation in impasse resolution, subsequent appeal should be made to "the final authority—the board of education." These AASA beliefs appear to be contrary, at least in spirit, to the intent of the NEA's Level III type of professional negotiations. The AASA also appears to be categorically opposed to sanctions which

---

[1] T. M. Stinnett, Jack H. Kleinmann, and Martha L. Ware, *Professional Negotiation and Public Education* (New York: The Macmillan Company, 1966), p. 18.

involve withdrawal of services. In contrast, the NEA not only supports withdrawal of services, but its Board of Directors has pledged the NEA's full support to locals that strike "under conditions of severe stress, causing deterioration of the educational program and when good faith attempts at resolution have been rejected." [2] Some writers have suggested that these and other differences between AASA and NEA policies may eventually result in a complete break between the NEA and the AASA.

COLLECTIVE BARGAINING

Charles Cogen has summarized the AFT's concept of collective bargaining.

> In general, the AFT favors the same sort of relationship between teachers and their boards of education as that which has been established for employees in the private sector through the National Labor and Management Relations Act.
>
> We favor the principle of exclusive recognition of a single bargaining agent. We are opposed to "members only" bargaining, in which two or more organizations have separate but equal rights to negotiate with the board. We are opposed to "joint committees," whether they are chosen on an organization basis or by direct election of individual committee members.
>
> We favor recognition of the organization which achieves a majority of those voting in a secret ballot election, where there are two or more organizations vying for such recognition. We are opposed to recognition on the basis of membership lists, except where only one organization is seeking exclusive recognition. Even here, due notice should be given so that any other organization could force an election upon making a sufficient showing of interest.
>
> We favor "continuing recognition" until such time as a significant proportion of the members of the negotiating unit petition for a new election. We are opposed to required annual or biennial elections of negotiating agents.
>
> We favor negotiating units composed of non-supervisory educational employees only. We are opposed to units composed of "all certificated employees," including principals and other administrators and supervisors.
>
> We would place no limit on the scope of negotiations, the items which are subject to the bargaining process. Anything on

[2] *Colorado School Journal,* September 5, 1967, p. 1.

which the two parties can agree should become a part of the agreement; anything on which they cannot agree will, of course, not appear.

We favor written agreements between boards of education and negotiating agents. These agreements should be legally binding.

We favor development of a code of unfair labor practices and definitions of what constitutes good faith negotiations.

We favor according teachers the right to strike; we are opposed to anti-strike laws, and we are opposed to the use of injunctions in teacher-board disputes.

We favor the use of skilled mediators to resolve impasses. We are opposed to compulsory arbitration of negotiable items.

We favor individual grievance procedures, with outside arbitration as the final step. We oppose grievance procedures which place the board or the superintendent in the position of final arbiter.[3]

Cogen responds to the NEA leaders who claim that labor-management concepts are not appropriate in the education area.

Teachers certainly are employees of the board of education, regardless of their professional status or the lack of it, and if one were to place a schematic drawing of the staff structure of a typical private business corporation of comparable size, the little boxes and circles would be about the same for each. The same stresses, strains, and conflicts which exist in such structures in private enterprise are also to be found in enterprises owned by the public, whether they be school systems, fire departments, or bus lines.

The "non-profit" argument, too, is fallacious. Schools are just as much in the marketplace for their share of consumer dollars as any manufacturer of automobiles or safety pins. People pay taxes because they want schools, just as they put up $3,000 for a new automobile or 10¢ for a packet of pins because they want these things. Boards of education and superintendents are elected and employed to produce education, and their obligation is even set forth by law. Their success, like that of private managers, is measured by an equation in which public approval is balanced against costs.[4]

[3] Charles Cogen, "The American Federation of Teachers and Collective Negotiations," in Stanley M. Elam, Myron Lieberman, and Michael H. Moskow, eds., *Readings on Collective Negotiations in Public Education* (Chicago: Rand McNally and Company, 1967), pp. 163–64.

[4] Cogen, "American Federation of Teachers," pp. 164–65.

The relationship existing now between supervisory personnel and teachers is superordinate-subordinate, not primarily collegial.

In normal employee-employer relations, those who have authority to hire and fire, settle grievances, or make specific job assignments are excluded from the employee bargaining unit. Placing these positions firmly on the management side acts to check possible abuses of power, and allows non-supervisory employees to make group decisions without being subjected to undue influence and undemocratic pressures from supervisors. We would see no objection to middle management administrators and supervisors forming bargaining units of their own, but these should be separate from those for non-supervisory personnel.

We in the AFT think it unwise—even downright silly—to ignore the experience which has been amassed in labor-management relations over the years. The principles and concepts which have evolved apply to industries of widest possible diversity, and there is no reason to segregate educational employees and attempt to establish a new body of rules for them. In fact, teachers can only lose from such a development.[5]

Robert Thornberry, Executive Director of the Indiana Federation of Teachers, contrasts what he believes are the NEA and AFT attitudes toward teacher-school board relationships.

The NEA has taken a "head in the sand" approach by pretending that the school board is not really an employer and the teacher really not an employee. The NEA has what I call a one-big-happy-family concept. "We are all in the business of educating children," the NEA says, "and therefore we should have no basic differences at all." The unions are more realistic. They know who hires and fires teachers. They know who makes it necessary for the principal to say, "I'm sorry about those six classes this year, Jones." They know who put 43 kids in Miss Smith's class so they won't have to hire that extra teacher.[6]

The NEA has held tenaciously to the theory that teachers and administrators have common interests to such a degree that they can negotiate most effectively on a joint basis as part of a single unified group. In contrast, the AFT has consistently supported the theory that teachers and administrators (particularly superintendents) have

---

[5] Cogen, "American Federation of Teachers," p. 166.
[6] Robert Thornberry, "All Is Not Right in School Board-Staff Negotiations; The Federations' Viewpoint," *The Teachers College Journal* (December, 1965), p. 129.

such conflicting interests that they cannot negotiate satisfactorily together with the same employer. The AFT's point is that since the
superintendent's job depends on the approval of the school board, not
that of the teachers, it is probable that he will not enthusiastically
support the teachers when a conflict arises. For the average school
administrator, there comes a limit to the extent to which he can go
in support of teachers for, in going further, he would jeopardize his
own position. It is fairly obvious, to the AFT, that an effective teacher
organization can go far beyond the limits of permissible administrative
action in order to improve teaching conditions.

The community-of-interest versus conflict-of-interest problem also
exists at state and national levels. Although unity of school boards,
administrators, and teachers apparently tends to strengthen a state
association's bargaining position, such unity imposes limits on association objectives. For example, it appears that Missouri has had no
teacher tenure or minimum salary laws because the Missouri State
Teachers Association has not wished to alienate its school board supporters. For a dated but in-depth analysis of the conflict-of-interest
problem, particularly as it relates to the AFT charge of "administrator
domination" of the NEA, the reader is urged to examine pages 280–
296 in Myron Lieberman's book *Education As a Profession.*

Cogen summarizes the AFT's view toward the problem of resolution of impasses in bargaining.

> We believe that work stoppages by teachers should be a last
> resort in attempting to resolve such impasses. Every possible
> effort to reach an agreement should be made before a work
> stoppage occurs. However, we also believe, as does the NEA,
> as evidenced by its sanctions policy, that work stoppages by
> teachers are morally justifiable under certain circumstances.
>
> AFT locals are urged to follow the normal procedure of
> collective bargaining. When an impasse occurs, they usually
> resort to some sort of public appeal—a public demonstration;
> informational picketing; leaflets; newspaper, radio, and television
> advertisements; and marshaling of support from the labor move-
> ment and parent and civic organizations. If these efforts fail to
> move the board from its position, the members often set a strike
> date.
>
> We strongly advocate the use of skilled mediators in at-
> tempting to resolve negotiating impasses. In addition to his
> experience and skill, the impartiality of the mediator must be
> above question. We do not think that most state superintendents
> of public instruction qualify for the mediation role on either
> count. Few have had mediation training or experience, and even

the "fairest" state superintendent is apt to have a pro-management bias. Perhaps standing educational mediation panels could be approved by state teacher organizations and the state school boards association. Mediators for any particular situation could then be chosen from this panel.[7]

A number of objections against collective bargaining in public education have been raised. These include the arguments that collective bargaining (1) would require an unlawful surrender of discretionary powers by school boards, (2) would be a threat to the stability and sovereignty of government, (3) would result in inefficiency, and (4) would be out of place in public employment because government is not operated for profit. After making a very telling analysis of these and other objections to collective bargaining in Chapter 2 of his book, *Education As a Profession*, Myron Lieberman concludes that none of these objections has any real merit. However, the reader is urged to examine Lieberman's analysis and determine for himself the adequacy of Lieberman's conclusion.

THE NATIONAL SCHOOL BOARDS ASSOCIATION POSITION

The National School Boards Association is a federation of 50 state school board associations comprising approximately 18,000 school boards who are, in turn, responsible for administering more than 95 per cent of the public school enrollment. What is the attitude of this very substantial and influential segment of the educational community toward professional negotiations and collective bargaining?

This statement from the NSBA "Beliefs and Policies" is indicative of the NSBA position:

> School boards, subject to the requirements of applicable law, should refrain from compromise agreements based on negotiation or collective bargaining, and should not resort to mediation or arbitration, nor yield to threats of reprisal on all matters affecting local public schools, including the welfare of all personnel. They should also resist by all lawful means the enactment of laws which would compel them to surrender any part of their responsibility.[8]

---

[7] Cogen, "American Federation of Teachers," pp. 169–70.

[8] Harold Webb, "The National School Boards Association and Collective Negotiations," in Elam, ed., *Collective Negotiations*, p. 199.

Harold Webb, Executive Director of the NSBA, has summarized the NSBA position:

> In summary, NSBA is opposed to collective bargaining and any other method of reaching compromise agreements with boards based on threat of sanction, strike, or appeal to third-party decision makers because, in the view of the most experienced and enlightened board members in the country, these approaches to the resolution of differences between boards and staff do not meet the best interests of the children and do not serve the welfare of the community.
>
> NSBA's leaders feel that the existing machinery is adequate to meet the challenges of the times—and that all who are a part of our great system of public education must meet our responsibilities in preserving this institution.
>
> Once we attack the essential elements of the great institutions in our society, we attack the very bedrock upon which we have built our way of life.[9]

To many educators, the NSBA is ignoring not only the need for change in employment relations in education, but also the changes that have occurred.

> The NSBA is clearly out of touch with big-city boards and with a large number of others as well. In a Neanderthalian statement which no other responsible group in American life would ever dream of issuing, they completely repudiate collective negotiations. Any school board which heeds this senseless policy deserves all the trouble it will get.[10]

It is fairly apparent that the NSBA, representing a very substantial segment of the educational community, is sincerely opposed to any form of collective negotiations. In fairness to the NSBA, it should be noted that present NSBA policies merely reaffirm its long-standing position that teachers have the right to "discuss" matters of mutual concern with the board, but the NSBA rejects the principle of negotiating these matters with teachers. Obviously, both the NEA and AFT positions are far from being generally accepted by many school boards.

---

[9] Webb, "National School Boards Association," pp. 201–2.

[10] Book review of Myron Lieberman and Michael H. Moskow's *Collective Negotiations for Teachers,* by Dan Griffiths, *Phi Delta Kappan* 48, no. 1 (September, 1966): p. 42.

THE COLLECTIVE NEGOTIATIONS ALTERNATIVE

Although the previously presented materials indicate that, to many NEA and AFT members, there are clear-cut differences between professional negotiations and collective bargaining, some critics claim that there are no basic differences, or only relatively unimportant ones. For example, in regard to membership in the negotiating unit, the NEA talks about welcoming all certificated personnel and the AFT talks about excluding managerial personnel. However, in reality, in one place or another the NEA excludes "management" personnel and in certain locals the AFT welcomes them. Also, state and local affiliates of both the NEA and AFT have pragmatically departed from stated policies when they thought it would be best to do so. For example, when he was Superintendent of the New York City Schools, Dr. Bernard E. Donovan noted that these days he could not tell the NEA and AFT apart when they campaigned. Arvid Anderson, Commissioner of the Wisconsin Employment Relations Board, said:

> Basically, both the NEA and AFT are talking about the same conditions of employment, regardless of whether they "negotiate" or "bargain." I also have difficulty finding substantive differences between "withholding of service," "organization-declared professional study days," "strike," and "sanctions." [11]

It is interesting to note that in the glossary of their book, *Collective Negotiations for Teachers*, Myron Lieberman and Michael Moskow use the term "collective negotiations" as being interchangeable with "collective bargaining" and "professional negotiation." They indicate that NEA and AFT propaganda statements have resulted in collective bargaining and professional negotiations being stated in persuasive definitions designed to resolve policy questions, rather than to facilitate objective analysis of issues.

> The essential point is that all such collective procedures, regardless of whether they are labeled collective negotiations, professional negotiations, collective bargaining, cooperative determination, democratic persuasion, or anything else, must answer certain questions: What persons seek to be represented? What shall be the scope of negotiations? For how long shall any agreements be made? Who should interpret agreements in case of conflicting interpretations? How do teachers change their representative? What are the rights of majority and minority organizations, and

---

[11] Arvid Anderson, "State Regulations of Employment Relations in Education," in Elam, ed., *Collective Negotiations*, p. 106.

of individual teachers under the procedures to be established? How should impasses be resolved? [12]

CONCLUSION

Although there are internal disagreements, uncertainties, and confusion in both the NEA and AFT, both organizations are working toward more adequate concepts of educator participation in school policy decisions. The appalling lack of teacher effectiveness in dealing with local school administrators and school boards is being vigorously attacked by both organizations. In spite of the National School Boards Association's "stand pat" policies, teacher unrest in many places is pushing out the traditional paternalistic concept of employer-employee relations. Some critics claim that there are no significant operational differences between the NEA's professional negotiations type of pushing and the AFT's collective bargaining pushing.

As the redistribution of educational power is forced on them, both school boards and administrators probably will have exaggerated fears of teacher encroachment on traditional management prerogatives. Since neither NEA nor AFT has been an exceptionally effective protector of teacher rights, and since teachers apparently can only be protected by effective organizations, it is probable that effective teacher organizations will differ markedly from the present structures and programs of both NEA and AFT.

SELECTED REFERENCES

Elam, Stanley M., Myron Lieberman, and Michael H. Moskow, *Readings on Collective Negotiations in Public Education.* Chicago: Rand McNally and Company, 1967. A companion volume to Lieberman and Moskow's *Collective Negotiations for Teachers.*

Guidelines for Professional Negotiations. Washington, D.C.: National Education Association, 1965. The NEA's official handbook on professional negotiations.

---

[12] Myron Lieberman and Michael H. Moskow, *Collective Negotiations for Teachers* (Chicago: Rand McNally and Company, 1966), p. 5.

Law, Kenneth L., Kenneth F. Melley, Thomas P. Mondani, and James P. Sandler, *The Manual for Teacher Negotiations.* Windsor, Connecticut: Educators' Press, 1966. A practical handbook for negotiators.

Lieberman, Myron, *Education As a Profession.* Englewood Cliffs, New Jersey: Prentice-Hall, Inc., 1956, Chap. 11. A dated yet relevant and provocative presentation.

———, *The Future of Public Education.* Chicago: University of Chicago Press, 1960, Chap. 8. A stimulating analysis.

——— and Michael H. Moskow, *Collective Negotiations for Teachers— An Approach to School Administration.* Chicago: Rand McNally and Company, 1966. A basic text in this problem area.

School Administrators View Professional Negotiation. Washington, D.C.: American Association of School Administrators, 1966. The official viewpoint of AASA.

Stinnett, T. M., Jack H. Kleinmann, and Martha L. Ware, *Professional Negotiation in Public Education.* New York: The Macmillan Company, 1966. A basic NEA volume.

THOUGHT AIDS

1. Analyze current articles on collective bargaining and professional negotiations. Have these positions been fairly presented in this chapter? Why or why not?

2. Which do you feel is the better model on which to base teacher-administrator-school board relationships, the AFT's conflict-of-interest model or the NEA's identity-of-interest model? Why?

3. Do you believe that there are significant differences between professional negotiations and collective bargaining? Why?

4. Examine the AASA's booklet on professional negotiations. Do you believe that the AASA's position is in conflict with the NEA's position? Why or why not?

5. Do school administrators tend to give greater support to school board policies or to teacher desires? On what do you base your opinion?

6. Indicate arguments which would support and arguments which would undermine the following statement. "Machinery designed to resolve differences between non-professional personnel and management in the framework of private business is not well suited to solving the problems of professional personnel in a public school system." (AASA "Teacher-Administrator-Board Relations," resolution, 1966 convention.)

16

Are Teacher Strikes Anti-Professional?

Many educational writers, particularly those in the National Education Association, have implied that strikes are anti-professional. To them, strikes are in conflict with professional codes of ethics. They assume that the strike is an anti-professional, labor union weapon. Teacher organizations affiliated with organized labor, particularly the American Federation of Teachers, are implicated as favoring the right to strike. Many writers in NEA publications condemn strikes as anti-professional, "trade union" methods which thwart attaining the objectives of the education profession.

The NEA belief that teacher unions affiliated with organized labor favor the right to strike appears to be a bit paradoxical since the AFT has had an explicit anti-strike policy for many years, whereas the NEA has failed to establish an official policy in regard to teacher strikes. However, presence or absence of national policies seems to be irrelevant since there have been a number of strikes by affiliates of both organizations.

The basic question remains: Are teacher strikes anti-professional? In order to deal with this question, the next step probably should be to determine just what a strike is. A strike usually is defined as a withholding of services or a temporary work stoppage in order to express a grievance or enforce a demand. Such a withholding of services may involve breaking a contract or it may involve a "no contract—no work situation. It should be noted that most NEA writings about teacher strikes seem to involve the assumption that teacher strikes necessarily involve an illegal procedure, breaking a teaching contract. In contrast, many strikes in industry occur precisely because an acceptable contract has not been negotiated.

THE "STRIKES VERSUS SANCTIONS" FALLACY

A basic fallacy which seems to appear frequently, particularly in NEA-oriented writings, is the fallacious belief that strikes are different from "sanctions." It is believed that strikes are anti-professional, whereas sanctions are professional. From a review of the writings about sanctions, starting with the sanctions invoked against California's Little Lake City School District, sanctions appear to involve teachers not accepting contracts in districts, or states, against which the NEA or certain of its affiliated organizations have declared sanctions to exist. Such a withholding of services is generally recognized in our society as a "no contract—no work" strike. Such a strike may be contrasted with a "wildcat" or contract-breaking strike, but obviously may not validly be contrasted with strikes in general.

There are a number of arguments for and against both wildcat strikes and no contract or sanctions strikes. Contract-breaking strikes have been supported, particularly by certain AFT members, as being widely publicized and as often having effective results due to the immediate pressure brought to bear on a school district. Such wildcat strikes are criticized, usually by NEA writers, as being illegal, as creating animosities, and as generating a poor public image of teachers. The sanctions or no contract type of strike has been praised, by the NEA, as being professional, and as offering a united front by educators against educational problems. Such strikes have been criticized as being cumbersome, harmful to students because they may drag on for a long time, and as sometimes being ineffectual.

Although arguments may be offered for and against various types of strikes, including the no contract or sanctions type of strike, the basic question still remains: Are teachers strikes, whatever the type, anti-professional?

STANDARDS OF GENERALLY RECOGNIZED PROFESSIONS

In order to determine whether or not strikes or work stoppages by teachers are anti-professional, the codes of ethics of generally recognized professions, such as medicine and law, may be used as standards in determining if professional practitioners are ethically obligated not to withhold their services. In essence, are there any situations in which professional practitioners of medicine and law are obligated by the codes of ethics of their professions to stop dispensing their services?

Section Six of the 1957 Principles of Medical Ethics of the American Medical Association states:

> A physician should not dispose of his services under terms or conditions which tend to interfere with or impair the free and complete exercise of his medical judgment and skill or tend to cause a deterioration of the quality of medical care.[1]

The Code of Professional Responsibility of the American Bar Association States:

> Employment should not be accepted by a lawyer when he is unable to render competent service or when he knows or it is obvious that the person seeking to employ him desires to institute or maintain an action merely for the purpose of harassing or maliciously injuring another.[2]
>
> A lawyer representing a client before a tribunal, with its permission if required by its rules, shall withdraw from employment, and a lawyer representing a client in other matters shall withdraw from employment, if:
>
> (1) He knows or it is obvious that his client is bringing the legal action, conducting the defense, or asserting a position in the litigation, or is otherwise having steps taken for him, merely for the purpose of harassing or maliciously injuring any person.
>
> (2) He knows or it is obvious that his continued employment will result in violation of a Disciplinary Rule.[3]

It can be seen from the preceding quotations that both the medical and legal codes of ethics not only permit but recommend that under certain conditions professional practitioners should withdraw their services or not accept employment. Since many physicians and lawyers do not work for a single employer, there usually is no reason for them to withdraw their services simultaneously. This does not, however, relieve them of the professional obligation to go on strike if they find themselves in situations which involve invasions of their professional autonomy. Physicians in other countries have found occasions

---

[1] *The Journal of The American Medical Association* (June 7, 1958), p. 31.

[2] *American Bar Association Code of Professional Responsibility and Canons of Judicial Ethics.* Printed by Martindale-Hubbell, Inc., 1969, p. 7.

[3] *American Bar Association Code of Professional Responsibility*, pp. 9–10.

in which they believed that they were obligated, as a group, to withdraw their services simultaneously.

PROFESSIONALISM AND TEACHER STRIKES

If each of the various teaching occupations had its own professional code of ethics, it is fairly apparent that such codes would obligate the practitioners in each teaching occupation to go on strike if their professional autonomy, usually termed academic freedom, was impaired or invaded. For example, if a school administrator or a school board attempted to invade decision-making areas of the high school social studies teaching occupation (such as determination of course content and requirements, curricular materials, teaching procedures, and teacher merit or competency), the practitioners in this occupation would be ethically obligated to withdraw their services. Just as a physician is ethically obligated to go on strike if those outside the medical professional occupation prescribe for his patients, so also a member of any of the various teaching occupations would be obligated to withdraw his services if persons outside his professional competency area, such as teachers in different teaching occupations, school administrators, or school boards, attempted to coerce him in his professional competency area. Just as physicians cannot take professional responsibility for medical outcomes when their professional autonomy is invaded, so also a practitioner in one of the various teaching occupations could not take professional responsibility for the intellectual and societal development of students in situations in which his professional autonomy is seriously impaired.

Anti-professional teaching practices are fostered in communities where teachers are coerced to avoid careful reflective analyses of major issues. Areas in which teachers often are forced to avoid careful reflective analyses include racial myths and prejudices, minority-group relations, alternative economic systems, sexual practices, social classes, religious beliefs, nationalism and national institutions, patriotism, and international institutions.

A professional teacher's ethical obligation to the public interest would be to resist public opinion and administrator and lay board decision making in areas of professional occupational decision making competency and autonomy. These might include what courses would be offered, what learning media and teaching procedures would be used, and what types of discipline would be carried out. If the various teaching occupations were professional, occupationally formulated teaching contracts probably would involve the professional autonomy provision that the contract is voided if the occupational organization determines, at any time during the period of the contract, that a practitioner's professional autonomy has been damaged to the point that drastic professional action, withdrawal of services, is necessary. Under professional occupational codes of ethics, which do not as yet exist, practitioners in the various teaching occupations would be obligated not to work in communities and states which refuse to conform to contracts specifying professional conditions of employment.

An argument often advanced against teacher strikes is that they would be strikes against students; such strikes would harm learners. This argument seems to ignore the probability that teaching under anti-professional conditions may do more harm to the students than would no teaching at all.

Why do many teachers, and many of the NEA's leaders, equate professionalism with subservience, obedience, and acquiescence to policies made by persons outside the various teaching occupations? Why is professionalism often regarded as being directly opposed to effective positive action by organized teacher groups? Why is the strike, an ethical tool of the generally acknowledged professions, rejected by many NEA writers? Why does the NEA Code of Ethics fail expressly to involve the professional obligation to go on strike when professional conditions of employment are violated?

A probable major reason for the present state of affairs is the traditional NEA policy of placing employers—school administrators—in the same organization with the employees—the teachers. A closely related probable reason is that the NEA groups all the various educational occupations under the "united education profession," and labels as "divisive" any attempts to develop strong practitioner-controlled organizations within the various occupations. Lest the writer be branded as an AFT "union" supporter, it appears that the AFT is almost as confused as the NEA in the area of professional strikes. Both the NEA and the AFT have failed to foster the establishment of clear professional requirements which would obligate teachers to withdraw their services, to go on strike, when their occupational autonomy is invaded.

CONCLUSION

If teachers were to develop strong organizations in the various teaching occupations, each occupation would establish professional standards of ethical behavior. Further, if the codes of ethics of generally recognized professions, such as medicine and law, are accepted as valid standards for ethical practices in the various teaching occupations, it is apparent that under certain intolerable conditions, as defined by particular occupational organizations, practitioners in those occupations would be professionally obligated to withdraw their services. If practitioners in the various teaching occupations would set up codes of ethics similar to those of the generally accepted professions, in certain prescribed situations teachers' strikes would be professional.

SELECTED REFERENCES

Barstow, Robbins W., Jr., "Teachers and Boards of Education Need to Work Jointly to Determine Policies of Common Concern," *NEA Journal* 50, no. 7 (October, 1961): 61–64. A statement of the NEA position at that time in regard to the AFT, teacher strikes, and relationships between teachers and lay boards of education.

Lieberman, Myron, "Professionalism and the Voodoo of Education." *Proceedings of the Seventeenth Annual Meeting of the Philosophy of Education Society*. Philosophy of Education Society, 1961, pp. 53–65. Note his discussion of teacher strikes and his concluding criticisms of philosophers of education.

_____, "Some Reflections on Teachers Organizations," *The Educational Forum* 24, no. 1 (November, 1959): 71–76. The NEA belief that teacher strikes are unprofessional is criticized.

_____, "Teacher Strikes: An Analysis of the Issues," *Harvard Educational Review* 26, no. 1 (Winter, 1956): 39–70. A comprehensive analysis of the teacher strike question.

Liesch, James R., "Strikes and Sanctions: A Moral Inquiry," *Educational Theory* 18, no. 3 (Summer, 1968): 253–61. A perceptive examination of the morality of teacher militancy.

Oakes, Russell C., "Should Teachers Strike? An Unanswered Question," *Journal of Educational Sociology* 33, no. 7 (March, 1960): 339–44. A thought provoking discussion of this problem area in the professionalization of teaching.

Roach, Stephen F., "School Boards and Teacher Strikes," *The American*

School Board Journal 135 (November, 1957): 54. Note that only strikes involving breaking contracts are discussed.

THOUGHT AIDS

1. Indicate possible reasons for and against public school teachers having the right to strike.
2. Prepare analytical reports on several of the references presented in this chapter.
3. Present and evaluate the concepts seemingly involved in the following quote. "But if the professional concept of teacher-board of education relationships is to prevail in contrast to the labor concept, our procedures in economic considerations must exclude the traditional trade-union weapon of the strike." (Robbins W. Barstow, Jr. "Teachers and Boards of Education Need to Work Jointly to Determine Policies of Common Concern," *NEA Journal* 50, no. 7 (October, 1961): 63.)
4. Some NEA writers indicate that the strike is basically a means for enforcing economic demands. Contrast this point of view with the professional concept of strikes which is involved in the medical and legal codes of ethics.
5. Do you agree with the concepts emphasized in the following quote? Why or why not? "Why do teachers equate professionalism with giving up the right to strike, to conduct boycotts, and to exercise other sanctions actually used by the acknowledged professions? Probably the major reason is that the organizations of teachers are employer dominated and employers find it advantageous to equate professionalism with acquiescence to administration and public opinion." (Myron Lieberman. "Professionalism and the Voodoo of Education." *Proceedings of the Seventeenth Annual Meeting of the Philosophy of Education Society.* Philosophy of Education Society, 1961, p. 58.)
6. Use *The Education Index* as a guide to recent articles on teacher strikes. Do the articles tend to support the NEA position? Why or why not?
7. On the basis of the NEA Code of Ethics, is it ethical for teachers to go on strike? Why or why not?
8. Is it necessary that an adequate code of ethics for professional teachers must involve the basic characteristics, such as mandatory strike or withdrawal of services requirements, of the medical and legal codes of ethics?
9. Do you believe that the following quote indicates the typical school administrator reaction to the question of whether or not teachers

should strike? Why? "Should Teachers Strike? The typical reaction of professional workers is found in the resolution adopted by the American Association of School Administrators in convention assembled: 'We disapprove of the use of the strike as a means of securing the right of professional workers. This type of conduct will react ultimately to the detriment of teaching as a profession.' " (Chris A. De Young. *Introduction to American Public Education.* New York: McGraw-Hill Book Company, 1955, p. 565.)

10. Evaluate the following quote. "In nearly all communities there will be no need for teacher strikes if interested committees representing the public, the board of education, and the teachers work together on problems of teacher salaries, working conditions, living arrangements, and other matters of teacher welfare. Informed and alert citizens will see that justice is done to the teaching profession and to the children of America." (De Young, p. 565.)

11. Should teachers be denied the legal right to strike because they are publicly employed? Why or why not? For one side of the argument, see Myron Lieberman, "Teachers Strikes: An Analysis of the Issues," *Harvard Educational Review* 26, no. 1 (Winter, 1956).

12. Do strikes by public school teachers necessarily deny the authority of government? Why? (For one answer, see the above Lieberman article.)

13. Are strikes by public school teachers contrary to the public welfare? Why or why not?

14. Analyze the following statement on the basis of concepts emphasized in this chapter. "When the number of teachers engaging in them is considered, strikes constitute during recent years one of the most serious violations of the codes of ethics of the teaching profession." (Ward G. Reeder. *A First Course in Education.* New York: The Macmillan Company, 1958, p. 571.)

15. Do you agree with the assumption that the commonly-accepted dualism of "strikes versus sanctions" really is a logical fallacy? Why or why not?

17

How Professional Is the National Education Association Code of Ethics?

The NEA has had a code of ethics since 1929; it was revised in 1941, in 1952, in 1963, and again in 1968. Although developed chiefly under the direction of the NEA, the code is meant to be the code of ethics of the "education profession." The present code, due to its acceptance by the NEA Representative Assembly, appears to be widely accepted as the code of ethics of the education profession.

Other than in Myron Lieberman's books and articles, the various versions of the NEA Code apparently rarely have been examined or evaluated systematically. Lieberman has criticized the 1952 revision of the code as being "an atrocious collection of cliches, platitudes, evasions, and ambiguities." To Lieberman, that code was so inadequate, it "will serve only to delay the development and enforcement of an adequate code of ethics for teachers." After examining Lieberman's analyses of the 1952 version of the code, which are noted in the reference section at the end of this chapter, the reader may perhaps conclude that Lieberman's harsh words do not have sufficient bases in fact, particularly when the current version of the code is examined. However, it is fairly clear that there are contradictory opinions as to the professional adequacy of the NEA Code of Ethics. Therefore, it appears that the code merits thoughtful examination.

THE NEA CODE OF ETHICS

CODE OF ETHICS OF THE EDUCATION PROFESSION

PREAMBLE

The educator believes in the worth and dignity of man. He recognizes the supreme importance of the pursuit of truth, devotion to excellence, and the nurture of democratic citizenship. He regards as essential to these goals the protection of freedom to learn and to teach and the guarantee of equal educational opportunity for all. The educator accepts his responsibility to practice his profession according to the highest ethical standards.

The educator recognizes the magnitude of the responsibility he has accepted in choosing a career in education, and engages himself, individually and collectively with other educators, to judge his colleagues, and to be judged by them, in accordance with the provisions of this code.

PRINCIPLE I

Commitment to the Student

The educator measures his success by the progress of each student toward realization of his potential as a worthy and effective citizen. The educator therefore works to stimulate the spirit of inquiry, the acquisition of knowledge and understanding, and the thoughtful formulation of worthy goals.

In fulfilling his obligation to the student, the educator—

1. Shall not without just cause restrain the student from independent action in his pursuit of learning, and shall not without just cause deny the student access to varying points of view.

2. Shall not deliberately suppress or distort subject matter for which he bears responsibility.

3. Shall make reasonable effort to protect the student from conditions harmful to learning or to health and safety.

4. Shall conduct professional business in such a way that he does not expose the student to unnecessary embarrassment or disparagement.

5. Shall not on the ground of race, color, creed, or national origin exclude any student from participation in or deny him benefits under any program, nor grant any discriminatory consideration or advantage.

6. Shall not use professional relationships with students for private advantage.

7. Shall keep in confidence information that has been obtained in the course of professional service, unless disclosure serves professional purposes or is required by law.

8. Shall not tutor for remuneration students assigned to his classes, unless no other qualified teacher is reasonably available.

PRINCIPLE II

Commitment to the Public

The educator believes that patriotism in its highest form requires dedication to the principles of our democratic heritage. He shares with all other citizens the responsibility for the development of sound public policy and assumes full political and citizenship responsibilities. The educator bears particular responsibility for the development of policy relating to the extension of educational opportunities for all and for interpreting educational programs and policies to the public.

In fulfilling his obligation to the public, the educator—

1. Shall not misrepresent an institution or organization with which he is affiliated, and shall take adequate precautions to distinguish between his personal and institutional or organizational views.

2. Shall not knowingly distort or misrepresent the facts concerning educational matters in direct and indirect public expressions.

3. Shall not interfere with a colleague's exercise of political and citizenship rights and responsibilities.

4. Shall not use institutional privileges for private gain or to promote political candidates or partisan political activities.

5. Shall accept no gratuities, gifts, or favors that might impair or appear to impair professional judgment, nor offer any favor, service, or thing of value to obtain special advantage.

PRINCIPLE III

Commitment to the Profession

The educator believes that the quality of the services of the education profession directly influences the nation and its citizens. He therefore exerts every effort to raise professional standards, to improve his service, to promote a climate in which the exercise of professional judgment is encouraged, and to achieve conditions which attract persons worthy of the trust to careers in education. Aware of the value of united effort, he contributes actively to the support, planning, and programs of professional organizations.

In fulfilling his obligations to the profession, the educator—

1. Shall not discriminate on grounds of race, color, creed, or national origin for membership in professional organizations, nor interfere with the free participation of colleagues in the affairs of their association.

2. Shall accord just and equitable treatment to all members of the profession in the exercise of their professional rights and responsibilities.

3. Shall not use coercive means or promise special treatment in order to influence professional decisions of colleagues.

4. Shall withhold and safeguard information acquired about colleagues in the course of employment, unless disclosure serves professional purposes.

5. Shall not refuse to participate in a professional inquiry when requested by an appropriate professional association.

6. Shall provide upon the request of the aggrieved party a written statement of specific reason for recommendations that lead to the denial of increments, significant changes in employment, or termination of employment.

7. Shall not misrepresent his professional qualifications.

8. Shall not knowingly distort evaluations of colleagues.

PRINCIPLE IV

Commitment to Professional Employment Practices

The educator regards the employment agreement as a pledge to be executed both in spirit and in fact in a manner consistent with the highest ideals of professional service. He believes that sound professional personnel relationships with governing boards are built upon personal integrity, dignity, and mutual respect. The educator discourages the practice of his profession by unqualified persons.

In fulfilling his obligation to professional employment practice, the educator—

1. Shall apply for, accept, offer, or assign a position or responsibility on the basis of professional preparation and legal qualifications.

2. Shall apply for a specific position only when it is known to be vacant, and shall refrain from underbidding or commenting adversely about other candidates.

3. Shall not knowingly withhold information regarding a position from an applicant, or misrepresent an assignment or conditions of employment.

4. Shall give prompt notice to the employing agency of any change in availability of service, and the employing agent shall give prompt notice of change in availability or nature of a position.

5. Shall not accept a position when so requested by the appropriate professional organization.

6. Shall adhere to the terms of a contract or appointment, unless these terms have been legally terminated, falsely represented, or substantially altered by unilateral action of the employing agency.

7. Shall conduct professional business through channels, when available, that have been jointly approved by the professional organization and the employing agency.

8. Shall not delegate assigned tasks to unqualified personnel.

9. Shall permit no commercial exploitation of his professional position.

10. Shall use time granted for the purpose for which it is intended.

AN ANALYSIS OF THE NEA CODE

Emphasis in the analysis of the code will be centered on the following questions: (1) Is the NEA Code a professional code? (2) If it is a professional code, how adequate is it? The particular section or statement being analyzed will be presented in italic type, followed by the evaluation of it. Let us first examine the title of the code:

Code of Ethics of the Education Profession

NEA leaders traditionally have held tenaciously to two basic beliefs: (1) Teaching is a profession, and (2) The NEA is a professional organization. However, as noted in previous chapters, if a profession must be an occupation, since a profession may be taken to be a professional occupation, and if "education" is not an occupation but a group label covering a number of related occupations, the NEA's assumption that there is an education profession must be recognized as faulty. Since the words "profession" or "professional" appear at least thirty times in this code, it would seem that clear operational definitions for these terms would be essential. However, since such definitions are not presented in the code, it appears that these words are merely high sounding "purr" words which are devoid of operational meaning. After examining the generally accepted professional occupations of medicine and law, it appears that at least one of the basic operational traits of a profession is that the practitioners in the occupation control training for, entrance into, and expulsion from the occupation. The NEA traditionally has labeled all such attempts by occupations within the educational area to control themselves as being "fragmentizing" and "divisive." More specifically, does the NEA code foster control over teaching in a particular discipline by teachers in that discipline? Let us reserve judgment on this point until we have examined the code more thoroughly.

PREAMBLE

The educator believes in the worth and dignity of man. He recognizes the supreme importance of the pursuit of truth, devotion to excellence, and the nurture of democratic citizenship. He regards as essential to these goals the protection of freedom to learn and to teach and the guarantee of equal educational opportunity for all. The educator accepts his responsibility to practice his profession according to the highest ethical standards.

What has the NEA done effectively to protect the "freedom to learn and to teach?" Historically speaking, it appears that the NEA has supported lay board control over the various teaching occupations. As chronicled by scholars studying infringements on academic freedom, such lay board control has been a hindrance to democratic freedoms to teach and to learn reflectively. Therefore, it would appear that the NEA's traditional policy of supporting lay board control over education is in conflict with this preamble to the code.

The educator recognizes the magnitude of the responsibility he has accepted in choosing a career in education, and engages himself, individually and collectively with other educators, to judge his colleagues, and to be judged by them, in accordance with the provisions of this code.

The code repeatedly talks vaguely about "educators," and not about occupational "colleagues." The code leaves the door wide open for the highly anti-professional practice of educators in the social-studies teaching occupation being judged by their colleagues in other educational occupations. Who is to determine the standards for judging colleagues in the same occupation? Anti-professional practices might include determination of such standards by lay school boards, the boards' administrative representatives, and colleagues in other occupations. It appears that the vagueness of this code would allow, and perhaps even encourage, such anti-professional practices.

PRINCIPLE I

Commitment to the Student

1. Shall not without just cause restrain the student from independent action in his pursuit of learning, and shall not without just cause deny the student access to varying points of view.

Who is to determine what "just cause" means, practitioners within each occupation, or school administrators who serve as the representatives of lay school boards? This is the type of crucial differentiation which is repeatedly avoided by this code.

4. Shall conduct professional business in such a way that he does not expose the student to unnecessary embarrassment or disparagement.

Who is to determine which business is "professional" and which embarrassment or disparagement is "unnecessary?" At these points, in which operational clarity is crucial, this code consistently is hazy. In the absence of any clear-cut criteria, it appears that the code would allow the generally prevalent anti-professional practice of school boards and their administrative representatives determining what business is or is not professional.

6. Shall not use professional relationships with students for private advantage.

Who is to determine which relationships are "professional"?

8. Shall not tutor for remuneration students assigned to his classes, unless no other qualified teacher is reasonably available.

Who is to determine whether or not a person is "qualified" to participate in any one of the various occupations in the teaching area? The determination of qualifications for participating in the various teaching occupations traditionally has been in the anti-professional hands of state lay boards of education. In school systems with "merit pay" plans, the power to determine merit usually has been in the non-proſessional hands of school administrators. It appears that the NEA Code fails to condemn such anti-professional practices.

PRINCIPLE II

Commitment to the Public

The educator believes that patriotism in its highest form requires dedication to the principles of our democratic heritage. He shares with all other citizens the responsibility for the development of sound public policy and assumes full political and citizenship responsibilities. The educator bears particular responsibility for the development of policy relating to the extension of educational opportunities for all and for interpreting educational programs and policies to the public.

Which principles of our "heritage" are "democratic" and which are not? Who is to decide this? Is the educator's "responsibility for the development of sound public policy," particularly in the educational area, the same as that of a member of the lay public? If it may be assumed that the public establishes the general policies governing professions (for example, obligating physicians to reduce sickness and suffering and to prolong life, and then professional practitioners determine what specific practices are to be carried out in order to implement the general policies), it appears that the code fails to distinguish clearly between publicly- and occupationally-determined policies. Is the public to participate only in the formulation of general educational policies, such as, for example, obligating educators to foster democratic student abilities to raise and resolve significant conflicts, or does this section allow the public, through their school boards, to invade professional decision-making areas? If it is highly anti-professional for the public to determine policies which would be occupationally determined in professional occupations, the code's lack of clarity apparently would permit such anti-professional practices.

PRINCIPLE III

Commitment to the Profession

The educator believes that the quality of the services of the education profession directly influences the nation and its citizens. He therefore exerts every effort to raise professional standards, to improve his service, to promote a climate in which the exercise of professional judgment is encouraged, and to achieve conditions which attract persons worthy of the trust to careers in education. Aware of the value of united effort, he contributes actively to the support, planning, and programs of professional organizations.

Not only does this section present the questionable assumption that education is a profession, it also presupposes the "self-evident truth" that professional organizations are already in existence. The writer knows of no occupation in the teaching area in which the occupational practitioners control training for, entrance into, and expulsion from that occupation. Like the famous waggish question, "Have you quit beating your wife?" the NEA's assertion that professional organizations already exist appears to be contrary to fact.

6. Shall provide upon the request of the aggrieved party a written statement of specific reason for recommendations that lead to the denial of increments, significant changes in employment, or termination of employment.

Again the crucial question of who is to deny increments and change or terminate employment is not dealt with. It appears that traditional anti-professional practices in which school boards and their administrative representatives control increments and changes in or termination of employment would not be clearly in violation of this code. Therefore, such highly anti-professional practices would be compatible with this code.

PRINCIPLE IV

Commitment to Professional Employment Practices

The educator regards the employment agreement as a pledge to be executed both in spirit and in fact in a manner consistent with the highest ideals of professional service. He believes that sound professional personnel relationships with governing boards are built upon personal integrity, dignity, and mutual respect. The educator discourages the practice of his profession by unqualified persons.

Does this principle endorse traditional anti-professional practices of lay boards of education and members of the various school administration occupations having power to determine aspects of the working conditions of the various teaching occupations, such as class size, or does this principle endorse professional practices such as governing boards within each teaching occupation determining working conditions within each occupation? Diametrically opposed practices have just been noted. Which does the NEA Code endorse? It appears that the NEA Code is so hazy and ill-defined that it could be interpreted as endorsing either or both of these mutually incompatible positions. In brief, it appears that operational clarity as to which activities are approved and which are not is almost totally lacking.

A number of other ambiguities in the code could be pointed out, but this would be belaboring the point. The reader is encouraged to examine the code himself and determine how valid these various allegations are.

CONCLUSION

In our analysis of the NEA Code, we attempted to find answers to two questions: (1) is the NEA Code a professional one? and (2) if it is a professional one, how adequate is it? Basic traits of generally recognized professions—such as medicine and law—involve practitioner control over training for, entrance into, and expulsion from each occupation. The NEA Code seems to be so hazy and ambiguous that whether the NEA Code fosters such professional practices cannot clearly be determined. However, a fairly defensible position in regard to the NEA Code might be that, since the code allows present anti-professional practices to continue uncondemned, the net effect of the code is to bolster traditional, anti-professional educational practices. Therefore, in order that the NEA Code may become a professional code, it appears that drastic changes are necessary.

Lest the writer be accused of siding with the American Federation of Teachers, it should be emphasized that even though the net effect of the NEA Code seemingly tends to be basically anti-professional, the NEA has at least made a number of attempts to design what the NEA leadership thought was a professional code, whereas the writer knows of no code of ethics having been developed by the AFT.

Before the NEA Code can be made into a tool for fostering professionalism, it appears that the NEA leadership must come to grips with and correct at least three questionable beliefs presently supported by the NEA: (1) "There is an Education Profession;" (2) "The NEA is a Professional Organization;" and (3) "Strong organizations in the various teaching occupations are divisive and debilitating." Also, thorough analyses of the codes of ethics of generally recognized professional "unions" such as the American Medical Association and the American Bar Association probably would be valuable preludes to the formulation of professional codes of ethics by governing boards in the various teaching occupations.

SELECTED REFERENCES

Burrup, Percy E., *The Teacher and the Public School System*. New York: Harper & Row Publishers, 1967, Chap. 15. A good introduction to educational ethics.

Gauverke, Warren E., *Legal and Ethical Responsibilities of School Personnel*. Englewood Cliffs, New Jersey: Prentice-Hall, Inc., 1959. A comprehensive examination of the legal and ethical aspects of education.

Implementing the Code of Ethics of the Education Profession and Strengthening Professional Rights. Washington, D.C.: National Education Association, 1964. An explanation of the NEA's role in implementing the NEA Code of Ethics.

Interpretations of the Code of Ethics of the Education Profession. Washington, D.C.: National Education Association, 1963. Interpretations of each section of the code are presented.

Lieberman, Myron, *Education as a Profession*. Englewood Cliffs, New Jersey: Prentice-Hall, Inc., 1956, Chap. 13. Although dated, much of this searching analysis appears still to be applicable.

————, "Professional Ethics and the NEA," *Phi Delta Kappan* 44, no. 7 (April, 1963): 310–12. A biting analysis of the 1963 revision of the NEA Code of Ethics.

Marvin, John, "The Role of the Code in the Education Profession," in Donald Orlich and S. Samuel Shermis, eds., *The Pursuit of Excellence: Introductory Readings in Education*. New York: American Book Company, 1965, pp. 319–28. A defense of the NEA Code.

Opinions of the Committee on Professional Ethics. Washington, D.C.: National Education Association, 1964. Opinions of the Committee deal with cooperation in investigations, selling musical instruments, reporting grades to parents, proper use of sick leave, etc.

THOUGHT AIDS

1. Do you agree with the belief that the NEA Code of Ethics needs to be drastically revised in order to be acceptable as a professional code? Why or why not?

2. Study the codes of ethics of the American Medical Association and the American Bar Association. Do you believe that these codes have been interpreted validly in this chapter? Why or why not?

3. Is administrator invasion of teacher autonomy, such as administrator

determination of textbooks and adequacy of teaching, in conflict with the NEA Code of Ethics? Why or why not?

4. Evaluate the NEA Code of Ethics on the basis of the criteria for good codes of ethics presented by Myron Lieberman in his book, *Education as a Profession*, pp. 417–19.

5. Prepare analytical reports on the references presented in this chapter.

6. Do you believe that a professional code of ethics for teachers should be patterned after the codes of ethics of commonly recognized professions such as medicine and law? Why or why not?

7. Use *The Education Index* as a guide to recent articles on teacher ethics. Do the articles tend to support the NEA position? Why or why not?

8. If a teacher disagrees with present NEA concepts of professionalism and teacher ethics, does he necessarily have to be "trade union" oriented? Why or why not?

9. On the basis of the NEA Code of Ethics, is it ethical for teachers to go on strike? Why or why not?

10. Is it necessary that an adequate code of ethics for professional teachers must involve the basic characteristics, such as mandatory strike or withdrawal of services requirements, of the medical and legal codes of ethics?

11. Do you agree with the analysis of the NEA Code ot Ethics which was presented in this chapter? Why or why not?

12. Present the ethical problems in teaching which you believe are important. Give specific examples of each problem.

13. Indicate possible arguments for and against the belief that all professions should subscribe to one professional code of ethics.

18

Should Merit Rating Be Fostered?

The basic question is whether or not a teacher's salary should, to some degree, be dependent on a judgment of his competence.

Prior to 1900, the salaries of public school teachers primarily were dependent on the bargaining ability of the individual teacher and on the judgments of school board members and their administrative representatives. After the turn of the century, formal merit pay plans multiplied, reaching a peak of popularity in the 1920's. During the decades of the depression and World War II, the single salary schedule became popular and merit pay programs were dropped by most of the districts which had used them. Under the single salary schedule, teacher salaries were determined solely on the basis of levels of training attained and years of experience. However, interest in merit pay plans was renewed in the 1950's.

Merit salaries have been paid in one or more of these ways: (1) special salary scales; (2) more rapid movement toward maximum salary levels through larger or doubled increments; (3) bonus payments; and (4) additional salary steps beyond the established maximum.

Thomas Stirling has summarized some of the basic arguments in the conflict over merit pay:

For

1. In a democracy, a person should be judged and rewarded upon his individual worth.

2. A good teacher should be paid more than an average one.

3. It is not difficult to recognize a merit teacher.

4. The morale of excellent teachers can be raised by recognition and monetary reward.

5. Merit rating encourages teachers to evaluate themselves and to improve.

6. Merit rating would result in greater service to the school by teachers.

7. All teachers should be rated by the same criteria.

8. If classroom teachers are rated, then all licensed personnel should be rated.

9. Only a relatively few teachers should attain merit status.

10. Improvement of instruction through supervision would be enhanced because teachers would be anxious to improve.

Against

1. It is undemocratic for one person to be categorized by the opinion of another.

2. Merit salary would result (finally) in average teachers being underpaid.

3. It is impossible to identify the merit teacher.

4. Staff morale will be lowered when certain teachers are singled out for increased salaries for similar duties.

5. Merit rating stifles a free exchange of ideas and techniques when teachers are in competition with one another.

6. Non-merit teachers would tend to shun extra duties by saying, "Let the merit teacher do it."

7. It is impossible to rate a gym teacher and a physics teacher by the same criteria.

8. A non-merit supervisor would be in an untenable situation to rate others.

9. Parents would object to having their children placed in the classes of non-merit teachers.

10. Constructive supervision would be destroyed because teachers would tend to cover up weaknesses rather than seek improvement through working with a supervisor.[1]

---

[1] Thomas Stirling, "What Is the Case for and Against Merit Rating for Teachers?" *Bulletin of The National Association of Secondary School Principals* 44, no. 255 (April, 1960): 93. For other lists of arguments for and against merit pay programs, see Stayner F. Brighton and Cecil J. Hannan. *Merit Pay Programs for Teachers* (San Francisco: Fearon Publishers, 1962).

ARGUMENTS FOR MERIT RATING

George Holloway lists arguments for merit rating programs:

1. Attracts and holds better teachers.
2. Is in harmony with the American tradition of paying on basis of value received regardless of years of experience or training.
3. Stimulates and encourages individual improvement.
4. Encourages teachers to be critical of their own work.
5. Improves morale.
6. Permits the teacher who wishes to work from 8 to 4 to be paid a lesser amount and not feel inferior.
7. Keeps the better teachers in the classroom and does not make it necessary for them to seek administrative positions in order to obtain greater remuneration.
8. Necessitates more administrators and this in itself is good; schools have always been understaffed administratively.
9. Enables the teacher to know where he or she stands in the eyes of administrators.
10. Will make the public more willing to support higher salaries.[2]

Richard Stauffer and Clarence Withers also list arguments for merit rating:

1. Teaching will be improved.
2. The professionalization of the teacher's calling will result from rating.
3. Teachers will be motivated to improve.
4. The supply of teachers will be increased.
5. The value of the salary paid teachers will be increased.
6. The community's respect for teachers will be improved.
7. Teachers will receive rewards more commensurate with their training and skill.
8. Teacher rating plans will increase the amount of money which the public will invest in education.
9. Snap judgments by supervisors are eliminated.
10. Such policies emphasize good personnel administration.
11. Teacher self-evaluation will be increased.
12. Incompetency is discouraged.
13. Professional status is raised.
14. Tenure increases importance of evaluation.[3]

---

[2] George E. Holloway, Jr., "Objective Look at the Merit Pay Issue," *The School Executive* 78, no. 8 (April, 1959): 21.

[3] Richard F. Stauffer and Clarence M. Withers. "What Are the Advantages and Disadvantages of Teacher Merit Rating Plans?" *Bulletin of the National Association of Secondary School Principals* 42, no. 237 (April, 1958), p. 216.

Studies indicate that successful merit pay plans have involved a number of the following factors.

1. A basic salary schedule well above the average.
2. A willingness on the part of teachers, administrators and board members (citizens too if possible) to work together in developing the plan and the evaluative procedure.
3. A common understanding of the objectives of the school system.
4. An understanding that no percentage ratio will be placed on the higher salaries.
5. A willingness to try a plan and revise it after more intensive study.
6. School board recognition that the plan will cost more money.
7. Do not adopt a merit plan from some other district; develop one which is tailor-made to your community and your staff.
8. Be careful to select the areas to be used in evaluating teaching competence.
9. Be prepared to study the problem.
10. Proceed slowly.[4]

1. Plans developed locally in terms of local conditions.
2. Teachers, administrators, school board members, and patrons worked co-operatively on the project.
3. Merit awards, or bonuses, superimposed upon a good single salary schedule.
4. Merit awards sufficiently high to be worth working for.
5. A co-operatively developed rating instrument that emphasizes performance and pupil progress rather than teacher traits used along with personnel record files.
6. Sufficient "supervisory" assistance to allow for adequate observation and teacher counselling.
7. An appeal committee and procedure through which a teacher may appeal what she considers an unfair appraisal.
8. An arbitrary limit on the number of teachers who can achieve merit status, although standards are high enough so that only a few teachers actually make superior ratings.
9. Ratings and files kept confidential, but access to them is always available to the individual teacher.
10. The program made a matter of constant review, evaluation, and improvement.[5]

1. A professional high level basic salary schedule must apply to all teachers.

---

[4] Holloway, "Objective Look at the Merit Pay Issue," p. 21.
[5] Brighton and Hannan, *Merit Pay Programs for Teachers*, pp. 15–16.

2. The staff must have a hand in developing any experimental plan.
3. Factors to be judged and procedures to be followed must be clearly understood by all.
4. Everyone must have an opportunity to qualify for higher salaries—no percentage restrictions.
5. Merit rating must be related to a larger plan of instructional improvement.
6. Administrators must devote more time to improving instruction and evaluating outcomes.
7. There must be periodic appraisal of the merit plan.[6]

ARGUMENTS AGAINST MERIT RATING

Over the last two decades, there has been a decline in the number of school districts having quality provisions in their salary schedules. At various times during the last quarter century, most of the largest city school systems have tried merit rating, but all have discarded such plans.

Clarence M. Withers notes these arguments against merit pay:

1. The merit rating system will increase the hostility between teachers, supervisors, and administrators.
2. It will cost more to initiate and implement than it can ever be worth.
3. Teaching is an art that never can be measured mathematically.
4. Teachers will be less willing to help one another.
5. Teachers are individuals who teach different pupils and different subjects and cannot be measured by the same yardstick.
6. It will cause a form of class distinction within the teaching profession.
7. Merit rating will not necessarily increase the economic status of teachers.
8. Such a system is difficult to administer.
9. It will not eliminate the poor teacher.
10. It cannot, by itself, increase the supply of good teachers to any appreciable extent.
11. There is no accurate means of measuring quality of teaching.
12. Great variations in philosophies of quality of teaching make the plan difficult to administer.
13. Merit rating tends to lower morale.

---

[6] Howard R. Jones, "Workable Merit Rating," *School and Society* 86, no. 2130 (April 12, 1958): 178.

14. Such plans tend to produce conformity to preconceived ideas of some person or group which may suppress initiative.
15. Experimentation is discouraged.
16. Democratic procedures in problem solving are retarded.
17. Pupil differences make evaluation of quality of instruction difficult and unfair.
18. Merit plans control educational costs and do not promote better teaching.
19. There is no best method of teaching and the difficulty of rating is increased.
20. Cooperation between teachers and administrators is reduced.
21. Teacher attitudes are conditioned, which will be detrimental to pupils.
22. The administrator becomes an inspector, not a professional leader of instruction.
23. A large, adequately educated staff for supervision is required.
24. The cost to have a just administrative system is prohibitive.
25. There are too many subjective factors which are difficult to evaluate.
26. There is a detrimental effect on administration as it substitutes force of rating for courageous administration.
27. Merit salary schedules give false impression of salaries actually paid teachers.
28. Cooperative discussion between teacher groups and boards of education regarding salary matters are inhibited.
29. Undue parent and board pressure on certain teachers might occur.
30. The feeling of insecurity might be magnified in the average or poor teacher and his effectiveness still further lowered.
31. School boards would be tempted to substitute merit raises for a generally improved salary schedule.
32. Parents and board members might resent the fact that their children were not placed with "superior" teachers.
33. Discriminations and injustices become almost inevitable.[7]

Carl Megel, president of the American Federation of Teachers, presents these arguments against merit rating:

1. It cannot fairly evaluate the true effectiveness of teaching.
2. It rewards conformity.
3. It puts a premium on the absence of teacher problems.
4. It fosters a competitive rather than a cooperative spirit.
5. It strikes at the security of the teacher.
6. It disregards the type of environment in which a teacher teaches.

---

[7] Stauffer and Withers, "Teacher Merit Rating Plans," pp. 216–17.

7. It cannot improve the quality of education.
8. It is a dangerous mirage and cannot and will not relieve the teacher shortage.
9. It does not reward good teachers for superior work.[8]

Many educators believe that good teachers, expending their best energy for their students, would not discover more energy under a merit pay plan. Therefore, it is much more important to raise the general level of teaching through in-service training programs than to reward a few individuals. Alternatives to merit pay, as ways to improve instruction, include better selection of teacher candidates, intensified in-service programs, more stringent professional growth requirements, and salary differentials based on differentiation of teacher function, such as higher pay for team teaching leaders.

PROFESSIONAL MERIT RATING

If one of the basic traits of professional occupations is determination of competency by practitioners themselves, practically all of the writings, both pro and con, about merit pay for teachers are based on the patently anti-professional belief that school boards and their administrative representatives should evaluate the merit of practitioners. In other words, the traditional merit pay debate is over whether a system of non-occupational, and therefore anti-professional, merit rating should be fostered. The professional concept of occupational practitioners rating the competency of their own occupational comrades basically is ignored.

The only known notable exception to the general ignoring of professional systems of merit rating is Myron Lieberman's proposal in his book *The Future of Public Education*. He suggests national specialty boards being established by the national organizations of teachers in certain fields, such as the National Council of Teachers of Mathematics, which would be comparable to the national specialty boards in medical specialties. Just as the American College of Surgeons controls the diplomate in surgery, Lieberman suggests that teachers in a given field could control the diplomate in that field.[9]

If, as has been noted in previous chapters, an occupation is best defined as a job or vocation in which the practitioners have basically

---

[8] Carl J. Megel, "Merit Rating Is Unsound," *Phi Delta Kappan* 42, no. 4 (January, 1961): 154–56.

[9] Myron Lieberman, *The Future of Public Education* (Chicago: University of Chicago Press, 1960), pp. 259–70.

equivalent skills and abilities—they can competently interchange positions—teaching appears to be an area encompassing many non-interchangeable occupations, and thus is not itself an occupation. Since Lieberman apparently fails to recognize clearly such distinctions, he also fails to observe that teachers and physicians are not validly comparable. As previously noted, teaching does not seem to be an occupation, whereas, to be licensed, physicians must demonstrate basically equivalent skills and abilities. However, Lieberman does make a very commendable attempt at exploring aspects of occupational determination of merit. Further explorations into various dimensions of occupational judgments of practitioner competency appear to be justified by the almost total lack of attention to this aspect of the merit pay question.

CONCLUSION

During the last two decades, the pros and cons of school boards and their administrative representatives judging teacher merit have been expressed in numerous articles. Articles favoring merit pay generally were accepted by journals such as *The Nation's Schools* and *The American School Board Journal.* Articles opposing merit pay predominated in the educational associations' journals.

Only about 10 per cent of current teacher salary schedules analyzed by the Research Division of the National Education Association included compensation for superior service.[10] Professional merit rating, rating of occupational members by other members, basically has been ignored. Myron Lieberman has been the one notable exception to this generalization. Intensive examination of the potentialities of professional merit rating appears to be justified.

SELECTED REFERENCES

Brighton, Stayner and Cecil Hannan, *Merit Pay Programs for Teachers.* San Francisco: Fearon Publishers, 1962. This handbook is the most comprehensive introduction to the merit pay problem. The extensive

---

[10] *Phi Delta Kappan* 51, no. 1 (September, 1969): 55.

bibliography is an essential tool for serious students of the merit pay problem.

Kleinmann, Jack H., "Merit Pay—The Big Question," *NEA Journal* 52, no. 5 (May, 1963): 42–44. A resumé of the NEA's position on merit pay.

Lieberman, Myron, *Education as a Profession*. Englewood Cliffs, New Jersey: Prentice-Hall, Inc., 1956, "Merit Rating," pp. 393–402. An excellent introduction to merit rating problems.

————, *The Future of Public Education*, "A Foundation Approach to Merit Pay." Chicago: The University of Chicago Press, 1960, pp. 259–70. An interesting attempt to move beyond the traditional arguments over merit pay.

Link, Frances R., "Merit Rating: Have the Issues Changed?" *Educational Leadership* 22, no. 5 (February, 1965): 322–26. An analysis of trends in merit rating.

Merit Rating—Dangerous Mirage or Master Plan? Chicago: American Federation of Teachers, Research Department, 1958. This booklet is an examination of merit rating from the "union" viewpoint.

Vander Werf, Lester S. *How to Evaluate Teachers and Teaching*. New York: Holt, Rinehart and Company, 1958. This booklet is an introduction to the area of teacher appraisal.

Weissman, Rozanne, "Merit Pay—What Merit?" *The Education Digest* 34, no. 9 (May, 1969: 16–19. Merit pay programs are analyzed in historical perspective.

THOUGHT AIDS

1. Use *The Education Index* to locate current articles on merit rating.
2. Why do you think articles supporting merit pay appear more frequently in journals such as *The Nation's Schools* and *The American School Board Journal,* and articles opposed to merit pay predominate in educational association journals? What, if anything, do you feel should be done about this?
3. Examine the possible strengths and weaknesses of the professional merit rating plan presented by Myron Lieberman.
4. What are the current trends in the merit rating problem area?
5. Do you agree that the merit rating conflict should be classified as one of the problems in the educational power and professionalism area? Why or why not?
6. Obtain and analyze teacher rating scales from school districts using merit pay programs.
7. Analyze the two following viewpoints on merit pay presented in *Saturday Review* 44, no. 50 (December 16, 1961): 47.

a. (Resolution adopted by the Representative Assembly of the National Education Association at its annual convention, June, 1961.)

The National Education Association believes that it is a major responsibility of the teaching profession, as of other professions, to evaluate the quality of its services. To enable educators to meet this responsibility more effectively, the Association calls for continued research and experimentation to develop means of objective evaluation of the performance of all professional personnel, including identification of (a) factors that determine professional competence; (b) factors that determine the effectiveness of competent professionals; (c) methods of evaluating effective professional service; and (d) methods of recognizing effective professional service through self-realization, personal status, and salary.

The Association further believes that use of subjective methods of evaluating professional performance for the purpose of setting salaries has a deleterious effect on the educational process. Plans which require such subjective judgments (commonly known as merit ratings) should be avoided. American education can be better served by continued progress in developing better means of objective evaluation.

b. (The following is from a speech by Carl J. Megel, president of the American Federation of Teachers.)

The American Federation of Teachers, representing classroom teachers, has vigorously opposed this specious practice (merit rating) for more than thirty years. Our organization has seen merit rating fail in city after city. We have seen school board after school board abandon it as unworkable and not conducive to improved educational practice.

The American Federation of Teachers knows that merit rating is a device designed to wreck the single salary schedule and to make teaching rewards appear higher than they are. We know that merit increases will be given to a relatively few teachers in order to blunt demands for across-the-board increases for all teachers.

Ideally, to speak of basing teachers' salaries on merit rating sounds completely plausible. But it is the impossibility of fairly judging and rating one teacher above another on a dollar-and-cents basis which makes the merit system unworkable. Experience has shown that the only way to protect the superior teacher from unfair, inadequate, inept, or vindictive rating is by the use of an adequate single salary schedule based upon training and experience.

19

Should Loyalty Oaths Be Supported?

Public school teachers in about half of the states are required, as a condition of employment, to sign legislatively prescribed loyalty oaths. Many of the oaths require teachers to swear or affirm that they will support and defend the United States Constitution and the constitution of the particular state. Some also require the signer to affirm that he is not and never has been a member of The Communist Party or any other subversive organization and that he is opposed to any belief that fosters the overthrow of the United States government. Should teachers be required to sign loyalty oaths?

ARGUMENTS FOR LOYALTY OATHS

There are a number of reasons given for supporting loyalty oaths. First, the loyalty oath is a valid legal means of protecting society from disloyal members. The courts have ruled that, since public school teaching is a privilege, not a right of citizenship (individuals having the right as citizens to believe as they please), public school teachers may be required as a condition of employment to support a belief in the validity of present state and federal governmental and

economic institutions. In this age of protracted conflict with an un-
scrupulous enemy, Americans should use any and all available means
to protect themselves against insidious forces. Requiring loyalty oaths
is one of the many effective ways of fighting the foreign powers that
would subvert the "American Way of Life."

Second, with all other Americans, teachers should be eager to
affirm their loyalty to America. Teachers should stand up and be
counted among those who are valiantly supporting the nation.

Third, since teachers mold the hearts and minds of youth, they
have more influence on the future of America than do most groups.
Since teachers transmit the verities and convictions which are the
bases of our culture, subversive teachers can do incalculable harm. In
order to preserve adequately basic American beliefs, teachers who are
commissioned to transmit these beliefs should be more carefully investigated and screened than should members of other occupational
groups.

Fourth, loyalty oaths stimulate teachers to renew their efforts to
inculcate loyalty to America into their students. Such oaths serve as
reminders to teachers of their high and sacred obligations to the
youth of America.

Fifth, loyalty oaths serve to satisfy the public in general, and
legislators in particular, that teachers as a group are doing their part
to win the struggle with communism.

Sixth, oaths to support the government are taken by many other
public officials. Like all other governmental employees, including military personnel, teachers are expected to carry out the policies which
are approved by the public.

Seventh, loyalty oaths provide a legal basis for dismissal of subversive teachers. Teachers who violate such oaths may be convicted
of perjury.

ARGUMENTS AGAINST LOYALTY OATHS

Before entering into a presentation of arguments against loyalty oaths,
it should be noted that those groups who object to loyalty oaths
usually agree with the principle that every American should be a loyal
citizen and should be willing to indicate his allegiance to the highest
American ideals. These groups usually are opposed to loyalty oaths
precisely because they believe that such oaths *tend to subvert* loyalty
and allegiance to the highest and most prominent American ideals.

The first argument against loyalty oaths is that they are futile and ineffective. Subversive teachers would sign them just as readily as would loyal teachers. Disloyal teachers would not hesitate to perjure themselves by signing such affidavits; therefore, the task of finding subversive teachers would still exist.

Second, the implication that teachers must sign loyalty oaths because they tend to be more disloyal than other influential groups has no basis in verifiable fact. Other groups, such as parents, influence the behavior of youth more than do teachers, but parents are not required to subscribe to such oaths. Other groups, such as farmers, often receive public funds, yet their loyalty is not questioned. Loyalty oaths place conscientious teachers on the horns of a dilemma. If the teachers refuse to sign such oaths, they raise the suspicion that they are unworthy of public trust. If the teachers sign the oaths, they are endorsing the validity of the belief that teachers are a particularly suspect segment of the population. Loyalty oaths, like the waggish question, "Have you stopped beating your wife?" involve fallacious prejudgments or presuppositions. Teachers are falsely prejudged to be a suspect group and are humiliated by being forced to swear that they are loyal.

Third, loyalty oaths will not guarantee loyalty. Requiring support of existing American institutions is not one of the basic factors in the development of loyal citizens. Responsible loyalty arises out of a galaxy of influences, not the least of which is a reflective awareness of the changes that profitably could be made in existing institutions.

Fourth, other laws are more effective when a person is proven to be a subversive. Subversive teachers violate laws which involve more severe punishment than those which could be meted out for perjury, for falsifying an affidavit of loyalty.

Fifth, members of certain religious groups refuse to take any type of oath. Loyalty oaths violate their freedom to worship as conscience dictates.

Sixth, those persons who believe that teachers are public servants who should be required by oath to carry out policies fail to understand the functions of teachers in democratic societies. Democratic teachers are not commissioned to indoctrinate presently approved beliefs or values. Their basic task is to foster reflective thinking, which may involve both critical analyses of existing policies and recommendations for changes in such policies. The public official swears to perpetuate certain policies and institutions. The democratic teacher must be free to foster reflective evaluation of present policies and institutions. The teacher's task is to indicate ways of improving present policies. In contrast, requiring teachers to foster and perpetuate present governmental policies is a tool of totalitarian powers. Teachers in such societies are required to renounce criticism of existing institutions. Therefore, loyalty oaths are compatible with totalitarian governmental concepts of thought control, not with democratic teaching procedures.

Seventh, groups who foster loyalty oaths seem to lack sufficient faith in the ideals of the nation. Such groups imply that American ideals are not adequately defensible in the open competition of the free market place of ideas. They imply that American institutions would lose in a fair and unbiased intellectual inquiry; therefore, teachers must be required to "support" existing institutions instead of fostering reflective analyses of them. If American beliefs are not defensible, shoring them up by insisting on specially privileged teacher support is dubious behavior.

Eighth, loyalty oaths tend to serve as bases for excluding teachers who are non-conformists, dissenters from the status quo. It is precisely just such teachers, those with restless and inquiring minds, who need to be encouraged, not intimidated. It might validly be claimed that the future existence of the United States as a nation is basically dependent upon how well non-conformists are fostered and encouraged, since many of them probably will be the creative thinkers who will go beyond the present limits of knowledge. It is the non-conformists who spearhead progress. Loyalty oaths perpetuate conformity to the status quo and tend to inhibit the progress our nation so desperately needs in this time of world struggle.

Ninth, loyalty oaths violate the modern scientific method. For example, many loyalty oaths require teachers to take an oath of allegiance to the United States Constitution. Teachers are required to value a conclusion, that the Constitution merits allegiance, more than the modern scientific method of inquiry. Such oaths put loyalty to existing institutions above the reflective search for better institutions. This is like requiring plumbers to support a particular brand of plumbing fixtures, regardless of the results of careful examination of alternative types of brands. Governmental institutions, like plumbing fixtures, are usually necessities, but to require support of one type over any other, regardless of the results of careful scrutiny, is a negation of intelligent behavior.

Tenth, one of the basic arguments against loyalty oaths is that they thwart democratic education. Democratic education is based on the principle that beliefs and conclusions must be arrived at through reflective study. There are no predetermined beliefs or conclusions which the teachers and students are required to accept. Only conclusions which, after examination, deserve merit are acceptable. Students and teachers must be free to arrive at the conclusions most warranted by available evidence.

To see how loyalty oaths tend to destroy democratic education, the previously noted loyalty oaths requiring support of the United States Constitution will again be used as an example. To many groups, such oaths imply that teachers must support the Constitution, even if reflective study in the classroom warrants the conclusion that the Constitution does not merit support and should be replaced by a more adequate document. This oath requirement forces teachers to negate reflective thought by requiring them to force students to accept specially privileged beliefs in the value of the present Constitution, in spite of possibly valid evidence to the contrary. It should be noted in passing that nineteen of the framers of the Constitution had such reservations about the adequacy of the Constitution that they refused to support it. Even the sage Benjamin Franklin stated publicly that he signed it only because he thought it would lead to something better.

Rather than involving the inculcation of predetermined conclusions, such as that the present United States Constitution is worthy of unqualified support, education for democratic living would involve fostering abilities to arrive at reflective conclusions based on available evidence. In democratic educational processes, reflective thought may turn its withering gaze on any "sacred cow." Any specially privileged belief may be toppled. The highest ideals of loyalty to American democracy emphasize persistent criticism of existing institutions, no matter how firmly established and how sacrosanct they may be. Instead of "stacking the cards" so students will be duped into accepting predetermined conclusions, democratic teachers foster the ability to judge beliefs not on the basis of their origins or popularity, but on the basis of reflective evidence for and against such beliefs. It appears that most loyalty oaths subvert the American belief that all arguments and conclusions must stand or fall on their own merits.

To democratically-oriented teachers who oppose legislatively prescribed loyalty oaths, the only valid teacher commitment is that exemplified by Thomas Jefferson when he swore hostility against every form of tyranny over the mind of man.

Eleventh, loyalty oaths violate reflective academic freedom. They tend to thwart the teachers and students who supposedly are embarked on intellectual ventures in which the range of inquiry should be boundless. Teachers become aware that there are great risks involved in being unorthodox and failing to conform to standardized tradition patterns of thought. Instead of fostering freedom of dissent and unhampered inquiry, legislatively prescribed loyalty oaths force teachers to present only innocuous and noncontroversial beliefs.

Twelfth, legislatively prescribed loyalty oaths are an unwarranted invasion of the professional autonomy of teachers. If professionalism involves the concept that practitioners within an occupation must be free to determine the standards for occupational competency, legislative determination of teaching competencies through the enactment of loyalty oaths is a clear invasion of professional autonomy. However, it is professionally proper for the practitioners in a professional occupation to set their own standards of competency. Thus, professional occupations could set up their own professional loyalty oaths. Professional codes of ethics, if they are ever developed, would be, in essence, professional loyalty oaths specifying acceptable standards for participation in the particular educational occupations.

CONCLUSION

In recent years, several state loyalty oaths have been struck down by the courts for being too vague. Such legal actions do not, however, invalidate the major arguments for and against loyalty oaths. The basic question still remains: Are teacher loyalty oaths good or bad?

SELECTED REFERENCES

Callahan, Raymond E., *An Introduction to Education in American Society.* New York: Alfred A. Knopf, 1960, pp. 435–38. A strong attack on loyalty oaths.

Kerber, August and Wilfred Smith, *Educational Issues in a Changing Society.* Detroit: Wayne State University Press, 1964, Chap. 10. Good introductory selections on the loyalty oath problem.

Lieberman, Myron, *Education as a Profession.* Englewood Cliffs, New Jersey: Prentice-Hall, Inc., 1956, pp. 102–4. A discussion of loyalty oaths.

John F. Kennedy, "For the Repeal of the Loyalty Oath," in Allan Nevins ed. *The Strategy of Peace*, Section 21. New York: Popular Library, 1961, pp. 217–20. Arguments against the loyalty oath provision of the National Defense Education Act which were presented when former President Kennedy was in the United States Senate.

THOUGHT AIDS

1. Read current articles on loyalty oaths which may be found through *The Reader's Guide to Periodical Literature* and *The Education Index,* and present a summary of your findings.
2. Write to state governments for copies of state teacher loyalty oaths. Analyze the basic principle embodied in these oaths.
3. Debate the issue, "Resolved: Teachers should be required to sign loyalty oaths."
4. Do you agree that legislatively prescribed teacher loyalty oaths are anti-professional invasions of the professional autonomy of teachers? Why?
5. What might be the motivations for setting up state teacher loyalty oaths? How valid to you are these motivations?
6. Could professional codes of ethics be professional loyalty oaths? Why or why not?

20

Which Is Best, Local, Federal, or Professional Control of the Public Schools?

To many Americans, to question seriously the traditional local lay control structure of American public education borders on blasphemy. Local control of education is generally accepted as an essential ingredient in the culture. Former President Kennedy reaffirmed this popular traditional belief about control of our schools when he indicated that "the direction of our public school systems must remain in local hands. The local authorities should determine both academic content and standards."[1] The National Education Association has gone on record as indicating that control of education should remain in the hands of state and local authorities. The NEA attitude toward federal control was stated in a recent pamphlet: "Everybody agrees that this is bad, un-American, unpatriotic, unworkable."[2]

In contrast to the NEA position that "everybody" favors local rather than federal control of education, some educators claim that local control is, intellectually speaking, a corpse which needs to have an autopsy performed on it and then be buried promptly. To these

---

[1] "President Kennedy's Views on Federal Aid," *School News*, Department of Education, State of Colorado, Denver, Colorado, March, 1961, p. 1.

[2] *The Nonexistent Dragon*. (Washington, D.C.: National Education Association Legislative Commission).

educators, local lay board control prevents equality of educational opportunity, weakens national survival, thwarts adequate teaching, is anti-professional, and basically fosters totalitarian protection of specially-privileged dogmas.[3]

ARGUMENTS FOR LOCAL CONTROL

1. *Local Control of Education is the Traditional American Way.* The fundamental direction of American education has been and must remain a local function. Our traditions of public school education rest on the family, implemented through local community effort, assisted by the states.

Our tradition of leaving responsibility for education at the local level has resulted in American education being the envy of the world. Our present educational needs do not justify a radical departure from the successful established policy. In fact, our present need is to preserve and perpetuate the traditional structure.

Encroaching federal controls are tending to destroy this tradition. There is concern that the traditional rights and home government rule with respect to public education are gradually being insidiously undermined. Our schools are one of the few remaining bulwarks of local self-government and democratic community enterprise.

Local control advocates agree with Abraham Lincoln's belief that the federal government should do for the people only those things the people can't do for themselves. It is abundantly clear that the local communities have done and are doing wonderfully well for themselves in education. The national interest in education, like many other national objectives, is best served by local administration and control.

2. *Local Control is Constitutional.* Local, community control of education is based on the constitutional law of the land. It is sanctioned by the Constitution of the United States, for education is one of the powers reserved to the states and to the people by the Tenth Amendment. There are only two major areas which the central government can handle constitutionally: defense and foreign affairs. The resources and capacities of the national government must be conserved and reserved to the above areas, and not fragmented on matters that are not genuine federal business, such as education.

3. *Local Control is Democratic.* Local control is democratic because the people themselves support and guide their schools. One of

---

[3] Myron Lieberman, *The Future of Public Education,* Chapter 3, "Local Control of Education" (Chicago: University of Chicago Press, 1960)

the matchless strengths of the United States is that our schools have always been primarily a local concern. Each individual citizen is responsible, with his neighbors, for the quality of the educational system. This democratic control is best since there is no place where both the strengths and deficiencies in an educational system can be better understood than locally where a community has the opportunity to judge the product of its own schools. Since in a democracy the communities should truly manage their own schools, they should control and make all the basic educational policy decisions in regard to the education of their children, including determination of teacher qualifications, course content, and acceptable teaching procedures. Local democratic control of the schools is in harmony with the dictum that it is best to use the level of government closest to the community for all public functions which can be handled there.

In contrast, federal control of education tends to be a direct denial of the democratic process. After a community has expressed a negative judgment on a project it fully understands, national officials could override the local verdict if federal bureaucrats wished it. State and local lay school board members know their own problems far better than any bureaucrats in Washington. The fundamental issue is big government versus democratic home rule, local democratic rights versus "Welfare Statism."

4. *Local Control Fosters Freedom of Thought.* Local control of education fosters freedom of thought and prevents totalitarian thought control. The present decentralized system of management and direction of the public schools is a reliable bulwark against the easy capture of the schools by economic, social, or political forces. The local school system with lay boards as direct representatives of the communities and as intermediaries between governmental officials and professional educators provides its greatest strength. The closer the control and operation of the American educational system is to the people, the greater is the chance to avoid the totalitarian control of what is taught to the next generation of Americans. The hallmark of intellectual freedom is the diversity involved in our present system of local control. The variety of differences between our locally-controlled schools is an important guarantee of the freedom to learn. In summary, it will always be much more difficult to regiment a system controlled locally than one controlled on a nationwide level.

National control of education is a characteristic of totalitarian countries, and federal control of education ultimately would open the door to such a totalitarian government. In totalitarian countries, the basic belief is "Everything for the state; nothing outside the state; nothing against the state." Nationally controlled systems of education condition the people to unquestioning obedience and submissiveness to the will of those in power. John Stuart Mill in his essay, "On Liberty," deplored totalitarianism in the following words: "A state-controlled system becomes a mere contrivance for moulding people to be exactly like one another . . . in proportion as it is efficient and successful, it establishes a despotism over the mind, leading by natural tendency to one over the body." A centralized educational system in the United States would provide an opportunity for a pressure group, such as a political party, to seize control of the schools, and by inculcating its point of view, maintain itself in power.

The basic issue regarding control of American education is clearly drawn: keep it free of centralized control and let it serve the objectives of our free society or surrender it to federal domination. When the federal government pays the salaries of the public school teachers, it will determine what they shall teach. As Thomas Jefferson wisely stated many years ago, "If we let Washington tell us how to sow and when to reap, the Nation shall soon want for bread."

5. *Local Control Fosters Individual Initiative and Free Enterprise.* Local control of education fosters the traits of individual initiative and free enterprise which have made America the greatest nation on earth. Local initiative rather than federal paternalism and domination is the only means of protecting the economic, governmental, and educational climate which has made this nation the envy of all others. Because it involves direct investment of money and effort, local control of education stimulates community interest in the schools and a desire to make the most effective use of school facilities.

The overwhelming majority of the American people have exercised their individual initiative by indicating that they want to keep educational control at the local level. Not one of the tens of thousands of state and local lay boards of education has favored anything other than local control of education. Local initiative is favored by businessmen, bankers, industrialists, farmers, doctors, legislators, governors, school board members, taxpayer associations, women's clubs, chambers of commerce, and the American Legion and other patriotic societies.

Federal control means a decay and demoralization of individual and community initiative and enterprise, the loss of individual independence of action. The more "good" the federal government undertakes to do for the people, the more damage it is likely to do to them since such federal paternalism destroys individual initiative. Federal control undermines the fiscal capacity and the administrative responsibilities of the local school districts. Federal control of education supported through a federal income tax would impose a severe penalty upon individual effort and economic success. This would further weaken personal incentives and would materially retard economic growth in the United States.

6. *Local Control is Efficient.* As a simple matter of exerting control over the public purse, it is good, sound, and efficient business for those who will be spending money for any given function to have to raise it themselves. The further the spending authority is from the taxing authority, the easier it is to ask for money and, once received, to spend it inefficiently. It is a logical contradiction to assume that the people can be better and more efficiently served by getting their own money back from Washington as grants-in-aid than they would be served by taxing themselves directly for their own good. The money returned to the states and communities by Washington is simply local money that first has been collected through federal taxes, shrunk through the federal government skimming off its costs, and finally sent back as a federal dole or handout. Federal financing of education is something like sending a leaky bucket of water on a round trip to Washington. It is a very inefficient way to get a drink, or to finance education.

ARGUMENTS FOR FEDERAL CONTROL

1. *Federal Control Will Provide Equality of Educational Opportunity.* The traditional American concept of equality requires that all students in all states and school districts should have equal opportunity for an adequate education. It is undemocratic for educational opportunity to be determined by capricious factors such as race, geographical location, or economic status. A child's chances in life should not depend upon whether his parents or his local community were willing and able to give him an adequate education.

In contrast, local control of education has resulted in tremendous inequalities in educational opportunities. Some states have four or five times as much taxable wealth, on the average, as other states. The differences between school districts, often between districts in the same state, are even greater. In our modern age of high mobility, many students who have been deprived of an adequate education by their local community may move and spend their adult lives in other communities and states. Since, on the average, every American moves to a different state two times during his life, the development of skilled and effective citizens must be related to national and not to local circumstances. Some children in wealthy communities are being denied a decent education because their communities refuse to **support** their schools adequately. The child who fails to receive an adequate education because his community refuses to tax itself for an adequate educational program is just as educationally deprived as the child who fails to receive an adequate education because his community lacks resources to be taxed. It is apparent that the national welfare, in education as well as other significant areas, must be placed above the financial condition or educational caprice of states and local communities. No child in the United States should be sentenced to mediocre or inferior educational opportunities because of the community in which he is born.

One of the basic bulwarks of inequality of education controlled at the local level is the antiquated property tax system of school support. Under the archaic property tax structure, the real income of the community is not adequately taxed. The property tax system of school support throws too great a financial burden on only one type of community wealth. In addition, under the present property tax support system, the persons who would be badly hurt by a substantial property tax increase are more effective politically than the diffuse majority whose children would benefit from a more adequate educational program. Under the local property tax system, the financing of the public schools is controlled by groups other than those most needing an adequate educational program.

What is the most effective system of financing education in order to ensure equality of educational opportunity? Only through federal taxation of real income can taxes be collected where the wealth *is* and be made equally available for education where the students *are*. Taxing powers can be most equitable on the federal level because the poorer states can share in the financial resources possessed by the richer states. For many years, authorities on school finance have been pointing out that the poorest states and local school districts usually devote a much higher proportion of their resources to education than do the wealthier ones. A difficulty with the present local control and support system is that, in the school districts which can boast of great taxable wealth, many high income persons and corporations would move away if tax rates were raised substantially. If many local communities raised their school taxes, businesses would move to areas less concerned about education. In contrast, national income taxation cannot be dodged by crossing state lines, creates no interstate competition, and tax revenues increase in proportion to the growth of national income.

What is the most effective system of financing education? A current cliche accepted as an unquestionable truth by the advocates of local control is that it is more efficient for local communities to administer their own money rather than to send it to the federal government. This "local administrative efficiency fallacy" is the belief that it is more efficient to keep the people's money at home rather than to send it on a round trip to Washington where the bureaucrats will squander part of it before sending back what is left. Well documented statistics on the cost of collecting, administering, and distributing tax monies clearly support the fact that the federal government is the most efficient and economical administrator of tax funds. For example, federal taxes are collected at an average cost of 44 cents per $100 collected. This is 99% per cent of efficiency. The average cost of collecting state taxes is over $1.00 per $100, more than twice as expensive as federal taxes. The collection costs of local taxes range from $5.00 to $10.00 per $100 collected. It is cheaper to send a dollar to Washington than it is to send the same dollar to the state capital, the county court house, or the local city hall. The federal tax dollar is the most efficient dollar because it is the one collected at the least expense and in the most equitable manner.

2. *Federal Control of Education Will Strengthen the Nation.* In this time of struggle, the strength of our nation is dependent on concerted action in all the phases of life that are involved in national survival. In contrast, under our present system of local control of education, the nationally vital adequacy of our educational program is now dependent on the most conservative and least forward looking elements in our local communities. Our present system is cumbersome, unwieldy, and non-adaptive. National survival now requires educational policies and programs which are not subject to local veto. The mobility and interdependence of modern life have completely undermined the notion that local communities should have autonomy in education. It is apparent that the arguments against federal control of education could with equal force be used, for example, to object to federal control of foreign relations and the armed forces. Since the local control exponents do not argue against federal control of these vital areas, they have shown their hand. They have shown that they consider the armed forces and foreign relations to be too important to be left to control by local communities and the states, and that they do not consider education to be critical enough to require concerted national effort. Federal control must be set up in order that national interests override the present system of localized self-interests of individual groups. Without direction and mobilization of our educational resources on the federal level, we shall continue to muddle through, providing inferior education for many students, and counte-

nancing needless confusion, waste, duplication, conformity, and stagnation.

Federal control of education strengthens the nation because it fosters educational experimentation and research. One of the most persistent arguments offered by local control advocates is that a federal school system would not permit experimentation and would foster total conformity. In refutation of this assertion, it should be noted that several federal agencies, such as the defense and agriculture departments, support programs of research and experimentation which make present educational research programs look ludicrous by comparison. Generally speaking, only large urban educational systems allocate funds to research, and most of the research is limited to questions of local concern. The present local control structure of education is well designed to obstruct rather than to support research. Most schools do not experiment; they just exist. As an example of how the present local control structure obstructs research, the problems involved in educational research may be related to those in agricultural research. Individual local farmers cannot support experimentation because it would cut their own profits, while the results of their research usually would be immediately available to all farmers who did not invest in it. It would also be financially impractical for a local school system to support research which benefits all schools. As in agriculture, the federal government logically should and can support adequate educational research.

Supporters of the local control system of education have repeatedly claimed that federal control of education is unconstitutional. To them, our decentralized school system was the result of an inspired stroke of genius by the framers of the Constitution. However, education was not described in the Constitution as a federal function because the concept of a universal free system of education had not even occurred to the founding fathers. In recent decades, the majority American opinion has held that the federal government has implied powers and is not limited to the powers enumerated in the Constitution. It is generally accepted that the people as a whole have the right to foster their own general welfare. The failure of the founding fathers to have foresight in the area of education has been and is being corrected through federal programs involving varying degrees of federal control over education. The constitutionality of these controls has not been questioned. For example, the National Defense Education Act and the aid to federally impacted areas (i.e., government support or subsidization around military installations) have not been criticized as being unconstitutional. Ironically, the conservative legislators who have opposed federal control of education, because they have claimed that it is unconstitutional, have failed to warn the public of the "unconstitutional" federal interference with and control over local education resulting from the hundreds of millions of federal tax dollars poured into local school systems in the legislators' home districts as a result of the NDEA and impacted areas legislation. They know that it would be political suicide to oppose such "gifts." It would appear that the "unconstitutional" label is brought forth only to stigmatize programs the conservative legislators believe they can effectively oppose.

3. *Federal Control Fosters Democracy.* Probably the most influential argument advanced by local control partisans is that our democratic way of life is threatened as soon as federal control of education is considered. Local control advocates charge that a centralized system of public education would provide an opportunity for specially privileged totalitarian groups to seize control of the schools and maintain themselves in power by indoctrinating their point of view. In contrast, it appears that the present system of local control is much more conducive to totalitarianism than a federal school system. Such a contention appears on the face of it to be patently absurd. The diversity and variety fostered by the present local lay board power structure of American education is such that no single pressure group is able to indoctrinate its dogmas in all the school systems. A totalitarian system of education develops a massive uniformity of outlook. Where, then, is the massive uniformity under our present system? It should first be noted that a totalitarian educational system involves protection for specially privileged points of view that are not required to stand the test of reflective analysis. The previous discussions of reflective academic freedom brought out the point that our American public schools seem to be basically totalitarian. The totalitarianism is not often recognized because not all school systems protect the same dogmas. Since the purposes of education presently are determined locally, the dominant pressure groups in the communities establish educational programs which foster their own particular political, economic, social, or religious points of view. The crucial factor which causes the local lay board system of control to foster indoctrinative or totalitarian education is that, at the local level, it is relatively easy for dominant pressure groups to enforce protection of their beliefs in the public schools. For example, racial segregation has been protected in the South, communities dominated by fundamentalist sects restrict the teaching of evolution, school boards dominated by conservative businessmen exclude reflective comparative analyses of economic systems, super-patriotic groups achieve the dismissal of teachers who encourage their pupils to examine American life critically, and some communities even have prohibited the study

of the United Nations or of UNESCO. Under local control, many teachers are quietly and stultifyingly intimidated. Those who remain in teaching tend to be retiring, timid, and often frightened for their jobs. They avoid controversial social questions and teach only what is in accord with the beliefs of the local lay school boards. In many school systems, to enter teaching means to become a quiet, proper, and orthodox agent of the community status quo. The democratic spirit of invigorating reflective inquiry is smothered by an overlay of conformity and acceptance. Schools become conveyor belts for the transmission of safe and antiseptic beliefs and facts. As a result, most students in the public schools have little opportunity to develop and exercise the intellectual skill of reflective criticism which is basic to competent participation in a democratic society. In brief, local control has resulted in the same type of intellectual protectionism that is the basic characteristic of education in totalitarian countries.

Federal control of education can foster effective democratic or reflective education and can end the totalitarianism fostered by the present local control system because, at the federal level, no pressure group has nearly enough power to interfere with educational programs that such groups can muster on a local level. Massive interference in a federal school program by a pressure group would be checked by others, and these groups could not dominate education the way they now dominate the programs of many local school systems. Rather than being circumscribed by local lay boards, teachers would be free to teach in a reflective manner since they would not be subject to local censorship. Under federal control of education, the operation of the public schools would be removed as far as possible from the influence of bigoted and selfish interests.

It should be noted that teachers in England, which has a national system of education, are opposed to local control of education precisely because it would undermine their professional autonomy. France and the Scandinavian countries also have national systems. There is far more reflective freedom to teach and to learn in all of these national school systems than there is in the many totalitarian local control educational systems in the United States.

ARGUMENTS FOR PROFESSIONAL CONTROL

Practically all of the writers dealing with the question of who should control American education have assumed the dualistic position that there are only two alternatives—either local control or federal control.

If incompetent or anti-professional control of an occupation is defined as control by persons or groups not in the occupation, both local and federal control are based on the various educational occupations being controlled by incompetents. Therefore, the traditional conflict between incompetent local control, by lay school boards and their administrators, and incompetent federal control, by federal government bureaucrats, is merely a conflict between types of incompetency.

1. *Professional Control of Education is Competent Control.* If teachers repudiated the NEA and AFT by forming strong national occupational organizations, each educational occupation would control training for, entrance into, and expulsion from the occupation as well as the basic teaching conditions within each occupation. Just as those who are competent in surgery, the surgeons, control surgery, those competent in high school social studies teaching, the high-school social studies teachers, should control their own programs. In brief, the conditions in each educational occupation should be under the control of the expert practitioners in each occupation, instead of under incompetent local or federal control.

2. *Professional Control of Education Will Make Education a Nationally Important Area.* As strong educational occupational organizations develop nationally, the occupations will, either singly or jointly, probably negotiate with the federal government and the representatives of local and state school boards. In such a counter-vailing power system, the professional occupational associations would serve as bulwarks against excessive concentrations of power, either in local boards or in the hands of federal bureaucrats. Because the various professional associations will be making decisions which will vitally affect every state and community, educational leaders will play important roles in the development of effective national educational programs. Public education will come close to the people as a whole in a much more adequate way than it does now under the present anti-professional and incompetent local lay control system.

The National Education Association's position in the control of education debate should be noted. The NEA has repeatedly gone on record that its policy is to strengthen and maintain the present system of state and local lay board control of public education.[4] The NEA continually makes the self-assertive claim that it is THE professional organization in education and that it fosters the professional goals of teachers. In contrast, it is fairly apparent to the advocates of na-

---

[4] For one among many statements of the NEA policy see, *The Case for Federal Support of Education—1961* (Washington, D.C.: National Education Association, 1961).

tional professional control, that the local and state lay board educational power structure, which the NEA traditionally has supported, effectively undermines the professional autonomy of the various teaching occupations. In such a contradictory situation, the most charitable thing that can be said about the NEA is that it appears to be very confused. To the NEA's credit is the fact that it is now supporting the policy of collective bargaining of teachers with local lay boards, which process it euphemistically labels as "professional negotiations." This is at least an attempt to move away from a basically anti-professional power structure in which lay boards control basic decisions affecting local public schools. It also should be noted that the American Federation of Teachers is almost as open as the NEA to the charge of anti-professionalism, since the AFT also has accepted the traditional anti-professional educational power structure of lay board control.

CONCLUSION

Arguments for local control of education have indicated that it is the traditional "American Way," is constitutional, is democratic, fosters freedom of thought, fosters individual initiative and free enterprise, and is efficient. Arguments for federal control have indicated that it will provide equality of educational opportunity, strengthen the nation, and foster democracy. The very few supporters of professional control argue that it involves control by those competent to make educational decisions and that it will make education a nationally important area. Which is best, local, federal, or professional control of the public schools?

SELECTED REFERENCES

Brembeck, Cole, *Social Foundations of Education*. New York: John Wiley and Sons, 1966, Chaps. 17 and 18. These chapters appear to be oriented to descriptions of the status quo.

Campbell, Roald, Luvern Cunningham, Roderick McPhee, and Raphael Nystrand, *The Organization and Control of American Schools*, 2nd. ed.

Columbus, Ohio: Charles E. Merrill Publishing Co., 1970. An excellent introduction to the problems of educational control.

Decisions For A Better America (By The Republican Committee on Program and Progress). Garden City, New York: Doubleday and Company, 1960, pp. 30–37. A defense of the local control position.

Educational Issues in a Changing Society, August Kerber and Wilfred Smith, eds. Detroit: Wayne State University Press, 1964, Chaps. 13 and 14. Articles analyzing the federal role in education are presented.

Goldwater, Barry, *The Conscience of a Conservative.* New York: Hillman Books, 1960, Chap. 9. A defense of the local control position.

Lieberman, Myron, *The Future of Public Education.* Chicago: University of Chicago Press, 1960, Chap. 3. Local control of education is criticized and points in favor of centralized control are presented.

New Horizons For The Teaching Profession (A report of the task force on New Horizons in Teacher Education and Professional Standards), Margaret Lindsey, ed. Washington, D.C.: National Education Association, 1961. Local and state lay control of education is supported.

Nixon, Richard M., *The Challenges We Face.* New York: Popular Library, 1961, Part 5, Section 4. A defense of the local control position.

Orlich, Donald and S. Samuel Shermis, *The Pursuit of Excellence: Introductory Readings in Education.* New York: American Book Company, 1965, Part 3. Articles on the educational control problem.

Schwartz, Lita Linzer, *American Education—A Problem-Centered Approach.* Boston, Mass.: Holbrook Press, 1969, Chap. 4. The Wallace and Schneider article, "Do School Boards Take Education Seriously," is particularly germane to the control problem.

The Case Against Federal Aid to Education. New York: Research Department, National Association of Manufacturers, 1961. A number of articles supporting local control are presented.

The Case for Federal Support of Education—1961. Washington, D.C.: National Education Association, 1961. Statistics supporting the NEA position are presented.

The Human Encounter—Readings in Education, Sheldon Stoff and Herbert Schwartzberg, eds. New York: Harper & Row, Publishers, 1969. A number of relevant articles are presented.

THOUGHT AIDS

1. Indicate possible arguments for and against control of education being in the hands of national professional teacher associations.
2. Indicate possible strengths and weaknesses of the position exemplified by the following statement: "But, it is important that federal funds be

made available in a way that will strengthen state and local control of schools. State and local school boards know the deficiencies of their schools. What these boards need are the financial resources to develop quality school programs." (*A Message to Parents . . . Will Your Child Get a Quality Education?* National Education Association, 1960.)

3. Could federal control of education result in a highly anti-professional educational power structure? Why or why not?

4. Do you agree with the contention in the latter part of this chapter that the NEA is advocating an anti-professional policy by supporting local and state lay board control of education? Why or why not?

5. Collect newspaper articles dealing with the control of education question. The editorial pages of conservative newspapers are fruitful sources of local control arguments.

6. Present an analysis of Barry Goldwater's viewpoint on education in his book, *The Conscience of a Conservative,* pp. 78–87.

7. How might the various teaching occupations achieve professional status without elimination of the present school laws which give educational decision-making power to nonprofessional local and state boards of education? Give examples.

8. Invite a qualified representative of the NEA to explain the NEA position in regard to control of education.

9. Indicate possible strengths and weaknesses of the position exemplified by the following statement: "In general, state departments of education are composed of a state board of education comprised of laymen, a professional chief state school officer, and a professional staff. The boundaries of power and responsibility vested in these departments are established by state legislatures. Thus, the wishes of the people with regard to education may always be made known through representative government. That this continue to be true is fundamental." (*New Horizons For The Teaching Profession,* A report of the task force on New Horizons in Teacher Education and Professional Standards—1961, Margaret Lindsey, Ed. Washington, D.C.: National Commission on Teacher Education and Professional Standards, National Education Association, 1961, p. 211.)

10. Evaluate critically Myron Lieberman's analysis of the control of education issue in his book *The Future of Public Education,* pp. 34–55.

11. Obtain materials on the control of education question and the federal aid question from the NEA and from the National Association of Manufacturers. Give a report on the similarities and differences between the viewpoints of these two organizations.

12. Prepare a report on the American Federation of Teachers viewpoint on the control of education.

21

Should Public Schools Be Integrated?

On May 17, 1954, the Supreme Court discarded the 58-year old doctrine of "separate but equal" schools for Negroes and ruled that segregation of children in public schools solely on the basis of race is unconstitutional. Although this ruling may be the law of the land, it is far from the practice of the land, even in many cities outside the South. Many "integrated" districts have satisfied the letter of the law through "token" integration, leaving most Negro students in basically segregated schools. Housing restrictions maintain Negro ghettos in many cities, forcing Negro students to attend predominantly Negro schools. Now, more than a decade and a half after the Supreme Court's ruling, a vast majority of Negro students still are in segregated schools.

What are the reasons why many Americans, both southerners and northerners, still resist integration in the schools? Based on an analysis of segregationist writings, the following arguments appear to be the main points emphasized in the case against integration.

THE CASE AGAINST INTEGRATION

1. *The Supreme Court's integration ruling is unconstitutional.* The Constitution reserves decisions on school matters to the states

or to the people. The Tenth Amendment in the Bill of Rights states: "The powers not delegated to the United States by the Constitution, nor prohibited by it to the States, are reserved to the States respectively, or to the people." The Supreme Court usurped the constitutional right of the states to operate their public schools in accordance with local wishes and without outside interference.

2. *Forced integration is undemocratic.* The forced mixing of races in public schools destroys the democratic right of people to make their own decisions. The Court's edict is contrary to the general sentiment of communities with large concentrations of Negroes. The integrationists are forcing white parents to accept black students when they have democratically decided that they do not want their children in schools with blacks. The Supreme Court has invaded the democratic rights of local option and community determination through the raw exercise of federal bureaucratic power.

3. *Forced integration violates the right to freedom of choice and association.* A fundamental American right is the freedom to choose one's friends and associates. The 1896 Supreme Court formula for race relations preserved this right: "Natural affinities, a mutual appreciation of each other's merits, and a voluntary consent of individuals." Association must be voluntary and based on earned respect, and the desire for association must be mutual. The Negro is demanding social equality with a group that does not desire his company. Also, parents should have the right to supervise the associations of their children. The Supreme Court has denied to the family the freedom of choice as to where and with whom its children should attend school.

4. *Forced integration is part of the Communist conspiracy.* It is a well-documented fact that one of the major goals of the Communist Party is racial amalgamation. To achieve this aim, Communists and their sympathizers have infiltrated the National Association for the Advancement of Colored People and other radical integrationist groups. Both Communists and integrationists are opposed to local government and the states-rights provisions of the Constitution. The socialistic, equalitarian integrationists who loudly proclaim their opposition to Communism are in reality lending much aid and comfort to the enemies of our form of government, since Socialism is a halfway step to Communism. The "authorities" cited by the Supreme Court in support of the integration ruling have long records of association with Communist causes. For example, one of the books cited was Gunnar Myrdal's *An American Dilemma.* Certain segregationists called him a foreign socialist who associated with leading Communist

sympathizers while he was in this country. Myrdal stated that the Constitution is "impractical and unsuited to modern conditions" and that its adoption was "nearly a plot against the common people." As Senator James O. Eastland of Mississippi noted in a Senate speech on May 26, 1955, the integration ruling was based on the writings and teachings of extreme left-wing collectivists who are part and parcel of the Communist conspiracy to destroy our country.

5. *Forced integration is unchristian.* Christ's commandment to love your neighbor is not a requirement to consider your neighbor your equal, or yourself his equal. In contrast, the integrationists tend to equate Christian love with a form of equality which obliterates all differences and distinctions between the races. As is noted in Acts 17:26, safeguarding the boundaries between the races certainly is not contrary to the will of God: "And he made every nation of men to live on the face of the earth, having determined allotted periods and the boundaries of their habitation." God never intended that the races should be mixed, since if He had intended to have only one race, He would have made such. Christian love requires that racial integrity be preserved and that schools be geared to the unique needs of each race.

6. *States are competent to deal justly with their own citizens.* Through generations of experiences, certain states developed a way of life which took the Negro's limitations into consideration with a minimum of friction and a maximum of kindness. The responsibility for gradually resolving the race-mixing problem, over many future decades, should remain with the people most concerned with the problem. However, meddling outsiders are now dictating to those who have experience and vital concern.

7. *Integration harms the physical and moral status of our country.* As a race, Negroes have very low standards of health, morality, and social conduct. Although Negroes constitute only about one tenth of the population of the United States, they commit about half of the total number of murders and manslaughters. They commit the bulk of all crimes of violence. They have a very disproportionate share of sexual assaults, drunkenness, dope addiction, and communicable diseases. Illegitimacy among Negroes runs as high as one-third of all Negro births. The incidence of venereal disease among Negroes is many more times as high as among whites. Negroes tend to be shiftless. Chronic family disruptions are the rule. They are a heavy welfare burden because they comprise the majority of those on relief. Is it any wonder that, when white men observe all this, they refuse to accept commingling of their children with black children who

have been raised in such amoral and unhealthy environments? Though it has been argued that white men share a major portion of the blame for the Negroes living in such conditions, the fact remains that these conditions exist, and no reasonable white man wants to subject his children to such conditions.

8. *Integration undermines the standards of white schools.* To expose young white children, in their most formative years, to negative Negro influence has an immediate adverse effect. The white children quickly pick up poor habits and attitudes. Is it any wonder that white parents are reluctant to undermine attempts to foster adequate personal standards among their own children by exposing them to youngsters whose standards are demonstrably lower in every respect?

9. *Integration violates the facts of anthropology.* In contrast to the equalitarian, pseudo-scientific hoax that the races are equal, authoritative anthropologists have found that the Negro race is hereditarily inferior to the white. Structural differences, such as the average Negro having a smaller brain, have counterparts in the Negro's relatively poor record for enterprise and initiative in the areas of self-control, judgment, character, and intelligence, all of which are highly important to our Western civilization. On the character-intelligence index, the index of capacity for civilization, it is an anthropological fact that the Negro has limited racial adaptability to Western civilization. Most integrationists believe that the present cultural differences between Negro and white races are caused by enforced cultural disadvantages; not by any natural, innate limitations. However, the cultural level the Negro achieves when left on his own resources can be clearly seen and measured today in his native habitat in the Congo. All comparative studies of the intelligence of the Negro and white races have arrived at the same conclusion: The average intelligence level of the Negro is markedly lower than that of the white race. About six times as many whites as Negroes were found to fall in the gifted category and less than twenty per cent of the Negroes examined exceeded the white average. The regularity and consistency of markedly lower test scores by Negroes points to a gap of inherent abilities between the races.

10. *Integration will irreparably damage our civilization.* School integration is social integration. Social integration always and everywhere has led and does lead to interbreeding, which is the destruction of the pure strain of the white race. Such amalgamation with Negroes invariably produces deterioration in any white civilization that tries it. Egypt, the highest of ancient civilizations, deteriorated through the

mongrelization of whites with Negroes. In more modern times, when the Portuguese colonized Brazil they interbred with the Indians and with the Negro slaves imported from Africa. In spite of its age, size, and enormous natural resources, Brazil is still a backward country. Segregationists are battling to preserve our civilization for all white Americans. These fighters for racial integrity often are pictured by the equalitarians as fighting against "progress." Such progress would make America over in the image of a mongrelized race. Such progress would destroy the heritage of a thousand years of Western civilization. Some integrationists ask, "Since some Negroes contribute more to our Western civilization than some whites, should not people be sorted by worth rather than by race?" In his book *Race and Reason*, Carleton Putnam presents an excellent answer to this question:

> In all the ordinary judgments of life, in dealings between individuals we should. But in those matters which involve social association, and hence the possibility of intermarrying, the element of race inevitably enters because each individual carries in his genes the heritage of his race and this will be passed on in the breeding process. As one Southerner put the point: "However weak the individual white man, his ancestors produced the greatness of Europe; however strong the individual black, his ancestors never lifted themselves from the darkness of Africa." [1]

11. *Integration will destroy both the white and Negro races.* Interbreeding and amalgamation of the races, which inevitably follows the social intercourse created by integrated schools, is nothing short of racial suicide. There is no case in all history in which whites and Negroes have lived together in large numbers, without segregation, and have failed to interbreed. Since mongrelization is the invariable and inevitable end product of integrated schooling, the integrationist is unmasked. It can clearly be seen that education is secondary to him; his real mission is to destroy the white race through amalgamation of the races.

THE CASE FOR INTEGRATION

1. *The Supreme Court's ruling is constitutional.* The Fourteenth Amendment to the Constitution prohibits any state from depriving any person of "life, liberty or property without due process of law," and

---

[1] Carleton Putnam, *Race and Reason—A Yankee View* (Washington, D.C.: Public Affairs Press, 1961), p. 42.

from denying any person "the equal protection of the law." When the Supreme Court ruled that segregation in public schools violated the Fourteenth Amendment, it was not legislating; it was performing an interpretative function assigned to it by the Constitution. Those who support integration contend that this ruling is constitutional. The Court was acting wholly within its constitutional powers when it ruled that a state may not deny to any person, on account of race, the constitutional right to attend any public school that the state maintains. The Supreme Court has deprived no state of a single right it possesses under the Constitution, since no state has the constitutional right to deprive a citizen of his rights to full American citizenship. In fact, the Constitution was expressly written as a rejection of the states-rights or state-sovereignty belief. It was designed to form a nation, not a confederation of states.

2. *Integration is democratic.* The basic trait of democratic societies is that they provide equality of opportunity for all members of society to participate equally in determining what the society will do. Such equality of opportunity to participate in governing can be effectively implemented only when the people are knowledgeable. Segregated schools have kept Negroes as second-class citizens, deprived of equal opportunities. Also, integration is democratic because it is what the overwhelming majority of the American people desire. Ignorance, conceit, and unreasoned prejudice lead many Southerners to believe that only they are competent to deal with the Negro problem, even though many Northern cities have a higher percentage of Negroes than do the eleven Confederate states.

3. *Integration enhances the right to freedom of choice and association.* Instead of setting up the arbitrary restrictions on association which segregationists desire to preserve, integrated schools would provide additional opportunities to choose associates. A person may have much more freedom in choosing his friends, since he is not restricted to one racial group alone. Artificial barriers to friendship, understanding, and respect are removed.

4. *Integration thwarts totalitarianism, both communistic and fascistic.* Communists and racist fascists are alike in that they would deny first-class citizenship to certain groups. In contrast, integrationists would foster the ability of all persons in society to participate equally in the benefits of society. The hoax that integrationists are communists needs to be exposed. J. Edgar Hoover gives the NAACP a clean bill of health in his book on communism, *Masters of Deceit.* Racists continually equate integrationists and communists, since both groups support integrated public schools. The logical fallacy in equating

basically conflicting groups who share one common factor has been exposed many times.

5. *Integration is Christian.* Christ's mission to mankind is summarized in the book of John, "I am come that man might have life and have it more abundantly." Since segregated schools have hindered the education of the Negro and since an adequate education is one of the main things leading to the achievement of abundant living, it is apparent that school integration is in harmony with Christ's central mission. Jesus taught that men should love one another. He fought against prejudice. He taught that each person deserves a fair chance in life. What do you think Christ would have said if a group of segregationists had come to Him and told Him that they had decided, for their own convenience, that the lives of certain children would be restricted, their educational opportunities reduced, and their futures stunted?

<u>6.</u> *School integration is supported by the facts of cultural anthropology.* The segregationists' notion that Negroes, as a race, are congenitally mentally inferior to white people can best be refuted by quoting a resolution passed by unanimous vote at the November 17, 1961, annual meeting of the Council of Fellows of the American Anthropological Association:

> The American Anthropological Association repudiates the statement now appearing in the United States that Negroes are biologically and in innate mental ability inferior to whites, and reaffirms the fact that there is no scientifically established evidence to justify the exclusion of any race from the rights guaranteed by the Constitution of the United States. The basic principles of equality of opportunity and equality before the law are compatible with all that is known about human biology. All races possess the abilities needed to participate fully in the democratic way of life and in modern technological civilization.[2]

The segregationist argument that Negroes are mentally inferior is, unbeknown to him, the most eloquent argument for integrated schools, since he is admitting that, as long as Negroes are shunted into second-rate schools and into restricted cultural opportunities, they will remain scholastically inferior. The grotesque hypocrisy of the segregationists speaking with horror about mongrelization and with fervor about racial purity also should be exposed. It was the white man's lack of sexual morality that created widespread "mongrelization" in the South. This was his exclusive contribution to the "Southern Way of Life."

---

[2] *Washington Post,* December 2, 1962, Editorial Section.

One Southerner was recently quoted as saying, "We figure we're doing you people a favor to get some white blood in your kids."

In answering the charge that integration will lead inevitably to intermarriage, integrationists note that in states that do not have laws against intermarriage, the incidence of intermarriage is infinitesimally small. Also, since intermarriage is a private matter between two individuals, integrationists are neither for or against it.

7. *Integration strengthens our international position.* Since we have repeatedly told the rest of the world that under our laws citizens have equal rights and that we have no second-class citizens, segregated schools are intolerable. The racial situation is not only a blot on our whole country, but it causes us to be viewed, especially by the non-committed bloc of African and Asian countries, as being hypocrites who do not practice what we preach about equality and human freedom.

CONCLUSION

Legal segregation is gone, but traditional attitudes and segregated housing keep many Negro children in basically segregated schools. Open-enrollment plans in which school authorities move Negro children to distant white schools are being tried. This alternative is questioned not only on the basis of high transportation costs but also because it would undermine the long cherished concept of the "neighborhood school." Now, more than a decade and a half after the Supreme Court ruling, most Negro students still are in basically segregated schools. If, in the words of the Court at the time of the ruling, segregation created "a feeling of inferiority as to their status in the community that may affect their hearts and minds in a way unlikely ever to be undone," it still does.

SELECTED REFERENCES

Benedict, Ruth and Gene Weltfish, *The Races of Mankind.* New York: Public Affairs Committee, Public Affairs Pamphlet No. 85, 1951. A presentation of the generally accepted anthropological concepts of race.

The Citizen. Jackson, Mississippi: The Citizens' Councils of America. The monthly official journal of the Citizens' Councils. An expression of southern resentment toward integration.

The Countdown on Segregated Education, William W. Brickman and Stanley Lehrer, eds. New York: Society for the Advancement of Education, 1960. The past, present, and possible future of segregated education in the United States and other countries are analyzed.

Essays on Segregation, T. Robert Ingram, ed. Houston, Texas: St. Thomas Press, 1960. Segregationist clergymen explain why, to them, segregation is Christian.

Griffin, John Howard, *Black Like Me.* New York: Signet Books, New American Library, 1960. A white man darkens his skin and travels through the South. A gripping psychological journal.

Hunt, Maurice and Lawrence Metcalf, *Teaching High School Social Studies.* New York: Harper & Row, Publishers, 1968, Chap. 18. Contradictions and confusions in American thought and practice in the area of race relations are examined.

Kluckhohn, Clyde, *Mirror for Man.* Greenwich, Conn.: Fawcett Publications, 1961, Chap. 5. The concept of distinct races, which is the foundation of the segregationist's position, is questioned.

Michael, W. E., *The Age of Error.* New York: Vantage Press, 1957. A lawyer supports the segregation position.

Myrdal, Gunnar, *An American Dilemma.* New York: Harper & Brothers, 1944. A classic study of the Negro problem.

Putnam, Carleton, *Race and Reality—A Search for Solutions.* Washington, D.C.: Public Affairs Press, 1967. A very effective defense of the segregation position.

———, *Race and Reason—A Yankee View.* Washington, D.C.: Public Affairs Press, 1961. An excellent presentation of the segregation viewpoint.

Schwartz, Lita Linzer, *American Education—A Problem-Centered Appoach.* Boston, Mass.: Holbrook Press, 1969, Chap. 8. Contemporary readings and reports on the desegregation issue are presented in historical context.

Stewart, Maxwell S., *The Negro in America.* New York: Public Affairs Committee, Inc., Public Affairs Pamphlet No. 95, 1944. A summary of Gunnar Myrdal's *An American Dilemma.*

The Human Encounter—Readings in Education, Sheldon Stoff and Herbert Schwartzberg eds. New York: Harper & Row, Publishers, 1969. A number of current articles are presented, including selections from James Baldwin's *The Fire Next Time.*

Waring, Thomas, "The Southern Case Against Desegregation," *Harper's Magazine* 212, no. 1268 (January, 1956): 39–45. An excellent summary of segregation arguments.

Weyl, Nathaniel, *The Negro in American Civilization.* Washington, D.C.:

Public Affairs Press, 1960. Evidence is offered in support of the segregation position.

Workman, William D., Jr. *The Case For the South.* New York: The Devin-Adair Company, 1960. A thought provoking defense of segregation.

THOUGHT AIDS

1. Criticize the presentation of the cases for and against integrated schools.
2. Report on the arguments for segregation presented in the monthly issues of *The Citizen.*
3. Look in social problems books for chapters dealing with "the Negro problem."
4. Was the Supreme Court's integration ruling constitutional? Why or why not?
5. Listen to the record, "Race and Reason Day in Mississippi." This analysis of the race problem by Carleton Putnam may be obtained from the Citizen's Council Forum, Jackson, Mississippi.
6. Do you believe that the public schools should be integrated? Why or why not?
7. Read some of the references on both sides of the integration controversy.
8. Debate the issue: "Should public schools be integrated?"
9. Does Christian love require integrated schools? Why or why not?
10. Do you believe that the segregation-integration controversy is an important educational problem? Why or why not?
11. Analyze the following statement: "The issue here is that school integration is social integration, that social integration, always, everywhere, has and does lead to intermarriage in the long run and that intermarriage, under our population ratios in the South, will destroy our society." (Carlton Putnam. *The Road To Reversal.* National Putnam Letters Committee, p. 14.)
12. Since each person is a unique entity, do "Blacks" really exist or is "Black" just a word—an arbitrary verbal category—in our minds?
13. Every year thousands of persons labeled as "Blacks" move elsewhere and are no longer categorized as being "Black." They have "passed over." If you believe that Blacks really exist, in what ways are those persons who have passed over still really Blacks?

22

Should Religion Be Taught in the Schools?

When the students' church preference cards were sorted out after fall registration at a college, it was noted that in the blank after "Church Preference:" one student had written "Gothic." Differences in meaning are quite important when dealing with the question of whether or not religion should be taught in the public schools. Answers to this question are dependent on which of a vast variety of meanings are given to the two key words: "religion" and "teaching."

Religion and education are intertwined in American historical traditions. The Puritans established schools as safeguards against the devil, as evidenced by their "Ye Olde Deluder Satan Law" of 1647. The first American colleges, such as Harvard and Yale, were established to train ministers. Due to the establishment of various conflicting religions in the colonies, the founding fathers achieved national unity by providing in the First Amendment of the Constitution that "Congress shall make no law respecting an establishment of religion, or prohibiting the free exercise thereof." The development of a diverse and pluralistic American society led to the traditional policy of using public funds to support only secularized or nonsectarian schools, which all children would be allowed to attend. However, over the years, various religious practices, such as Bible reading, prayers, religious choral works, and Christmas programs have become traditional.

Recently, the Supreme Court ruled against certain types of prescribed prayers in public schools. Certain denominations, particularly the Roman Catholic Church, are now campaigning for public school funds to be "fairly" distributed so that public tax funds would go to the schools, either public or parochial, where parents, exercising their freedom of choice, choose to send their children. Would such use of public tax funds violate the First Amendment? Should prayers and Bible reading be banned from the public schools? A humorous reaction to the Supreme Court's ruling against certain prescribed prayers in public schools was this sign near a school basement radiation shelter: "In case of nuclear war, prayers may be said in this school." Also, must public schools be hostile toward denominational beliefs? Even if devotional services are banned from the public schools, does this necessarily mean that objective cultural studies of religious beliefs and practices are also banned? Could the public schools really produce cultured and knowledgeable citizens if the religious aspects of history, social studies, literature, art, and music were banned from the schools? And, if all study of religion were banned, should the public schools continue to attempt to inculcate and reinforce generally accepted moral and character values?

PUBLIC FUNDS FOR PAROCHIAL SCHOOLS?

The case for providing public funds for parochial schools has many supporters, particularly in the Roman Catholic Church. From this point of view, government enters the area of education at local, state, and federal levels, in order to "promote the general welfare." The government has the mandate or obligation delegated to it by the society to provide equal educational opportunities for all students, regardless of race, religion, geographical location, or any other arbitrary circumstance. Not only is the government obligated to promote the general welfare in the educational area by providing equal educational opportunities, it is constitutionally prohibited from establishing one religious outlook in a preferential position. As the First Amendment states, "Congress shall make no law respecting an establishment of religion, or prohibiting the free exercise thereof." Constitutionally, the government is not allowed to discriminate against certain religions and assist others. There is no specific mention in the Constitution of a necessity to keep a "wall of separation" between state-supported schools and religion. The Constitution only requires that public funds not be used to establish or to give preference to one religion, since such discriminatory use of public funds would hinder the free practice of other religions.

Do the above conditions exist in our present tax-supported schools, or do certain religious viewpoints receive preferential treatment? The government builds and maintains schools and provides teachers, text-books, transportation, free lunches, and free health services for the children of both atheistic parents who do not believe in God and for the children of dogmatic liberal secularists who ignore or are in-different toward God. What governmental assistance is provided for children of parents who insist on including, rather than excluding, God? What education is provided for families who in good conscience wish to fulfill their obligations under state compulsory attendance laws by sending their children to religiously-oriented schools rather than secularly-oriented schools? What is provided for families who value God enough not to ignore or forget him? These families are harshly discriminated against. Little or no help is provided for these "second-class" families. They are victims of "double taxation," since they are required to pay taxes to support the established secular schools, which exclude God, and then on their own they must build and maintain educational systems in which God is respected and valued. In direct violation of the First Amendment of the Constitution and in direct violation of the "equal protection of the laws" guaranteed under the Fourteenth Amendment, secularism is established in a favored position in tax-supported schools. Secularism is enshrined in educational temples erected and sustained by the tax money of all Americans.

Since the basic purpose for using public-tax funds in the edu-cational area is to aid and assist parents in providing the kind of education they wish for their children, the present harshly discrim-inatory system tramples on the rights of parents to determine freely the education of their children. If parents insist on choosing a re-ligious atmosphere for the education of their children, they are pun-ished for this "wrong" choice by not receiving public funds. Genuine freedom of choice and equality of educational opportunity can be achieved only when tax funds for education are equally provided for all students, regardless of whether their parents choose to have them educated in secular schools or in parochial schools. Only on the basis of the child-benefit principle, under which public educational funds go equally to each student, can all parents freely exercise their demo-cratic and constitutional rights of educational choice.

The case against providing public funds for parochial schools also has been persuasively argued. From this viewpoint, during the century of 1830–1930, a satisfactory concept of American public education evolved. The public's conviction that an effective democratic government could only be based on universal enlightenment resulted in the establishment of free, public schools, supported by taxing all the people. These common public schools were maintained under state authority and administered by locally-elected, public school boards. A "wall of separation between church and state" was erected. No men could be compelled by the state to pay taxes to support programs of denominational indoctrination that outraged their convictions. In brief, parochial schools were not to receive public funds. Parental freedom of choice was preserved, however, since although parents were obligated by the state to see that their children were educated, the parents could choose to educate their children themselves, to send them to private schools, or to send them to the public schools. Recently, this traditional pattern of public funding of public education has come under attack by those desiring to have denominational indoctrination-programs subsidized by public funds.

The public schools traditionally have been credited with being one of the most potent unifying factors in our society. What would happen if denominational schools were supported by public funds? The Netherlands and Belgium are fitting examples. The public schools in these countries, amid tensions, rivalry, and strife, have been reduced to the level of minority programs. Exclusivism and separateness, with resultant divisiveness, suspicion, and lack of communication are everyday problems there. In contrast to our "public" schools, which are dedicated to educating and serving the public, their non-denominational schools are labeled as "state" or "government" schools. Also, as England and other countries have found, providing public support for religious denominations reduces the denominations' vitality and initiative. Do we want these things here in America?

Certain denominations argue forcefully that parental freedom of choice is a real freedom only if the parents' choices are subsidized from public funds. How valid is this principle that "freedom of choice" must be supported by the public treasury? If farmer Smith exercises his "freedom of choice" by driving diagonally across his farm, instead of on the county roads beside his farm which are provided through tax funds, is the county therefore obligated to build and maintain a diagonal road for farmer Smith? If I choose to write a book, is it "fair" to expect tax funds to be spent for publishing and distributing it? If I choose to take a trip from New York to California, may I validly expect the public to pay my airplane fare? If segregationists exercise their "freedom of choice" by choosing to set up their own all-white schools, may they validly expect to receive their "fair share" of school taxes? And may the militant black-power advocates expect similar "fair" treatment?

Once the barriers against any special-interest groups being supported from public funds are removed, it logically may be concluded that all special-interest groups should be supported by public funding as they make their "free choices." This would open a Pandora's Box of public financial support for special-interest groups in racial, political, economic, and social-class areas as well as in the denominational area. It would be tragic to fragmentize public education and divide it among various minority groups since, instead of developing the thoughtful and tolerant personality-qualities needed in a democracy, public school funds would be used to inculcate specially privileged, exclusivistic, sectarian dogmas. It should be fairly apparent that the whole case for public support of parochial schools rests on the false argument that the exercising of freedom of choice should involve an option on the public treasury.

The parochial argument for parental freedom of choice also is specious, since the intent of the ecclesiastical hierarchy, which is pushing for governmental aid to parochial schools, is to eliminate parental choice. The clergy are trying to get the parents to do as they are told by the hierarchy, and parental freedom of choice is merely a cover for clerical domination.

Released-time and shared-time programs have been offered as compromise alternatives to direct public aid to parochial schools. Under released-time programs, students are released to attend denominational classes, either on the school premises or at local churches. Under shared-time programs, students attend public schools for certain courses and go to parochial schools for others, but particularly for their religion classes. About a dozen states legally permit such programs and a similar number prohibit them. Proponents of shared-time programs claim that the "wall of separation" between church and state would not be breached, since there would be no religious observances in public schools. Also, students could have better facilities and staffs and public schools probably would gain more effective support from parochial school parents. Critics of such plans contend that support of shared-time programs would result in the proliferation of parochial schools and would be a giant step toward abandonment of public schools. Also, to certain critics such plans are not "compromises" since, where shared time is provided, there is no clear indication that parochial demands for public funds have ceased.

TEACHING RELIGION

The two key words in this problem-area seem to be "teaching" and "religion." In this problem-area, the word, "teaching," has been given a number of meanings ranging from conducting worship or devotional services, through indoctrinating certain sectarian beliefs, to objective analyses of the cultural significance of various religious institutions, beliefs, and practices. The teaching of religion can occur on at least three general levels: (1) Fact, (2) Skill, and (3) Behavior. On the factual level, religious information, such as the Ten Commandments, would be taught and students would be expected to demonstrate the ability to recall such information. On the skill level, students would be expected to demonstrate skills in dealing with or applying information, such as to be able to apply knowledge of the Ten Commandments to current social and personal problems. On the behavior level, students would be taught in such a way that they would demonstrate behavioral changes in attitudes, preferences, and values. Students would be disposed to think, feel, and act differently. For example, do students go out and consistently act in ways which are harmonious with the Ten Commandments? [1]

Perhaps "religion" has even more different meanings than does teaching. These range from meaning a church or denomination, through major world religions, and through belief in a supernatural divinity, to religion being what is of central value to a person, what he devotes himself to, even if it is eating, bowling, drinking, or playing bridge.

In its ruling against prescribed devotional services, the Supreme Court indicated that there is no legal barrier to "study of the Bible or of religion, when presented objectively as part of a secular program of education." This is in line with the belief that an educated person in our society should be knowledgeable about the history, literature, beliefs, and cultural impact of the major world religions and of the various Christian denominations. From this point of view, worship is the responsibility of both home and church, and religion belongs in

---

[1] For further discussion of these levels of teaching, see Thayer S. Warshaw, "Teaching About Religion in Public Schools: 8 Questions," *Phi Delta Kappan* 49, no. 3 (November, 1967): 129.

the public schools as an academic subject to be taught. Perhaps it might be better to say that religion should be examined and studied, not taught, since "teaching religion" often is given the implied meaning of propagating certain denominational dogmas.

Representative of the various attempts to deal objectively with religion in the public schools is Thayer Warshaw's integration of Bible-as-background studies into his English classes in the Newton, Massachusetts, public schools. He found that even his brighter students did not know the origins of literary allusions, such as a person being a "doubting Thomas" or having "the patience of Job." Warshaw's students study the Bible as literature.[2]

Although many argue that it would be practically impossible to deal adequately with many aspects of social studies, literature, art, and music without involving religion, much of the presently available instructional materials in the area of teaching about religion have been labeled as superficial and inadequate. Also, most teacher-education programs in the social studies and the humanities areas do not involve adequate preparation for teaching the religious history, literature, beliefs, and practices involved in these fields. For example, how many public school teachers have the ability to explain meaningfully the Calvinistic outlook on life involved in Hawthorne's *The Scarlet Letter,* or to explain the social significance of the Second Vatican Council? An additional problem is whether or not "religion" should be presented in separate courses or integrated into traditional course areas.

PATTERNS OF RELIGIOUS INSTRUCTION

In his book *Democratic Educational Theory,* Ernest E. Bayles examines seven generalized patterns of religious instruction. Pattern one is the parochial school pattern in which loyalties to particular moral and religious beliefs are inculcated into students in private schools which are supported by private financing. This pattern is acceptable to most Americans.

Pattern two involves the inculcation of denominational beliefs either through released time or with students freely choosing to go

---

[2] "Teaching the Facts of Faith," *Time* 88, no. 26 (December 23, 1966): 61. Also see Thayer S. Warshaw's articles on this same theme in *Liberty* 59, no. 2 (March–April, 1964), and *Liberty* 63, no. 2 (March–April, 1968).

to indoctrinative programs conducted in the school building by representatives of the various churches. The legality of such procedures, however, is open to question.

Pattern three is the non-promotive acquainting of students with the Bible as literature and history, world religions, comparative religions, religious doctrines and creeds, religion and culture, the history of religion, and significant religious literature of the world. This teaching about religion basically is social-studies instruction and does not represent a change from traditional school policies, even though few school districts include such studies in their programs. However, this is not the type of doctrinaire, sectarian instruction desired by those who are critical of the presumed "anti-religious" bias of the public schools.

Pattern four is an adaptation of pattern two in that, instead of the inculcation occurring in separate places with separate groups, it would be done serially in one large group. In this "debate" system, each denominational representative would be allowed time to argue as persuasively as possible for his own beliefs and to rebut the arguments offered by other representatives. Each student would be free to choose which, if any, of the denominations he desired to accept.

Pattern five would involve capable and knowledgeable teachers playing the roles of the various denominational advocates. The teacher would be expected to take pains to label clearly his own religious predilections so that students might guard against his giving undue advantage to them. As with pattern four, each student would be free to make his own choice or choices.

Pattern six would be based on group study of the comparative strengths and weaknesses of the various church doctrines. Through undetected, subtle manipulation of resources and activities, the teacher hoodwinks the students into accepting his beliefs while they think they are arriving freely at their own religious convictions. Such clearly authoritarian "soft sell" inculcation probably would have more influence on students than the blatant denominational propagandizing involved in patterns one and two.

Pattern seven might involve the procedures in patterns three through six for presenting the various denominational beliefs. As with pattern six, the relative adequacy of the various views would be examined. However, instead of the teacher subtly attempting to influence the students to agree with his beliefs, he takes a reflectively analytical position. He fosters reflective thought about pertinent religious outlooks, including his own, adopting varying criteria and noting the logical consequences that each entails.

As Ernest Bayles notes, patterns one and two are openly and un-apologetically dictatorial. Pattern six is also dictatorial, but cleverly and subtly so. Patterns three, four, and five seem to be anarchistically permissive. Bayles believes that pattern seven points toward a genuinely democratic approach to religious instruction in the public schools.[3]

MORAL VALUES AND CHARACTER EDUCATION

Although the teaching of religion in public schools has received much opposition, moral and character education traditionally has been accepted as a valid task of the public schools. However, just where religious education ends and character education begins has not been clearly defined. Perhaps certain types of "religious" education have been carried out for many years under the guise of "character" education.

Should schools be responsible for transmitting generally-accepted moral values? Some thoughtful critics have contended that causing people to do what is right, to act morally, is not a valid school task. To them, the inculcation of moral values is authoritarian and, in such a program, students are indoctrinated, not taught. In contrast, the task of the schools in a democracy should be to teach, not to indoctrinate. Other critics hold that society in general, and teachers in particular, are continuously fostering value-choices. Therefore, from this point of view, the question is not whether or not moral values should be taught, but which values.

Various tests have been devised to use in examining the attitudes, character traits, and moral values of students. Character traits that have been considered important include the following: conformity to rules and laws, respect for authority, obedience, friendliness, freedom from inner hostility, zestful spontaneous commitment to worthy causes, susceptibility to inner controls, understanding the implications of behavior, power of rational self-criticism, open-mindedness, fair-mindedness, ability to withhold a decision for a time, honesty, punctuality, courtesy, cooperation, generosity, neatness, thoughtfulness, dependability, kindness, resourcefulness, good sportsmanship, and mutual respect for human differences.

---

[3] For a more extensive presentation of these seven patterns, see Ernest E. Bayles, *Democratic Educational Theory* (New York: Harper & Row, Publishers, 1960), Chap. 9.

Delinquency and prejudice are generally recognized as character flaws. School-centered attempts to improve student attitudes in these and other personality-trait areas have been spotty, at best. Studies indicate that failures have outweighed successes in character-education programs. For example, many high school students reflect fascistic character traits and, if they had the power, would eliminate many of the provisions of the Bill of Rights. Perhaps the fostering of mature moral attitudes leading to responsible young adulthood is at least partially thwarted by the traditional assumption that students are dependent, non-involved, legal infants. It has been claimed that a college education, instead of fostering moral maturity, generally appears to encourage safe and irrational conformity to imposed rules. Studies indicate that college seniors are more addicted than freshmen to not rocking the boat. College students are more tolerant than high school students, but they do not register an increase in serious social commitment. It may be that responsible and mature, yet risky, commitment to an altruistic morality comes not from overt instruction in moral values, but from student participation in and responsibility for dealing with significant moral conflicts, both in the classroom and in the community.

CONCLUSION

The question of whether or not religion should be taught in the public schools often seems to produce more emotional heat than intellectual light. In attempting to put the problem in perspective, it should be noted that there is very little evidence that mature and responsible conduct is inevitably bound to acceptance of any particular set of religious beliefs. Studies indicate that formal religious instruction does not markedly foster moral behavior. In fact, "general goodness of life" appears to correlate negatively with church membership.[4] If the various studies are valid, they indicate that religion may be of much less value in our society, and in our schools, than advocates of classroom inculcation of traditional Christian beliefs would care to admit publicly. However, regardless of the many disagreements among writers about religion and education, they do agree that mature adults in our society should have an understanding of what is one of mankind's greatest continuing concerns.

---

[4] V. T. Thayer, *The Attack upon the American Secular School* (Boston: The Beacon Press, 1951), pp. 152–57.

SELECTED REFERENCES

Bayles, Ernest E., *Democratic Educational Theory.* New York: Harper & Row, Publishers, 1960, Chap. 9. An excellent introduction to problems in the religion and education area by an avowed democratic relativist.

Butts, R. Freeman, *The American Tradition in Religion and Education.* Boston: The Beacon Press, 1950. A lucid presentation of the historical foundations of the present conflict over the place of religious instruction in the schools.

Duker, Sam, *The Public Schools and Religion: The Legal Context.* New York: Harper & Row, Publishers, 1966. An examination of the U.S. Supreme Court decisions dealing with religion and the public schools.

Educational Issues in a Changing Society, August Kerber and Wilfred Smith, eds. Detroit: Wayne State University Press, 1964, Section 4. Articles express differing opinions on the role of religion in public education.

Panoch, James V. and David L. Barr, *Religion Goes To School.* New York: Harper & Row, Publishers, 1968. A practical guidebook for teachers of religion in the public schools.

Religion and Public Education, Theodore R. Sizer, ed. Boston: Houghton Mifflin Company, 1967. A number of articles by authorities in the field of relationships between religion and education.

Religion in the Public Schools. New York: Harper & Row, Publishers, 1964. A report by the Commission on Religion in the Public Schools of the American Association of School Administrators designed to help public school administrators deal with religious problems.

Schwartz, Lita Linzer, *American Education—A Problem-Centered Approach.* Boston, Mass.: Holbrook Press, 1969, Chap. 7. Emphasis is given to the issue of whether public funds should be used for parochial schools.

Social Foundations of Education, William O. Stanley, B. Othanel Smith, Kenneth D. Benne, and Archibald W. Anderson, eds. New York: Dryden Press, 1956, Chap. 9. Excellent articles present conflicting beliefs about religion and education.

Thayer, V. T. *The Attack Upon The American Secular School.* Boston: Beacon Press, 1951. Although somewhat dated, this book probably is the most succinct argument for the preservation of our traditionally secular public schools.

The Human Encounter—Readings in Education, Sheldon Stoff and Herbert Schwartzberg, eds. New York: Harper & Row, Publishers, 1969, Chap. 5. Articles range from Supreme Court opinions to John Gardner's "Education is Always Religious."

Warshaw, Thayer S., "Teaching About Religion in Public Schools: 8 Questions," *Phi Delta Kappan* 49, no. 3 (November, 1967): 127–33. Warshaw raises and examines a number of important questions about teaching religion in public schools.

THOUGHT AIDS

1. Should the public schools continue to attempt to inculcate and reinforce traditional moral and character values? Why or why not?

2. Should the public schools be allowed to undermine or destroy the religious faith and moral convictions of students through objective studies of The Bible, world religions, and religious history? Why or why not?

3. If religion is studied in the public schools, should parents be allowed to have their children excused from such classes? Why or why not?

4. Do you agree with Robert Ingersoll, the great "atheist" of the previous century, that "Real religion is usefulness"? On what do you base your reaction?

5. Relate Socrates' dictum, "The unexamined life is not worth living," to the concepts involved in this chapter.

6. Should schools observe Christian religious events, such as Christmas and Easter, or do these constitute violations of the rights of minorities? Why or why not?

7. If the majority of American parents desired, should they have the right to have their children taught to believe in God through religion classes in the public schools, or should a minority group of atheists be allowed to determine what is taught in the public schools? Why or why not? Or is this, to you, a valid type of question?

8. Should students be encouraged to consider Christian values as being highly desirable, even though certain scholars, such as Bertrand Russell, claim that religion has done more harm than good? Why or why not? (See C. D. Hardie. "Religion and Education," *Educational Theory* 18, no. 3 [Summer, 1968]: 199–223.)

9. Do you agree with Ernest Bayles belief that religion can be taught in a democratic manner in the public schools? Why or why not?

10. If religion were taught in the public schools, which level would you prefer that it be taught on: fact, skill, or behavior? Why?

11. React to this statement by John Gardner: "Most human societies have been beautifully organized to keep good men down."

12. Analyze the following statement: The Supreme Court's barring of state prescribed classroom prayer is another victory of "those forces which conspire to remove faith in God from the public conscience." (Billy Graham, "Speaking Out—Our Right to Require Belief," *Saturday Evening Post* 235, no. 7 [February 17, 1962]: 8.)

13. Do you believe that parochial schools should receive financial aid from public funds? Defend your position.

23

Should Sex Education Be Taught in the Schools?

Sex education in the schools has become the hottest political issue since "law and order." Controversies over sex education have mushroomed in three-fourths of the states. PTA and school board meetings dissolve into bitter shouting matches as charges of "Communist conspiracy" and "irresponsible fanatics" fill the air. Opposition to sex education is the single major plank of many school board candidates. Parents threaten to take their children out of public schools and some are suing their school districts for "breach of privacy." A number of state legislatures are considering bills to prohibit, control, or investigate sex education programs, and state support has been banned in other states. Certain parent groups and congressmen are attempting to restrict or eliminate federal financing of sex education projects. Unsubstantiated rumors, such as that a teacher stripped naked in front of her class, are trumpeted by far-right groups as being irrefutable evidence that pornography, promiscuity, and perversion are invading classrooms under the guise of sex education. Savage, emotional wrangles have left a residue of suspicion and hatred in certain now-divided communities.

From one camp come charges that sex education in schools is unAmerican, unhealthy, immoral and obscene, and that it will undermine American youth and usurp the duties of parents and churches. "Teach children to read, not breed," is the battle cry. From the other side come claims that right-wing extremists are behind the anti-sex-education campaign, that they are misleading well-intentioned parents with scare tactics and blinding them to the fact that physical and mental health depends on good, above-board sex education. "Take sex education out of the back room into the classroom" they argue.[1]

What is sex education? As could be expected, the combatants are not in agreement as to what they are quarreling about. A pamphlet written by the far-right Christian Crusade's education director, Gordon V. Drake, *Is The Schoolhouse the Proper Place to Teach Raw Sex?* has become the "Bible" of many of those opposing sex education. To them, the "raw sex" being pushed at young children includes how to perform the sex act, positions to take in intercourse, and very explicit contraceptive information. Young children are shown pictures of papier-mache models of chickens and dogs copulating, followed by a picture of "Mommy and Daddy" under bed sheets "doing the same things dogs do." [2] Impressionable kindergarteners are even expected to make clay models of sex organs. A film series, "Time of Your Life," shown to elementary children in California schools, "presents the male and female anatomy in detail, discusses the mechanism of erection and ejaculation and the role of the clitoris in sexual pleasure." [3]

Many supporters of sex education, particularly members of the Sex Information and Education Council of the U.S. (SIECUS), say that the most avid critics of sex education tend to look only at the physiological aspects of sexuality, thus equating sex education with reproductive biology, something involving only the genital organs. To sex educators, "this is not really sex education; a student can learn all about reproduction without gaining an understanding of sex." [4]

To some sex educators, "sex education" is a misleading term because sex education is more than sex information. Almost all programs include reproductive information only as a part of broader studies

---

[1] Carl T. Rowan and David M. Mazie, "Sex Education: Powder Keg in Our Schools," *The Reader's Digest* 95, no. 570 (October, 1969): 74.

[2] Gary Allen, "Sex Study—Problems, Propaganda, and Pornography," *American Opinion* 12, no. 3 (March, 1969): 8–9.

[3] "Too Much Too Soon?" *Nation's Schools* 84, no. 2 (August, 1969): 19.

[4] Paul Woodring, "What Is Sex Education?" *Saturday Review* 48, no. 51 (December 18, 1965), p. 55. *Also see* Dr. William H. Masters and Virginia E. Johnson, "Sex and Sexuality: The Crucial Difference," *The Reader's Digest* 90, no. 538 (February, 1967): 123–26 (Condensed from *McCall's* 94, no. 2 [November, 1966]).

of health, psychological development, moral and responsible human relations, social roles, and family life education. Sex education is learning "how to find meaning and value not only in sex relations but in life." [5] Dr. Mary S. Calderone, Executive Director of SIECUS, defines sex education:

> Enlightened sex education today is not just the facts of reproduction and certainly not education about the act of sex. It deals with one's total sexuality—maleness or femaleness, what makes you a man or a woman, the way you think, act, dress, marry. Sex is not something we do, but something we are, and the goal of SIECUS is simple: the use by every individual of his sexual faculties in mature, creative, and responsible ways in all his relationships, not just the sexual ones. [6]

Mrs. Patricia Schiller, director of a District of Columbia sex and family life education training program, differentiates sex from sexuality.

> It is sexuality, not sex, that is crucial. Human sexuality is what is personally important to the growing child, the adolescent, and the adult. Sexual identity is an important part of the self-image and affects every aspect of life. For example, sexuality involves the name we are given at birth, the toys we play with as a child, the clothes we wear, the friends we have, the things we like to do, the courses we take in high school and college, the careers we choose, the way we see our roles and responsibilities in our homes, and last but not least, the ways we satisfy and cope with our sexual needs and urges as responsible and committed human beings. [7]

Even though parental pressure originally led to the beginning and expansion of most sex education programs, much of the uproar against sex education is generated by parents' organizations with colorful titles such as SOS (Sanity On Sex), MOTOREDE (Movement to Restore Decency), and PAUSE (Parents Against Universal Sex Education). However, more than half of the public and parochial schools in the nation have some form of sex education; many programs have been functioning effectively for decades. Also, public opinion polls consistently indicate that over 70 per cent of American parents favor sex education.

---

[5] Jo Gorsuch, "An Experiment in Sex Education," *The Reader's Digest* 91, no. 547 (November, 1967): 142.

[6] Paul Friggens, "Shameful Neglect of Sex Education," *The PTA Magazine* 61, no. 9 (May, 1967): 5.

[7] Patricia Schiller, "Sex Education That Makes Sense," *NEA Journal* 57, no. 2 (February, 1968), p. 17.

CRITICISMS OF SEX EDUCATION

1. *Far-Right critics* particularly in the John Birch Society and the Christian Crusade, *believe that sex education is part of the Communist conspiracy.* To these critics, sex education is a "subversive monstrosity" through which Communists and their allies—the liberals, leftists, pinkos, and some duped "genuine" Americans—weaken the family, corrupt our youth, and destroy morality. The insidious plan of the Communists is to use diabolical, degenerate, and filthy pornography, peddled by perverted teachers, to prepare the minds of youth for Communist conquest. The schools are being used by sinister seducers and debauchers to foster rampant promiscuity, often under the lofty and deliberately deceitful euphemism of "Family Life Education."

Gary Allen outlines this leftist plot against America in an article in *American Opinion,* the official journal of Robert Welch's John Birch Society:

> As far back as May of 1919, Allied forces in Dusseldorf, Germany, first captured a Communist document entitled *Rules For Revolution.* Number One on that list of objectives was: "Corrupt the young, get them away from religion. Get them interested in sex. Make them superficial, destroy their ruggedness." [8]
>
> Historically, the destruction of morality has often been used as a technique to ready a country for Communist revolution. [9]
>
> It would test our credulity to propose that our schools and other influential institutions are deliberately aiding this hideous process. It is possible, however, to believe that such institutions are being used by conspirators to accomplish the aims of the worldwide Communist movement. [10]

Dr. Gordon V. Drake, educational director of Billy James Hargis' Christian Crusade, also attacked the subversive immorality of sex education programs:

> What the sex educators have in mind is simply this: Sex should be as easily discussed as any other subject in the curriculum, and any inhibitions or moral and religious taboos should be eliminated. This obviously drives a wedge between the family, church and school—bolstering the authority of the school while casting cynical doubts on the traditional moral teachings of the home and church. If this is accomplished, and the new morality is affirmed, our chil-

---

[8] Allen, *American Opinion* (March, 1969), p. 19.
[9] Allen, *American Opinion* (March, 1969), p. 19.
[10] Allen, *American Opinion* (March, 1969), p. 19.

dren will become easy targets for Marxism and other amoral, nihilistic philosophies—as well as V.D.! [11]

It should be evident that the sex educators are in league with sexologists—who represent every shade of muddy gray morality, ministers colored atheistic pink, and camp followers of every persuasion—off-beat psychiatrists to ruthless publishers of pornography. The enemy is formidable at first glance, but becomes awesomely powerful when we discover the interlocking directorates and working relationship of national organizations which provide havens for these degenerates. [12]

The "pornographic arm of the liberal establishment" [13] is the Sex Information and Education Council of the U.S. (SIECUS) who's directors are fostering "indoctrination in promiscuity." [14] SIECUS is encouraging moral decay and the destruction of right standards of conduct. Gary Allen, and all other true Americans, object to "putting the sexual morality of all children at the mercy of the atheists and pornographers and Communists who are supporting and directing S.I.E.C.U.S. . . ." [15]

2. *Sex education can best be taught by parents and the churches.* Concerned and sensitive parents know their own children as no one else does. They, and they alone, really know when the time is right to communicate sex information to their children. If parents are uninformed or inept in conveying needed knowledge, they are the ones who need sex education, not their children. Also, since human beings are more than mere animals, human sexual behavior is more than biology. Human sexuality must be dealt with in a religious, moral, and ethical context. In our pluralistic society, the home and the church are the proper places to relate sexual values to divinity.

3. *Sex education in the schools is not based on teaching values, morality, and ethics.* Many parents are upset by the SIECUS philosophy of "sex without morality" which results in amoral and anti-religious sex instruction. Gordon Drake has emphasized SIECUS's lack of morality: "There should be no attempts to build character; merely spell out the options available in the sensual grab bag of sexual delights." [16] "In order to uproot in the child's mind the notion that religion has anything important to say about sexual morality in today's

---

[11] Gordon V. Drake. *Is The School House The Proper Place To Teach Raw Sex?* (Tulso, Oklahoma: Christian Crusade Publications, 1968), p. 20.

[12] Drake, *Teach Raw Sex?* p. 31.

[13] Walter Goodman, "The Controversy Over Sex Education: What Our Children Stand To Lose," *Redbook* 133, no. 5 (September, 1969), p. 194.

[14] Allen, *American Opinion* (March, 1969), p. 18.

[15] Allen, *American Opinion* (March, 1969), p. 18.

[16] Drake, *Teach Raw Sex?* p. 16.

world, modern sexologists recommend that the moral view *must not be used, or given a hearing."* [17]

The so-called "antiquated morals" of Christianity are thrown out the window; teen-agers are given a "sexual smorgasbord" and told to take their choice. Such amoral education programs are conducted in Sweden, and most Americans are aware of the rampant immorality, lasciviousness, and soaring venereal disease rates which characterize Swedish society.

There are only two alternatives: either a teacher transmits a moral code based on accepting man's duties toward God, or the teacher encourages hedonistic permissiveness. This permissiveness has been dressed up and ticketed as the "new morality" or "situational ethics" by sex educators. They claim that the old sanctions don't necessarily apply anymore; each student is to build his own code of sexual ethics. Morality is taken by sex educators to be a matter of "personal opinion." Each student is told to let his conscience be his guide; each does what is right in his own eyes. Personal desires of the moment are put ahead of anything else. As Fritz Ridenour has noted: ". . . the new morality has often been used as a tool of expediency by those who want to live as they please and love every minute of it." [18] Situation ethics becomes a clever excuse for letting each student do what he really wanted to do in the first place. It is sugar-coated anarchy, lawlessness, and immorality. "The doors are left wide open for human nature, with its lust and desires, to express itself without restraint." [19]

An inordinately heavy burden of judgment and decision making is placed on uncertain and confused youth. Final moral choices are left to young minds far too immature to make such decisions. Is it any wonder that there has been a loosening of morals and an erosion of traditional sexual restraints?

4. *Sex knowledge will tempt students to experiment with sex.* When explicit, "how-to-do-it" sex information is thrust onto students, they will naturally want to go out and test their knowledge. The following is excerpted from a letter from one mother to the *Phoenix American* and is self-explanatory.

> We have a 12-year-old son who was taught this smut last spring, and about 9 weeks thereafter we had a near disaster in our home.

---

[17] Drake, *Teach Raw Sex?* p. 30.

[18] Fritz Ridenour, *It All Depends* (Glendale, California: G/L Regal Books, 1969), p. 12.

[19] William F. Dankenbring, "What's Behind the Furor Over Sex Education?" *The Plain Truth* 34, no. 11 (November, 1969), p. 21.

I walked in and caught him sexually molesting our 4-year-old daughter. He had been taught all about intercourse at school and wanted to "try it out" on his sister. (I caught him before he actually committed the act.)

Now, teaching young kids this in school is nonsense. . . . It's like giving someone a recipe to discourage cooking. It won't discourage, but rather encourage experimentation.[20]

5. *Too much is being taught too soon because the Freudian "Latency Period" is being ignored.* Sigmund Freud taught that there is a latency period from about the age of five until puberty during which children are not sexually curious and must be free to concentrate on socialization, play, and learning. Sexual interests are submerged and must not be stirred up. If children are catapulted into advanced sexual information during this period, they often develop anxieties, sexual fixations, and obsessions—growing up to be distorted and perverted adults.

Dr. Rhoda Lorand, author of *Love, Sex and the Teenager,* and a New York City psychologist and child analyst, is leading a campaign against sex instruction in the lower grades. "The ability to learn in school and to be spontaneous in play may eventually be destroyed for many children if they are not permitted to keep their minds off sexual matters during the school day." [12] Premature force-feeding of elementary children with stimulating knowledge of the mechanics of sex must be stopped. Innocent, unready minds must not be overwhelmed; neither parents nor teachers should anticipate curiosity.

6. *There are not enough skillful, sensitive, and mature sex education teachers.* Reports of insensitive and shattering approaches to sex education by teachers are legion. For example, a teacher's blunt approach to homosexuality caused a normal boy to conclude he was a homosexual. Psychiatric care was required to correct the teacher's blunder. Also, many sex educators seem to have as many, or more, sexual "hang-ups" as the parents they are supposedly replacing. In fact, sexually distorted teachers tend to gravitate to such programs.

7. *There is very little scientific evidence that sex education really does change behavior.* Practically speaking, there are no definitive studies on effects of sex education upon individual attitudes and behavior. No research studies have been carried out in order to distinguish "good" sex education from "bad." It has not been con-

---

[20] Allen, *American Opinion* (March, 1969), p. 11.
[21] Barbara Yuncker, "Sex Education: Should It Be Taught In School?" *Family Circle* (January, 1970), p. 70.

clusively proven that sex education programs really do reduce promiscuity, venereal disease, and premarital pregnancies.

IN DEFENSE OF SEX EDUCATION

It is easy to fall into the error of branding all critics of sex education as "rightist nuts." Although the well-organized and usually extremely vocal minorities often make more noise and attract more attention than their numbers warrant, they deserve a fair hearing in the market place of ideas. Therefore, a response will be given to each of the seven criticisms of sex education previously noted.

1. *Far-right critics believe that sex education is part of the Communist conspiracy.* The *Reader's Digest,* which has consistently taken a conservative, anti-communist stance, printed an article by Carl T. Rowan and David M. Mazie in which it was noted that the "Communist conspiracy" argument is not a terribly convincing one. "If the charges of communist leanings weren't so vicious, they would almost be amusing. It is difficult to think of the AMA, YWCA, and the U.S. Catholic Conference as part of a subversive plot." [22]

Clear distinctions need to be made between calm discussion by responsible critics and the smear sheets and scare tactics of die-hard conservatives which are designed to intimidate and silence opponents and to poison the air with fear and distrust. The emotional barrage by far-rightists is designed to destroy objective study and temperate criticisms. Rather than fostering genuine debate and fairly judging programs on their merits, extreme rightists are attempting to prevent careful examination of issues.

Rather than seeking to improve family life education programs, the Birchers are frankly out to destroy them through manipulating and exploiting the valid concerns and anxieties of parents.

> The present onslaught, however, is designed not to promote discussion but to destroy sex education by muddying the motives and reputations of its advocates, circulating frightening reports of doubtful reliability and arousing community passions.[23] . . . Sex education foes are not interested primarily in the child or sex education. They want to create fear, hatred, and suspicion in a community and take over the schools.[24]

---

[22] Rowan and Mazie, *The Reader's Digest* (October, 1969), p. 76.
[23] Goodman, *Redbook* (September, 1969), p. 197.
[24] Rowan and Mazie, *The Reader's Digest* (October, 1969), p. 78.

Irresponsible "blanket" attacks on sex education signal a return to the tactics of the late Senator Joseph McCarthy. The far-right plan of attack is a Pandora's Box of various demagogic techniques such as guilt-by-association, distortion, half-truths, falsehoods, and name-calling. Luther G. Baker, Jr., Professor of Family Life at Central Washington State College, has prepared a booklet which, in detail, refutes the contentions made by the Christian Crusaders and the John Birchers.[25] However, as was painfully learned in the Mc-Carthyism era, "refutations can scarcely keep up with accusations." [26]

2. *Sex education can best be taught by parents and the churches.* Sex educators agree with this concept; they also believe that sex education in the schools should, ideally, only supplement sex education received at home and in the churches. All approved sex education programs, which are established by community planning and curriculum committees, are designed to strengthen the family as a social institution. Studies of successful sex education programs indicate that one result of such programs is that children are motivated to communicate with their parents.

How many students, with or without sex education courses, are receiving sex education from their parents and in church? Although many parents readily admit the importance of sexual knowledge in their children's lives, studies indicate that a dishearteningly small percentage of students (usually less than ten per cent) receive meaningful sex knowledge from their parents, and that received in church is practically infinitesimal. Even though the vast majority of parents fail to communicate with their children, should their children be deprived of adequate sexual knowledge because of parental deficiencies?

Even in homes where adequate sex knowledge has been conveyed to children, as youth grow into the adolescent seeking of self-identity, it is normal and fairly common for them to grow apart from their parents. It is the rare high school student who feels free to talk to his parents. One high school girl pinpointed the problem: "When I tried to ask my parents about sexual questions, they got emotionally involved and became overly suspicious, so I stopped asking." Sex educators believe that skillful, sensitive, and mature teachers can serve as effective confidants for students seeking valid answers to

---

[25] Luther G. Baker, *The Rising Furor Over Sex Education.* Northfield, Illinois: SIECUS Publications. Also see the SIECUS pamphlet, *A Brief History of the Current Campaign Against Sex Education.*

[26] Goodman, *Redbook* (September, 1969), p. 194.

sexual questions. High school students also can benefit from the awareness that other students are facing similar problems.

3. *Sex education in the schools is not based on teaching values, morality, and ethics.* It appears that certain critics are again attacking a "straw man." They define the "new morality" and "situational ethics" as anarchistic, do-as-you-please permissiveness, and proceed to knock the stuffings out of that straw man. In contrast, as defined by sex educators, situational ethics means that persons should act humanely and responsibly in all situations. Rather than leading to anarchy, sex education programs are designed to foster personal and social responsibility. Rather than being based on authoritarian (absolutistic) moral codes, sex education programs are based on awareness that behavior has situational, personal and social consequences, and that self-control ultimately must be a personal responsibility.[27] Students must be educated to measure the future consequences of their actions. For example, rather than favoring promiscuity, sex educators note that the consequences of premarital sex usually are harmful.[28]

> The basic purpose of morality is not to tell people, "Do this, don't do that," but to help them to live together in a really humane way. We've got to realize that various behavior patterns are possible, that not everyone is going to behave according to the same set of rules. But as long as we can act like human beings toward each other we are observing the essence of morality.[29]

> The strongest opposition to sex courses comes from the middle-aged; more often than not, it reflects their discontent with the changes taking place in a world different from that in which they grew up. The schools, for their part, are obviously not responsible for creating today's sexual revolution; they are merely trying to help students cope with it. To eliminate these courses is to deny many children access to essential knowledge that can ease their difficult psychic transition from adolescence to adulthood.[30]

The charge that immorality and venereal disease are rampant in Sweden—as results of the sex education programs there—needs to

---

[27] Isadore Rubin, *The Sex Educator and Moral Values,* SIECUS Study Guide No. 10, 1969.

[28] Lester A. Kirkendall, "How Premarital Sex Hurts Girls," in *Guide to Sexology,* Frank S. Caprio, ed. (New York: Paperback Library, 1965, pp. 20–23. *Also see* Lester A. Kirkendall and Ruth F. Osborne, *Teacher's Question and Answer Book on Sex Education* (New London, Conn.: Croft Educational Services, Inc., 1969).

[29] "Sex Education: Blunt Answers for Tough Questions" (An interview with Lester A. Kirkendall by James Lincoln Collier), *The Reader's Digest* 92, no. 554 (June, 1968): 84.

[30] *Time* 94, no. 4 (July 25, 1969): 50.

be laid to rest. According to the United Nation's World Health Organization, the divorce rate in Sweden is one out of every six marriages, and the divorce rate in the United States is one out of three. The per capita rate for rape arrests in the United States is about five times that of Sweden. The United States rate for number of reported cases of early syphilis is over double that of Sweden.

4. *Sex knowledge will tempt students to experiment with sex.* Various defenses can be offered in response to this charge. For example, if there were no sex education programs in the schools, would sex knowledge and experimentation cease? Of course not! Sexual curiosity is a natural and normal thing. Studies indicate that the normal child will explore his own body and will be curious about the other sex. He also will receive information and stimulation, inaccurate and distorted as it may be, from peers and our sex-saturated society. Students cannot be insulated from sexual information and misinformation. They need not only accurate information but also to be made thoughtfully aware of moral values so they can learn to manage their normal sexual needs in healthy and mature ways.

The National Congress of Parents and Teachers is one of the many distinguished organizations supporting sex education. Elizabeth Hendryson, President of the National PTA, says:

> Some people object to sex education per se; they believe that information provokes sexual curiosity and stimulates sexual experimentation. The reverse is closer to reality. Ignorance is not a protection. Physicians and nurses report that many teenage girls have no idea how they became pregnant. And the curiosity of children and youth will not be denied or suppressed. When their questions are brushed aside or inadequately answered by parents or teachers, children and youth will seek answers elsewhere—from each other or from older boys or girls. The answers they get may be false and dangerous.[31]

The question of whether or not to provide sex education is a false one. It is being done anyway by peers and other potentially inaccurate sources in our culture. The real question is whether or not we want the often distorted and erroneous sex education children receive from their peers and others to be counteracted by accurate, positive, and effective sex education programs in the schools. As Dr. Clark E. Vincent, director of the Behavioral Sciences Center of the

---

[31] Elizabeth Hendryson, "The Case For Sex Education," *The PTA Magazine* 63, no. 9 (May, 1969): 21.

Bowman Gray School of Medicine in Winston-Salem, North Carolina, notes, "Your children are being 'sex educated' every day of the year ... The only relevant question is whether you are satisfied with what they are being taught." [32] Dr. G. G. Wetherill, director of health service for the San Diego, California, schools, asks: "Are you satisfied with the way your children are receiving their sex information now? If not, do you feel that we as teachers and parents are mature enough in our thinking about sex to do better? If you agree, we can begin planning a program." [33]

5. *Too much is being taught too soon because the Freudian "Latency Period" is being ignored.* Since critics who have not understood or been interested in Sigmund Freud's teachings often suddenly become "instant experts" on the latency period, sex educators may be pardoned for their suspicions as to the motives of such "experts." However, even if this argument is just one more emotionalized gimmick, it deserves a fair hearing. In response to the charge that sex education programs prematurely draw attention to sex, Dr. Mary Calderone makes the point that children are being exposed to sexual information from the time of birth. "Sex is so intrusive and our culture so permeated with sexual messages that planned and relevant sex education programs are vital now." [34]

Freud based his latency concept on what he saw in his patients who were living in the culture of that time, a culture that did not thrust sex upon children. In contrast, children today are exposed constantly to explicit sexual stimuli. If Freud were living now, he probably would reject the "sexual cocoon" concept and hold that education in sexuality is needed to counter the unrelenting cultural bombardment of negative and distorted genital sex. To Dr. Earle Marsh of the University of California Medical Center in San Francisco:

> The so-called "latency period" is one of Freud's concepts that has pretty much been abandoned. It's just ridiculous to think that there is a period when a human being cannot be taught. In fact, the rough-and-tumble of childhood is necessary for the development of a healthy sex life. Education at any stage of a person's life makes sense, it just depends on the language you use. [35]

---

[32] Walter Goodman, "The New Sex Education," *Redbook* 129, no. 5 (September, 1967): 135.

[33] Friggens, *The PTA Magazine* (May, 1967), p. 7.

[34] *Time* (July 25, 1969), p. 50.

[35] Ernest Dunbar, "Sex In School—The Birds, The Bees, and The Birchers," *Look* 33, no. 18 (September 9, 1969): 17.

Dr. Harvey J. Tompkins, a past president of the American Psychiatric Association and chief of psychiatry at St. Vincent's Medical Center, New York City, presents a view typical of most psychiatrists and child psychologists:

> I see no reason why sex education should not involve five- to 10-year olds. In fact, as society is now, they need it. Of course, it all depends on the teacher and the techniques he uses and the sensitivity with which he approaches it. But if it is presented well, it will not intrude but will enhance normal development.[36]

6. *There are not enough skillfull, sensitive, and mature sex education teachers.* Although this is not a criticism, per se, of sex education programs, it is a valid concern. Granting that effective sex education programs are needed, it is obvious that such programs can only be conducted by gifted teachers who are knowledgeable, perceptive, and secure—teachers who are comfortable in dealing with sexuality. This leads logically to the contention that much greater emphasis needs to be given to the selection, training and in-service progress of family-life education teachers.

The concern about emotionally-troubled teachers gravitating to such programs is also a valid one. It must be admitted that mistakes are being made in sex education programs and that there probably are sex-education instructors who have unresolved sexual problems of their own. However, we do have faith that most school administrators know their teachers and will screen them accordingly.

7. *There is very little scientific evidence that sex education really does change behavior.* May sex education programs validly be expected to reduce promiscuity, venereal disease, and premarital pregnancies? Although the few studies, admittedly inadequate, indicate that extensive sex education programs may produce these results, is it fair to expect such changes in behavior from sex education programs? Do we expect the same types of behavioral results in other fields? For example, do we expect social studies classes to produce active voters—do we expect student enlightenment? Studies indicate that culture tends to be far more influential in determining personal behavior than the influence exerted by the schools.

PROBLEMS IN SEX EDUCATION

Once the hurdle of whether or not sex education programs should be included in the schools has been cleared, a number of smaller, but no less significant, hurdles appear.

---

[36] Yuncker, *Family Circle* (January, 1970), p. 71.

1. *Should parents be allowed to exempt their children from attending sex education classes, or should attendance be compulsory?* If exemptions are allowed, what grounds should be established for such exemptions? SIECUS, often pilloried by extremist groups as trying to force sex education on objecting citizens, affirms the right of parents to withdraw their child from participation if they find that their own personal values are being subverted.[37] To some sex educators, the policy of seeking parental permission is branding sex education as being different. If it is as much a part of the school program as social studies, science, mathematics, music, and English, why should parental permission be needed? If the permission question cannot be ignored, most sex educators believe that it should be dealt with through carefully written school board policies indicating if and upon what grounds exemptions will be allowed.

2. *Should boys and girls be in separate classes?* Some argue that students will be more comfortable and become more involved in detailed discussions in segregated classes. Sex instruction in many districts is given in home economics and physical education classes where separation by sex is normal. Since girls and boys mature at different ages, and since many teachers are uncomfortable when trying to discuss sex in mixed classes, segregated classes are desirable for discussions of sensitive topics as menstruation, masturbation, and homosexuality. On the other hand, segregated classes may give a pornographic connotation that sexual topics should not be talked about in mixed groups. Experience indicates that, with a secure and competent teacher, students in mixed classes are mature enough to learn together.

3. *Should sex education be presented in separate courses or integrated into the traditional subjects?* The casual approach of dealing with sex questions as they arise in traditional courses emphasizes the "teachable moment" when students genuinely seek the knowledge a teacher has to offer. However, a "catch-as-catch-can" approach ignores the need of many students to be exposed systematically to information about the major aspects of sexuality.

4. *What is the best way to initiate sex education programs?* Some educators argue that most school districts already teach something about sexuality, even if it is only reproduction information in biology classes; rather than "starting" programs, existing programs should be formally expanded and made more comprehensive. Such an approach would reduce the fears of groups opposed to what is new. A manual

---

[37] Carlfred B. Broderick, "Parents Rights in the Sex Education Controversy," *SIECUS Newsletter* 5, no. 1 (October, 1969): 2.

developed by the National School Public Relations Association, *Sex Education in Schools*, presents detailed plans for involving community groups in studying community needs and then choosing what would be the content of their local sex education program.[38]

CONCLUSION

Both the public and educators are overwhelmingly in favor of sex education, so the major legitimate controversy probably should be over what constitutes good sex education. The spectacle of a shrill minority blocking programs supported by majority opinion should give pause to those who endorse democratic decision-making processes. Perhaps greater emphasis should be given to the almost ignored question of how to provide sex education for parents. How sex education programs might deal more effectively with the wide range of student differences also seems to merit more attention. Student lack of confidence in both school and parents is a significant, but practically unnoticed, phenomenon. A recent study indicated that only a minority of students would turn to either their parents or school counselors for help on sex problems. The community-by-community approach to implementing sex education programs has rarely been questioned. Might it be better to have nationally-established programs? If so, which agencies should be responsible for establishing them? What are the schools' social responsibilities to our society? John H. Gagnon, senior research sociologist, Institute for Sex Research, Indiana University, concludes that sex education programs may not be as influential as critics fear and supporters claim.

> There is, for instance, no good evidence that answering children's questions about sex enhances either their sexual or non-sexual lives; there is no evidence that enlightened children do not experiment with sex more than the unenlightened; there is no evidence that teaching in the school is more efficacious than learning from one's peers; and finally there is no evidence that the accuracy of either biological or psychological information about physical or mental sexual activities aids in either sexual or other adjustment.[39]

Perhaps a *Saturday Review* cartoon can also add a bit of perspective, if not levity. The cartoon depicts a man turning from reading

---

[38] *Sex Education in Schools* (Washington, D.C.: National School Public Relations Association, 1969).

[39] John H. Gagnon, "Content: Stereotypes—Style: Castrated Freud," *Phi Delta Kappan* 49, no. 9 (May, 1968): 543.

his newspaper to remonstrate with three women seated around a coffee table: "What's to worry about? They'll teach sex like they do the rest of the subjects and the kids will lose interest." [40]

SELECTED REFERENCES

Arnstein, Helene S., *Your Growing Child and Sex*. New York: Avon Books, 1967. This book is designed to give concerned parents a better understanding of the growth of sexuality from infancy to adulthood.

"Growth Patterns and Sex Education," *The Journal of School Health* (May, 1967). A suggested program for kindergarten through grade twelve.

Kirkendall, Lester A. and Ruth F. Osborne, *Teacher's Question and Answer Book on Sex Education*. New London, Conn.: Croft Educational Services, Inc., 1969. Particularly note the analyses of arguments against sex education programs.

Schulz, Esther D. and Sally R. Williams, *Family Life and Sex Education: Curriculum and Instruction*. New York: Harcourt, Brace & World, 1969. An extensive curriculum guide for a kindergarten to grade twelve sex education program.

Sex Education in Schools. Washington, D.C.: National School Public Relations Association, 1969. A practical guidebook to how to start sex education programs and what topics to deal with at various grade levels.

SIECUS Study Guides. Northfield, Illinois: Sex Information and Education Council of the U.S. Topics dealt with include sex education, film resources for sex education, and the sex educator and moral values.

The Individual, Sex, and Society—A SIECUS Handbook For Teachers and Counselors, Carlfred B. Broderick and Jessie Bernard, Eds. Baltimore, Maryland: The Johns Hopkins Press, 1969. Resource readings for sex educators.

THOUGHT AIDS

1. After carefully researching "situational ethics," indicate your reactions to this concept of morality.

---

[40] *Saturday Review* 52, no. 50 (December 13, 1969): 69. For a witty briefing on the war for sexual liberation and a guide to Who's Who in American Sex Circles, see "Who Killed The Stork?" *McCall's* 95, no. 4 (January, 1968): 38–39.

2. Do you believe that sex knowledge presented in the schools will tempt students to experiment with sex? Why or why not?
3. Does it appear to you that sex educators have effectively defended their programs against the criticisms presented in this chapter? If not, what criticisms have not been effectively countered? Why?
4. Watch the "Dear Abby" and "Ann Landers" columns for letters and comments about sex education and American cultural-sexual behavior.
5. What results, if any, do you believe should be expected from sex education programs? Why?
6. Explore possible answers to the following question. "How have discredited guilt-by-association techniques, outright slander, and sheer fabrication managed to arouse substantial numbers of people against school programs that have the backing of the overwhelming majority of the nation's educators, health experts and religious leaders?" (Walter Goodman. "The Controversy Over Sex Education: What Our Children Stand to Lose," *Redbook* 133, no. 5 (September, 1969): 196.)
7. Do you believe that there should be nationally-established sex education programs? Why or why not?

24

Which Is Better, Soviet or United States Education?

Starting with Sputnik, the Soviet Union's successes in rocketry and space science have resulted in a hue and cry being raised about the adequacy of education in the United States. Various critics, such as Admiral Rickover, believe that certain European educational systems, and the Soviet system in particular, are superior to ours. How good is Soviet education? Is Soviet education better than education in the United States? Is it true that their commitment to education is much greater than ours? Even if their whole educational system is not superior to ours, are there certain parts which we would do well to emulate in our system? Is United States education really as haphazard, aimless, and chaotic as the Soviets claim? And, in contrast, are the Soviet schools really effectively organized to achieve clear and realistic Soviet national objectives? Or, are the goals and structures of Soviet education so incompatible with ours that valid comparisons can not be made between the two educational systems?

A COMPARISON OF THE
SOVIET UNION AND THE UNITED STATES

Soviet Union   *United States*

LAND SIZE

Largest country in the world. Covers one-sixth of the earth's land area. More than twice as large as the countries next in size—Canada and China—and nearly three times as large as the United States. Area: 8,649,798 square miles. Most of Russia lies above 50° North Latitude.

Fourth in size in the world. Area: 3,615,211 square miles. Most of the United States lies below 50° North Latitude.

CLIMATE

Almost every kind of variation from sub-tropical to polar. Great temperature extremes in summer and winter. A great deal of area not arable.

Many variations, but tend to be more moderate than in Russia. Major areas arable.

POPULATION

More than 235 million persons. Ranks third, behind China and India. 24 persons per square mile. 50% of population live in rural areas.

About 200 million persons. Ranks fourth in population. 50 persons per square mile. 70% of population live in urban areas.

LANGUAGE

Russian is the official language. About 100 distinct ethnic groups speak about 200 languages and dialects. Newspapers published in 65 languages. Each of the 15 Soviet Republics has its own official language.

English is used almost universally. However, some minority groups, such as Indians and Spanish-Americans continue use of own languages.

GOVERNMENT

Dictatorship of the proletariat in socialist state of workers and peasants represented by Soviets

Representative democracy. All citizens free to participate in government. Two major political

Soviet Union	*United States*
of Working Peoples Deputies. Only the Communist Party, controlled by 4% of the people, is legal. All important government officials are members of the party.	parties and numerous smaller splinter groups.

ELECTIONS

One-party system; no choice among candidates; no secret ballot.	Multiparty system; free choice among candidates; secret ballot.

PUBLIC EXPRESSION

Press censored. Public opinion controlled.	Free press. Criticism of government permitted.

POLICE

Secret police may arrest or search without warrant or charge.	Law requires warrant or charge for arrest and search.

TRIALS

Prolonged jailing and terrorism, and execution without public trial.	Right to a speedy and fair public trial.

RELIGION

Worship permitted, but opposed.	Freedom to worship as one chooses.

PROPERTY

State owns nearly all property.	Private ownership fostered, but a mixed economy.

INDUSTRY

State owns means of production and distribution. Controls markets.	Private ownership of most means of production and distribution. Competitive market.

EMPLOYMENT

State restricts choice of training and jobs.	Free choice of training and jobs.

Soviet Union	*United States*

UNIONS

Unions are a tool of the state. Strikes banned.	Unions controlled by workers. Strikes permitted.

EDUCATIONAL LEVEL

Median schooling of all adults: 4 years.	Median schooling of all adults: 11 years.

EDUCATIONAL COMMITMENT

One-fourth of national budget committed to education and related fields. Gross national product is one-third that of United States. 8% of GNP spent on education. 2% of GNP spent on higher education and 15% of GNP spent on research and development.	Less than 5% of national income spent on education. 3% of GNP spent on education. 0.7% of GNP spent on higher education. 1.5% of GNP spent on research and development.

EDUCATIONAL GOALS AND PURPOSES

Education is primarily a political tool for constructing and strengthening the communist state. Education is designed to prepare each individual to serve the uniform and conforming collectivist state. Schools must serve the goals set for the state by the communist regime. Schools produce polished cogs for the state machine. The USSR is bent on becoming the leading world power, and education is the primary means of attaining this domination, the key that will unlock the door to world supremacy. The schools are to create an army of scientists and engineers who will build a superior physical power structure.	Education is to develop individuals for responsible citizenship. Americans believe that if each individual is given a chance to choose freely his own career, the good life can be achieved by all. Each individual has talents which must be sought out and identified. In order to be qualified to participate in a nation of intelligent voters, students should participate in a wide range of intellectual, social, economic, and political activities. The schools are to foster a fluid society with few barriers of class and hierarchies. Equality of respect and opportunity for all vocations are valued. The schools are to improve the lot of each

Soviet Union	*United States*
Being trained in the materialistic world outlook, students are to have knowledge and understanding of the fundamentals of socialist production and construction as they develop unified affection for and commitment to the ideals of collectivist service, physical health, obedience, industriousness, and the socialist motherland. The schools are to sort out at an early age those who are to govern, direct, guide, and "think" for society from those who are to be governed, directed, and guided, and who are to do the work.	citizen to survive and remain free by furthering science and the knowledge of man.[1]

SCHOOL ORGANIZATION

The central government, controlled by the Communist Party and backed by police, sets up educational objectives, enforces its directives, and allocates priorities and prestige. Courses of study, schedules, textbooks, examinations, certification of teachers, and numerous other administrative details are uniform and are precisely specified nationwide by central educational authorities. In this rigid, inflexible system the school is the die in which human material is cast into the state required mold. As a state monopoly, the schools move students into certain slots on the basis of centralized planning and control.	Public schools in the United States are directed by approximately 40,000 local school boards which operate as agencies of state governments, administering a great variety of school systems, with no central body in the position of specifying imperatives to all schools, either directly or indirectly. Local responsibility rather than centralized control is emphasized. However, in recent years, with the advent of financial aid programs by both state and federal governments, the influence of these vehicles is being increasingly felt both by publicly-supported and by privately-controlled educational institutions.

[1] Some of the sections in this comparison are based on Henry Chauncey's "Some Comparative Checkpoints Between American and Secondary Education," *Comparative Education Review* 2, no. 3 (February, 1959): 18–20.

Soviet Union	*United States*

CHANGES IN SCHOOL POLICIES AND CURRICULUM

School policies and curriculums are centrally planned and controlled on the basis of political, social, and economic considerations. The rigid chain-of-command fosters extreme conservatism. New syllabi are printed each year for each subject and are compulsory for every school.

School officials, educational leaders, school boards, teachers, parents, and the general public have a voice in the making of school programs.

STRUCTURE OF EDUCATIONAL PROGRAMS

All students take the same standard set of subjects during the first four years. These include Russian grammar, reading, writing, arithmetic, drawing, singing, history, geography, natural science, and physical education.

A wide variety of programs dictated by state and local preferences exists, with little noticeable similarity from locality to locality.

EDUCATIONAL OPPORTUNITIES

Elementary grades 1–4, beginning at age seven, and junior secondary grades 5 to 8 are free, universal, and compulsory. Additional education in general labor schools, vocational-technical schools, technicums, and secondary schools through grades 10 or 11 are optional. Only one-third of the students complete a 10- or 11-year course. Educational opportunities are much greater in the cities. About two-thirds of all rural schools are one-teacher, one-classroom schools. Soviet educational leaders predict that in 20 years all children will be in boarding schools since the cost is less than staying at home and

Elementary grades 1–6 and junior and senior high school grades 7–12 are free and universal, with movement toward such education for grades 13–14 in junior or community colleges. Compulsory education usually is to 16 years of age. 65% of students graduate from high school. Most school districts are consolidated. There are very few one-room schools left.

Soviet Union	*United States*

the state has much better control over the students in their formative years. All students are now trained for factory jobs in order that they may immediately join the labor force if they do not pass crucial examinations.

EDUCATIONAL SELECTIVITY

Program based on principle of selective education, since only those with demonstrated ability and motivation are allowed to enter higher education. The less competent are absorbed into technical schools or on-the-job training. Emphasis is on employment skills.

Program based on the principle of general education. All-inclusive, mass education is emphasized.

PRE-SCHOOL

Creches for 6-months to 3-year old children. Nursery schools or kindergartens for 3–7 year olds. Parents pay fees.

Free public kindergartens for 5–6 year olds in majority of school districts. Nursery schools usually private, except Head Start for disadvantaged children.

MENTALLY AND EDUCATIONALLY RETARDED

No ability grouping. Dullness is held to be environmental and retards children no more than three years. Mental, psychological, and psychiatric examinations are not used in the schools. There are some special schools for seriously retarded students.

Ability grouping is common in regular classes with special education classes and schools in most major school districts.

PROVISIONS FOR TALENTED

None in regular academic program, but gifted helped in extracurricular clubs and through academic competitions. There are special schools for art, dance, and music.

Enrichment programs and faster sections for the talented.

Soviet Union	*United States*

ELECTIVES

Practically all students take the straight academic program. In the higher grades, some electives and some independent study are being allowed. Rigorous and bulky academic program.

20–25% of high school age students take straight academic program. There is a variety of general-education courses and of special courses in various tracks designed to satisfy varying interests and abilities.

SCIENCE CURRICULUM

Great emphasis on science with at least 5 years of physics and 4 years of chemistry. 50% of high school students take mathematics and science.

No enforced emphasis on science with about 25% of high school students taking mathematics and science.

MATHETICS CURRICULUM

High school students take algebra, solid geometry, and trigonometry.

Advanced mathematics is optional in high school, with most students going only through elementary algebra.

FOREIGN LANGUAGES

Beginning in second grade, one language is taught for a period of 5 or more years. Most students are not conversant in the languages studied. In the non-Russian republics, 50–60% of foreign-language instruction is the teaching of Russian.

In high school, foreign languages are optional and usually not offered for more than 2–3 years. Very little foreign-language study in lower grades.

HUMANITIES CURRICULUM

Russian language and literature taught extensively.

English language and American literature taught extensively.

SOCIAL STUDIES

Geography well taught. Biases, omissions, and distortions are prevalent in history textbooks.

Geography is often neglected. Other social studies generally are offered with varying degrees of adequacy.

Soviet Union   *United States*

SHOP WORK

Extensive for all high-school students.

Only a course or two, except in vocational-technical programs.

SCHOOL SCHEDULE

200–210 days in school year, from early September to early June. Six-day school week, with shift to five-day week planned. Four hours of homework daily in high schools. Four-fifths of schools operate on a two-shift basis.

180 days in school year, from early September to early June. Five-day school week. Two hours of homework per night.

EXTRA CURRICULAR ACTIVITIES

Well-organized youth organizations educate youth in Marxism and Communism. The Young Octobrists is a loose organization for 7–10 year olds. They are taught songs, dances, and rituals, and participate in community activities. The Pioneer Organization of Lenin (Pioneers) enrolls almost all children of 10–15 years. Main activities at the more than 2,500 Pioneer Palaces are arts, sports, and technical training. Classes range from chess and airplane building to languages and writing. The Komsomol, enrolling those between the ages of 14 and 26, is an arm of the Communist Party. It supplies teachers for the Pioneers. Its members are from higher education, the armed forces, and industry.

Usually rare and spasmodic, except in major sports areas.

Soviet Union	*United States*

CULTURAL OPPORTUNITIES

Many artistic activities in Pioneer Palaces. Many of the vocational-technical schools even have trade union supported, compulsory "Houses of Culture" where workers participate in bands, choirs, and ballet.	Usually available in some areas of large cities.

SCHOOL BUILDINGS

Often are poorly constructed and lack architectural modernity. Most of the maintenance and cleaning is done by the students. Custodial care is generally poor and the buildings often are in severe need of repair. There are usually no provisions in new buildings for large-group instruction areas, ETV, or language laboratories. There are lighting and ventilation problems and lunch rooms often are unsanitary. Usually there is little playground space. Poor school buildings often are compensated for by spacious and modern Pioneer Palaces.	Most school districts are engaged in construction programs which are bringing modern, well constructed, and adaptable buildings. Custodial and maintenance services are provided by full-time personnel. Lunch rooms are usually required to be very sanitary. Certain slum and rural areas fall below these standards.

TEACHING-LEARNING METHODS

The state clearly specifies what shall be taught and how it will be taught, in detail. Pavlovian stimulus-response, rigid, authoritarian, formalistic, rote learning and regurgitation: "arise-recite-and-sit."	Teachers generally free to choose topics and methods. Most appear to use authoritarian, transmissive or "tell-'em" methods.

Soviet Union   *United States*

MEDIA

Textbook and chalkboard are chief instructional tools.

Wide variety of teaching aids available, but use is optional. They often are not correlated with textbooks.

EXAMINATIONS

Standardized tests are used to determine whether or not students should go to senior high school, to vocational-technical schools, or directly to the labor force. Both oral and essay tests are used. Teachers complain that the students cram for examinations rather than seeking understanding of the subject.

No standardized tests required. Teachers use both objective and essay tests. A wide variety are used.

TEACHER-STUDENT RELATIONSHIPS

"Family" concept; teacher serves as substitute parent: teachers exhibit concern, affection, and understanding of students. This does not fit the oversimplified stereotype of the unfeeling totalitarian teacher.

Wide variety of relationships exist. Many elementary teachers tend to be "mother" types, whereas many secondary teachers tend to stress subject matter, not students.

AVERAGE CLASS SIZE

17 students per teacher.

25 students per teacher.

TEACHING LOAD

18 hours a week on all levels. No required clerical duties, extra-curricular activities, or discipline problems. Due to the load, professors tend to fall behind in their fields.

24 hours a week in elementary and high schools with less than 10 hours per week in the universities. However, there are many clerical duties, etc., in many school districts.

Soviet Union	*United States*

GUIDANCE AND COUNSELING

No formal program and no aptitude or interest tests used. Students encouraged to develop special interests through participation in Pioneers.	Widespread individual guidance available in many schools with group guidance increasing. Extensive use of aptitude and interest tests.

DISCIPLINE

Often students are disciplined by their peer group. Parents are called to account if their children are out of order. Parental cooperation is compulsory.	Basic responsibility for classroom order rests with the teacher, assisted by administrators and guidance counselors. Parental cooperation is voluntary.

TEACHER RESPONSIBILITY

Teachers are held specifically responsible for the success of every student. Therefore, they teach the tests and pass almost all students, regardless of student achievement.	Teachers are only generally responsible for student classroom achievement.

STUDENT MOTIVATION

Uniformly high attentiveness and seriousness of purpose.	Marked variations from low to high, but students usually are passive.

SOURCES OF MOTIVATION

Students recognize that their future income, prestige, and success in life are dependent on success in education. It is the way to get ahead in Soviet society.	Motivation depends on family values and environment. A person's future income and success in life are only partially dependent on success in school.

HIGHER EDUCATION

12% of the population in the higher education age category is enrolled in higher education. Universities and institutes are	25% of total higher education age population enrolled in higher education. Open to all at student's expense, with low tuition

Soviet Union

free, with monthly living allowances, but only one place for every four applicants. Training is highly and rigidly specialized. Emphasis is on technical education, not liberal arts. Narrowness limits and constricts career flexibility. The aim is to develop narrow, specialized, applied, and functional skills. About 60% of all graduates are scientists, technologists, and engineers. With half the industrial capacity of the United States, Russia is producing twice as many scientists and technicians. There is heavy emphasis on part-time education and on-the-job training. Extensive programs in formal and informal adult education. Evening and correspondence courses account for half of the higher education participants. Workers' cultural clubs often have Houses of Culture near industrial complexes.

United States

at tax supported schools, plus scholarships. Of the top 20% of high school graduates, two-thirds do not finish college, primarily for economic reasons. A broad education, emphasizing underlying principles and systems and the humanities, is the goal. Graduates will not become technologically obsolete almost overnight. They will be able to roll with the future. The aim is to develop broad, creative intellects critical of society and its values. About 25% of all graduates are scientists, technologists, and engineers.

TEACHER EDUCATION

4 or 5 applicants for each place available. 2 years training after high school for primary teachers and 5 years after high school for secondary teachers. Training includes free tuition plus a stipend for living expenses. Emphasis is on content of subjects to be taught, theory of pedagogy, and specific methods of teaching individual topics. Most teachers are trained in separate pedagogical institutes for primary and secondary grades.

4 to 5 years training after high school for both elementary and high school teachers. Each student pays his own tuition and living expenses, except for the few on scholarships. Emphasis is on content of subjects to be taught, with particular attention being given to pedagogical theories. Most teachers are trained in multi-purpose colleges and universities.

Soviet Union	*United States*

JOB PLACEMENT

The teacher serves the government where he is sent and at the wage set by the government.	The teacher is at liberty to accept or reject any job offered to him.

IN-SERVICE TRAINING

Compulsory training occurs one day a week for 2 or 3 months every three years.	Training is optional and regulations vary in the various states and districts.

JOB SECURITY

No such thing, except when teacher is valued by the officials over him.	In most states, teachers are protected by state laws from unfair dismissal.

TEACHER STATUS

High for secondary teachers; much lower for primary teachers. The respect for professors borders on adulation. Particularly in rural and small town areas, teachers are active and influential political figures.	Most public school teachers have medium to low prestige. They tend to be in the "backwash" of society. Teachers usually are not community leaders and seldom are active in politics.

TEACHER PAY

Professors' salaries are among the top in Russia. Their salaries are higher than those of bureaucrats and plant managers. The primary and secondary teachers tend to be poorly paid. Waiters may earn 50% more than teachers and skilled factory workers may earn twice as much.	Professors' salaries are well below those of businessmen and physicians. Public school salaries tend to be about equivalent to those received by semi-skilled and skilled laborers.

EDUCATIONAL RESEARCH

Extensive research by certain pedagogical institutes and systematic experimentation in certain public schools. Teacher participation is encouraged. Due to	Research done in "bits and pieces" by researchers in various colleges and universities. Teacher participation is voluntary and very infrequent. Due to

centralized control, research results may be used to change
school programs within 3–5
years.

the strength of the belief in "local control," it may take 25 or
more years for research results
to be implemented in the majority of school districts.

ARE COMPARISONS VALID?

There appear to be at least two types of problems involved in making
comparisons between the Soviet Union's educational system and that
of the United States. First, many of the comparisons are over-general-
izations which often lead to false impressions. Second, since each nation's educational system has its own goals based on each nation's
value-system, it might be more valid to determine to what degree
each system meets its own goals, rather than to be misled by compar-
ing the two systems with each other.

Let us first note how certain of the previous comparisons can be
misleading. In terms of educational commitment, it was indicated
that the Soviets commit a much higher percentage of their gross national product to education than does the United States. However,
some observers claim that the Soviet education budget has been
overstated, since about one-third of their education budget goes for
things such as youth centers, summer camps, public libraries, art
exhibits, movie theaters, radio stations, and newspapers, which are not
expenditures for education as interpreted in the United States. When
the categories of education are adjusted to include the same things
in both countries, the relative educational commitments in both appear to be fairly comparable, with absolute expenditures higher in
the United States.

The comparison of pupil-teacher ratios indicates that the Soviets
are far ahead of the United States. However, the Soviets include
part-time teachers and administrative personnel in their "teachers"
category. When the numbers of what appear to be administrative
personnel and part-time teachers are subtracted from the Soviets'
figures, a ratio of one teacher to about 24 students in grades 1–10
seems to be more accurate than the ratios usually quoted.

Certain critics of United States education point with pride to the
much larger amount of time Soviet students are required to devote to
homework. However, since most Soviet city schools are on double
session with each student in school for only half a day, there is no
time for supervised study periods. Therefore, students must work on
their lessons at home.

Perhaps the most repeated comparison has been about how many more engineers the Soviets graduate. This is misleading, since professional titles in Russia often mean less in the way of educational qualifications than they do in the United States. For example, a Russian "engineer" might only qualify as a "technician" in the United States. Also, due to population differences, there are twice as many persons of university age in Russia than in the United States. The United States actually is producing more engineers and physical scientists, per thousand 22-year-olds, than is the Soviet Union. This is in spite of the fact that the Soviets place high priority on those scientific and engineering fields which primarily support industrial growth. In contrast, as a highly advanced and diversified industrial society, the United States needs diversified college graduates to satisfy sophisticated consumer needs, as well as producer needs in heavy and light industries.

Although certain foreign observers have concluded that Soviet teachers have higher status than teachers in the United States, teacher status is difficult to gauge. The deference of Russian pupils to their teachers is in the European educational tradition, but is not necessarily a sign of teacher status. The political positions accorded many teachers often appear to be honorary rather than functional. Also, there seems to be an extreme range of income, with university professors averaging about eight times the salaries of elementary school teachers. It must be remembered that public school teachers in the United States have many times the salary in terms of real income, and a much higher standard of living, than do public school teachers in Russia.

Certain critics of education in the United States have concluded that the Soviets are doing a much better educational job than we are. In support of the critics' contention that we should copy the Soviet system and get rid of all the "fads," "frills," and "soft courses"—meaning anything other than the 3 R's and science—they claim that less than 5 per cent of United States high school graduates could pass the final examinations of Soviet high schools. One critic titled his biting article, "It's Time to Close Our Carnival."

However, it should be remembered that the Soviet examinations are oral, the questions are known in advance so the teachers can "teach the test," and the number of failing students is extremely low because a teacher who fails a student is rated a poor teacher. The Soviet educational authorities regularly complain that many students are passed who really cannot answer the final examination questions. Also, it should be noted that many Soviet educational authorities are critical of their rigid public school system and are trying to move toward the comprehensive United States type.

Assessment of Soviet education, and accurate comparisons, are made difficult because, in the "closed society" of Russia, foreign educators are allowed to observe only certain schools in certain areas and are told only what the Soviets want to tell. Are visitors shown "show places" or "average" schools? Do the Soviet pedagogical journals and reports accurately indicate the present state of Soviet education? Are Soviet criticisms of the shortcomings of their system representative of what is really going on, or do they give a distorted picture of Russian education? It appears that all we can base educational comparisons on are varying levels of ignorance about what is really going on in the Soviet educational system.

The second major problem involved in making comparisons is that since the goals of education in Russia and the United States are so diverse, it would be more valid to check to see how successful each system is in achieving its own goals. The Soviet goals have included providing some form of secondary education for most of its youth, providing highly qualified, higher education specialists in certain science fields, and obtaining general student acceptance of the Soviet Communist Party's value-system. In terms of the goals which have been set for Soviet education, their system is unquestionably a success. They have changed a sleeping peasant giant into a roaring industrial superman. But their narrow focus on fostering the production of specialists and their authoritarian indoctrination of dogmas and amenity to rule by a specially privileged elite certainly do not appear to be models to be emulated by societies valuing democratic educational abilities—abilities to develop creative intellects who are critical of existing societies and their values. A system which considers students as cogs in a nationalistic machine apparently has little to offer to a society which is attempting to educate people to live together in liberty.

CONCLUSION

Granting that there are serious problems involved in attempting to compare Soviet and United States education, granting that the systems are designed to achieve thoroughly different goals, granting that many Soviet educational authorities want to shift to a system nearer to what is fostered in the United States, and granting that very little is known in the Western World as to what really is going on in Soviet education, what, then, can we conclude?

The Soviets took the traditional European pattern, of advanced liberal arts education for a specially privileged elite, and shifted it to a narrow, technical-centered pattern of advanced education for the Soviet intellectual elite. Such a system is clearly contrary to Marx's vision of egalitarianism. However, their "sorting out" system seems to fit their tightly controlled society. Their system seems to be an effective tool in achieving their goals. In contrast, under our mass education concept, are we really offering quality education to students able to benefit from such? Could we do a better job of sorting out our standards so that, for example, half of the students in the freshman classes at many major public universities will not have to be "washed out"?

The Soviets know that the world belongs to the most educated. The march through their schools is serious business to them, their "grand passion." They know that they are in a race against the United States for world domination, and they have a burning desire to win. Education is their prime tool for surpassing the United States. In contrast to their singleness of purpose, they view education in the United States as haphazard, aimless, and chaotic, with no clearly defined priorities. Can we move toward our goal of creating thoughtful and humane democratic citizens as efficiently and effectively as the Soviets appear to be moving toward their goal of creating highly competent "cogs" for their totalitarian society? Perhaps this is the basic challenge of Soviet education.

SELECTED REFERENCES

Benton, William, *The Teachers and the Taught in the U.S.S.R.* New York: Atheneum Press, 1966. A perceptive evaluation of the challenge of Soviet education.

Counts, George S., *The Challenge of Soviet Education.* New York: McGraw-Hill Book Company, 1957. By using Soviet texts, curriculum guides, and examinations, Dr. Counts analyzed the strengths and weaknesses of the Soviet educational system.

De Witt, Nicholas, *Education and Professional Employment in the U.S.S.R.* Washington, D.C.: National Science Foundation, 1961. A very comprehensive (856 pp.) study of the Soviet educational system and the employment of professional and specialized manpower in the U.S.S.R.

Educational Issues in a Changing Society, August Kerber and Wilfred Smith, eds. Detroit: Wayne State University Press, 1964, Chap. 16. A series of brief articles analyzing Soviet education.

Grant, Nigel, *Soviet Education.* Baltimore: Penguin Books, 1964. An excellent brief examination of the Soviet educational system against its geographical, historical, social, and political background.

Hechinger, Fred M., *The Big Red Schoolhouse.* Garden City, New York: Doubleday and Company, 1962. This volume by the education editor for *The New York Times* also is an excellent brief examination of the Soviet educational system.

Moos, Elizabeth, *Education in the Soviet Union.* New York: National Council of American-Soviet Friendship, 1963. A brief description of the Soviet educational system.

———, *Soviet Education—Achievements and Goals.* New York: National Council of American-Soviet Friendship, 1967. Another good brief introduction to the Soviet educational system.

———, *Soviet Education—1970.* New York: National Council of American-Soviet Friendship, 1970. A summary of changes occurring in Soviet education.

Rosen, Seymour M., "Problems in Evaluating Soviet Education," *Comparative Education Review* 8, no. 2 (October, 1964): 156–63. A perceptive presentation of a number of evaluational problems. This article also was reprinted in *Controversy in American Education,* Harold Full, ed. New York: The Macmillan Company, 1967, pp. 411–21.

Rudman, Herbert C., *The School and State in the USSR.* New York: The Macmillan Company, 1967. The management, decision making, and implementation processes in the Soviet educational system are explored.

The Changing Soviet School, George Z. F. Bereday, William W. Brickman, and Gerald H. Read, eds. Boston: Houghton Mifflin Company, 1960. An authoritative field-study of the Soviet educational system by 71 members of the Comparative Education Society.

THOUGHT AIDS

1. "They [the Soviets] believe the acceptance of their doctrines to be synonymous with enlightenment." (George Z. F. Bereday, *Comparative Method in Education,* p. 120.) Is this a good attitude to have? Why or why not? Do you believe that many persons in the United States have similar attitudes? Why or why not?

2. Do you agree with the Soviet view that education in the United States is haphazard, aimless, and chaotic? Why or why not?

3. It has been said that the Soviets have developed the most comprehensive educational operation to develop the superman and the supernation. Do you agree? Why or why not?
4. See the documentary film, "Meet Comrad Student." What do you think of the educational program presented in this film?
5. Do you believe that the Soviets are placing more emphasis on education for their purposes than United States citizens are placing on education for our purposes? Why or why not?
6. React to the following quote: "It is one of the great ironies of this century that a police state rather than a democracy thinks more highly of its teachers than of its policemen." (Fred M. Hechinger. *The Big Red Schoolhouse,* p. 113.)
7. Since the Soviets have clear national objectives and have organized their school system to achieve these objectives, should we also formulate clear national objectives and organize our public schools to achieve these objectives? Why or why not?
8. Some writers in popular magazines have compared exceptional Soviet students with average United States students and then have concluded that Soviet education is much better than education in the United States. What is your opinion of such journalistic tactics? What do you think such articles show about Soviet and United States education?
9. In one of his telling analyses of United States education, Admiral Rickover noted: "In no other Western country are educational institutions so precariously placed financially, so dependent on local politicians, on the whim of small communities where few have ever had a higher education . . ." (Quoted in Hechinger's *The Big Red Schoolhouse,* p. 164.) Assuming that Admiral Rickover's description is accurate, what do you believe should be done to correct this problem? Why?
10. What to you is the most important challenge of Soviet education to education in the United States? Why?

Index